Private Lives in the Public Sphere

Todd Kontje

Private Lives in the Public Sphere: The German *Bildungsroman* as Metafiction

The Pennsylvania State University Press
University Park, Pennsylvania

Library of Congress Cataloging-in-Publication Data

Kontje, Todd Curtis, 1954-
   Private lives in the public sphere : the German Bildungsroman as metafiction / Todd Kontje.
      p.   cm.
   Includes bibliographic references and index.
   ISBN 0-271-00823-7 (alk. paper)
   1. Bildungsroman. 2. German fiction—18th century—History and criticism. 3. German fiction—19th century—History and criticism.
   I. Title.
   PT747.E6K64   1992
   833'.609353—dc20   91-25763
                                                                         CIP

Copyright © 1992 The Pennsylvania State University
All rights reserved
Printed in the United States of America

It is the policy of The Pennsylvania State University Press to use acid-free paper for the first printing of all clothbound books. Publications on uncoated stock satisfy the minimum requirements of American National Standard for Information Sciences—Permanence of Paper for Printed Library Materials, ANSI Z39.48-1984.

Contents

	Acknowledgments	vii
1	The German *Bildungsroman* as Metafiction	1
2	Private Life in the Public Sphere: Heinrich Jung-Stilling's *Lebensgeschichte* (1777-1804)	19
3	Creative Destruction: Karl Philipp Moritz's *Anton Reiser* (1785-90)	33
4	The Aesthetic Alienation of Wilhelm Meister (1795-97)	51
5	Professional Romanticism: Ludwig Tieck's *Franz Sternbalds Wanderungen* (1798)	79
6	Nostalgic and Progressive Utopias in Novalis's *Heinrich von Ofterdingen* (1800)	97
7	Self-Engendering Fictions in Jean Paul's *Flegeljahre* (1804-5)	123
8	From Cultural Renaissance to Political Reaction: E.T.A. Hoffmann's *Kater Murr* (1819-21)	143
9	Conclusion	161
	Works Cited	167
	Index	181

Acknowledgments

I would like to thank the Alexander von Humboldt Stiftung for the generous support that enabled me to complete this manuscript during the academic year of 1989-90 at the Freie Universität Berlin. The Columbia University Council for Research in the Humanities provided support for initial research.

Part of Chapter 1 appeared in substantially different form in *Michigan Germanic Studies* 13 (1987), 140-55. Chapter 2 was published in *Colloquia Germanica* 21 (1988), 275-87; it is reprinted here with minor revisions. Chapter 5 appeared in *Monatshefte* 82 (1990), 34-50. I am grateful for permission to reproduce this material here.

In addition, I have been given generous permission to use the following copyrighted translations:

Goethe. *Wilhelm Meister's Apprenticeship.* Ed. and trans. Eric A. Blackall and Victor Lange. Goethe's Collected Works 9. New York: Suhrkamp, 1989.

Novalis. *Henry von Ofterdingen: A Novel.* Trans. Palmer Hilty. New York: Ungar, 1964.

Hoffmann. *The Life and Opinions of Kater Murr.* Vol. 2 of *Selected Writings of E.T.A. Hoffmann.* Ed. and trans. Leonard J. Kent and Elizabeth C. Knight. Chicago: University of Chicago Press, 1969.

All other translations are my own.

Rolf-Peter Janz sponsored my Humboldt fellowship and was generous with his time in Berlin. Frederick Amrine, Stanley Corngold, Walter Hinderer, and Andreas Huyssen all supported the project in its early stages. Special thanks to Dennis F. Mahoney, Keith Monley, and Kenneth Weisinger, all of whom read the entire manuscript and offered invaluable suggestions for revision. Most of all, I thank Elizabeth Bredeck for her insight and support in all aspects of the research and writing.

The German *Bildungsroman* as Metafiction

1

Late eighteenth-century Germany experienced a literary revolution that made up for its belatedness in its rapidity and scope. The nature and quantity of reading material produced, the social status of the writer, and the reading habits of the public changed dramatically within a few decades.[1] At the beginning of the century the new texts that appeared at the annual book fairs were primarily written in Latin and devoted to theology. By the end of the century the number of new publications each year had increased almost exponentially, with the novel leading the way. Reading societies sprang up, literary journals were founded and collapsed at a furious rate, and writers began the slow and often difficult attempt to become professionals who lived from the profits of their publications.[2] That such professionalism was at all possible depended in part on the change in reading habits of the German public, which Rolf Engelsing has described as a movement from "intensive" to

---

1. See Schmidt for a recent, detailed survey of changes in the German literary institution during this period (*Die Selbstorganisation des Sozialsystems Literatur im 18. Jahrhundert*).

2. See works by Haferkorn ("Der freie Schriftsteller"), Engelsing (*Der Bürger als Leser*), and Ward (*Book Production*) on the growth of the reading public and the emergence of the professional writer. Works by Becker (*Roman um 1780*), Hadley (*Novel in 1790*), and Heiderich (*Novel of 1800*) provide useful cross sections of the changing literary market in the late eighteenth century.

"extensive" reading.³ Intensive reading involved the repeated study of the Bible and a limited number of religious texts for the purpose of reinforcing both commonly shared beliefs and the social structure that supported them. Extensive reading, in contrast, challenged readers to expand their understanding of themselves and their society in encounters with the new secular literature that emerged in the second half of the century.

These developments signaled Germany's participation in the general European phenomenon that Jürgen Habermas has termed the "structural transformation of the public sphere." Habermas situates the public sphere of the eighteenth century between the private realm of the home and the official political institutions of the state. Coffeehouses, secret societies, newspapers, journals, and literature served as forums for public debate in which members of the middle class, although still limited in their direct access to political power, could at least begin to articulate their problems and formulate their hopes.⁴

The discursive community of the public sphere formed earliest and most actively in England, whose citizens enjoyed a gradual series of democratic reforms that stretched from the Glorious Revolution of 1688 through the restructuring of Parliament in 1832. By the first decades of the eighteenth century the infrastructure of the public sphere was in place, as a lively publishing industry produced newspapers, periodicals, and a socially critical literature.⁵ In prerevolutionary France, the public sphere developed under less propitious circumstances. Here the literary institution was divided into a narrowly restricted official culture on the one hand and a vibrant but illegal literary underground on the other.⁶ While the French Revolution reversed this situation nearly overnight, as freedom of the press was declared one of the inalienable rights of humanity, the immediate results were not entirely positive for the publishing industry. Rapidly evolving political events, combined with the complete deregulation of the literary market, drove many printers out of business. For a brief time, at least, France witnessed "a

---

3. Engelsing, "Die neuen Leser" in *Der Bürger als Leser,* 182-215. See also König, "Lesesucht und Lesewut."

4. Thus Habermas refers to the intimate family sphere in which reading took place as "das Übungsfeld eines öffentlichen Räsonnements" (*Strukturwandel der Öffentlichkeit,* 44). "Literature served the emancipation movement of the middle class as an instrument to gain self-esteem and to articulate its human demands against the absolutist state and a hierarchical society. Literary discussion, which had previously served as a form of legitimation of court society in the aristocratic salons, became an arena to pave the way for political discussion in the middle classes" (Hohendahl, *The Institution of Criticism,* 52).

5. Habermas, *Strukturwandel,* 76-87.

6. Darnton, *The Literary Underground of the Old Regime.*

temporary collapse of 'the book' itself," as more ephemeral literary forms could be produced more quickly and inexpensively.[7]

The situation confronting the German bourgeoisie was even more difficult. Still reeling from the devastating effects of the Thirty Years' War at the outset of the eighteenth century, Germany remained a provincial backwater until well into the next. Whereas France and England had the cultural advantage of being unified countries with central capitals, "Germany" existed only as a myriad of petty absolutist states whose subjects spoke different dialects of the same language. Germans could not look back on a long tradition of political reform, as could the English, nor did they experience the mixed blessings of political revolution, as did the French. Nevertheless, they *did* experience a revolution in print.

Due to the political situation in Germany, however, the transformation of its public sphere had little direct effect on the institutions of state authority. The gap between the two realms emerges clearly in Immanuel Kant's short essay in response to the question "What is Enlightenment?" Subsequent readers have tended to quote out of context his definition of Enlightenment as "the emergence of humanity out of its self-imposed immaturity."[8] Actually, the Prussian civil servant combines his clarion call for intellectual freedom with a tyrannical demand for absolute obedience to the state: "Reason as much as you want and about whatever you want, but obey!"[9] Friedrich Schiller would turn this demand for the complete separation of the public sphere and politics into the basis of his paradoxical program of aesthetic education. As he expressed it in his announcement of his new literary journal, *Die Horen,* in 1795, it was only by turning away from current political events to concentrate on the eternal verities of the human condition that Germans could hope to overcome the misery of modernity without suffering the chaos of political revolution.[10] Far from advocating art for art's sake, Schiller insisted that the proper sort of aesthetic experience could provide the only lasting solution to political problems, "for it is through beauty that we proceed to freedom."[11]

Yet even as Schiller envisioned humanity united in a future aesthetic state, financial pressures accompanying the capitalization of the book market began to undermine the homogeneity of the existing public

---

7. Hesse, "Economic Upheavals in Publishing," in *Revolution in Print,* ed. Darnton and Roche, 96-97.
8. Kant, "Was ist Aufklärung?" in *Werkausgabe* 11:53.
9. Kant, "Was ist Aufklärung?" in *Werkausgabe* 11:61.
10. *Werke* 5:870.
11. *Werke* 5:573.

sphere. While the professional writers became emancipated from the demands of noble patronage, they became increasingly dependent on the favor of the reading public. Schiller's announcement of an earlier literary journal provides a good example of this shift. Forced to flee his native Swabia when Duke Karl Eugen forbade him to continue writing, Schiller turned to the public for support: "The public is everything to me now, my study, my sovereign, my confidant. To it alone I now belong."[12] Schiller optimistically hoped to transcend the boundaries of rank and class in a direct appeal to the "human soul" of the united public. Yet the very dependence on the public for support among such writers as Schiller began to work against the emancipatory potential of the new literature. The book had become a commodity, and if writers hoped to profit from their publications, they had to give the public what it wanted, not what the writers felt it needed.[13]

By the 1790s such authors as Goethe and Schiller were no longer willing to cater to the tastes of the German public. "The only relation to the public that one cannot regret is war," writes Schiller to Goethe in a particularly aggressive mood in 1799.[14] As Martha Woodmansee has argued, the aesthetics of German Classicism were conceived in direct opposition to the mode of reception encouraged by popular fiction.[15] While readers identified with tales of Robinson Crusoe for vicarious adventure, sought edification in novels of education, or titillation in novels of romance, Moritz, Kant, Goethe, and Schiller favored self-contained works that rewarded repeated study, neither intoxicating the readers with sensory stimuli, nor browbeating them with moral lessons. We witness the attempt on the part of a few individuals to establish a new literary canon by applying old intensive patterns of reading to a select body of secular texts.[16] In the process, however, these authors

12. "Ankündigung der Rheinischen Thalia" (1784), in *Werke* 5:856.

13. See articles by Schulte-Sasse ("Das Konzept bürgerlich-literarischer Öffentlichkeit") and Christa Bürger ("Literarischer Markt und Öffentlichkeit") for detailed theoretical discussions of the inherent contradictions in the public sphere (in *Aufklärung und literarische Öffentlichkeit*).

14. *Briefwechsel Schiller Goethe*, 770. See Berghahn for a critical assessment of Schiller's relation to the public ("Volkstümlichkeit ohne Volk").

15. "As literature became subject to the laws of a market economy, the instrumentalist theory ... was found to justify the wrong works. That is, it was found to justify the products of the purveyors of strong effect, with whom more serious writers could not effectively compete. The theology of art fashioned by Moritz offered such writers both a convenient and a very powerful set of concepts with which to address the predicament in which they found themselves—concepts by which (serious, or 'fine') art's *de facto* loss of direct instrumentality could be recuperated as a (supreme) virtue" (Woodmansee, "The Interests in Disinterestedness," 46).

16. "Die intensive Lektüre wird von der extensiven nicht einfach abgelöst, sondern

drove a wedge between high and low culture that threatened to alienate the public from the very literature originally intended for its enlightenment.

Not surprisingly, therefore, Habermas has been accused of idealizing the eighteenth-century public sphere in order to sharpen his critique of the current age.[17] Nevertheless, he does offer a new perspective on the proverbial "rise of the middle class" by illustrating how public forums for the exchange of ideas helped to initiate social reform. Rather than viewing cultural developments as a mere reflection of economic change, Habermas understands public discourse as itself an event that transforms reality in the minds of its participants. As Terry Eagleton has put it, in his study of the English public sphere, "Discursive identities are not pre-given, but constructed by the very act of participation in polite conversation.... the rational are those capable of a certain mode of discourse, but this cannot be judged other than in the act of deploying it."[18] One of the key sites for the public deployment of discourse was literature. Thus Eagleton argues in a different context that "Richardson's novels are not mere images of conflicts fought out on another terrain, ... they are themselves a material part of those struggles, ... instruments which help to constitute social interests rather than lenses which reflect them." In short, he is "interested less in what that fiction 'mirrors' than in what it *does*."[19] Given the relatively progressive political climate in England, we can only conclude that literature in Germany had to do more.

It is during this period of rapid transformation in the literary institution that we witness the emergence of the *Bildungsroman*. As these cultural developments might lead one to suspect, most of the protagonists of

---

entsteht aus dieser und erlaubt immer wieder die Rückkehr zu ihr. Selbst der 'Werther' wurde intensiv wie ein Erbauungsbuch gelesen" (Sauder, *Hansers Sozialgeschichte*, 266). See also Vaget, "Die Leiden des jungen Werthers," 39, and Kittler, *Aufschreibesysteme*, 150. In his investigation of French readers of Rousseau, Darnton goes so far as to claim "that no such revolution [in reading habits] took place" (*Great Cat Massacre*, 251). I would disagree for two reasons. First, the very fact that French readers read Rousseau like earlier generations had read the Bible is revolutionary enough. Second, not all new fiction was read with the same intensity. There was simply too much material available by the end of the century to permit it. What we witness is indeed a revolution that involves *both* a change to a new, superficial sort of reading for most printed matter and a transferal of old religious reading habits to a select body of secular fiction.

17. Albertsen, "Internationaler Zeitfaktor Kotzebue," 230. See also Hohendahl, "Critical Theory, Public Sphere and Culture: Jürgen Habermas and His Critics."
18. Eagleton, *The Function of Criticism*, 15.
19. Eagleton, *The Rape of Clarissa*, 4.

these texts are avid readers.[20] Anton Reiser reads *Werther,* Wilhelm Meister reads *Hamlet,* and Murr has clearly studied his Shakespeare, Goethe, and Schiller. Moreover, most of these characters engage in some form of artistic production themselves, whether it be as writers, actors, or painters. Direct commentary on the contemporary cultural scene often plays an important role in these texts as well, ranging from the protagonists' attempt to take part in the establishment of a national theater in novels by Moritz and Goethe, through Jean Paul's criticism of incompetent publishers and reviewers in the *Flegeljahre,* to the satirical portraits of literary salons and foppish aesthetes in Hoffmann's *Kater Murr.*

In addition to reflecting on the world around them, the novels also turn inward to reflect upon themselves. Of particular interest are those moments when the extensive readers portrayed in the novels become intensive readers of their own lives. Seen in chronological perspective, these self-reflexive moments in the texts provide an indirect commentary on successive stages in the transformation of the German literary institution. Jung-Stilling and Moritz write fictional autobiographies whose protagonists are drawn away from their Pietist heritage through incessant extensive reading of current fiction. In the process it becomes first difficult, and then impossible, to interpret individual development in terms of the biblical paradigm of salvation history. Goethe's *Wilhelm Meisters Lehrjahre (Wilhelm Meister's Apprenticeship)* represents an attempt to recenter the fictionally inspired wanderings of the hero in the secular closure of classical aesthetics. The novel both exhibits the self-reflexive form that distinguishes the autonomous work of art from its popular counterparts, when for example Wilhelm reads the Tower Society's *(Turmgesellschafts)* version of his own apprenticeship, and also offers an implicit critique of the cultural aspirations of Weimar Classicism, in that Meister finds it impossible to turn from aesthetic contemplation of his past to decisive action in the present.

The motif of the book within the book recurs in several romantic novels, as when Heinrich von Ofterdingen encounters an illuminated manuscript that prefigures the events of his own life, or when the twin brothers Walt and Vult in Jean Paul's *Flegeljahre* spend part of their time writing and trying to publish another version of the same novel in which they appear as characters. On the one hand, these romantic

20. Schlaffer, *Bürger als Held:* "Es ist bedeutsam, daß Albano und Wilhelm Meister— wie die prominentesten Helden des modernen Romans seit Don Quixote—lesende Helden sind, genauer: Figuren, die erst durchs Lesen vergangener Poesie zu (allerdings problematischen) 'Helden' werden, indem sie vorbürgerliche Helden zum Vorbild eines unbürgerlichen Lebens in der bürgerlichen Realität nehmen" (49).

ironists widen the gap between art and life. By generating an endless series of reflections within the text, the novelists gesture toward the inexpressible, ineffable literary absolute. At the same time, however, Tieck, Novalis, Jean Paul, and Hoffmann ground the metaphysical striving of romantic irony in a critical commentary on the changing literary institution. In doing so, they already begin to question certain boundaries recently established in autonomy aesthetics: between serious and popular literature, between the artist and the public, and between literature and life.

On the most direct level, these writers investigate the strained relation between romantic notions of artistic creativity and the financial pressures on the professional artist. Franz Sternbald finds himself caught between his belief in the sanctity of the artistic calling and his need to earn a living. A series of abusive publishers reject the twins' manuscript in the *Flegeljahre,* and even Hoffmann's Murr, serene in the conviction of his superior genius, laments the prejudice with which editors regard his lucubrations. At such moments the distinction between autobiography and fiction becomes blurred, as authors use their novels to reflect on their own experiences. For this reason I devote particular attention to the authors' relations with the public, both in terms of the popularity and profitability of their own books, and their reflections on the general surge in literary production and consumption around 1800. Historical changes do not proceed uniformly and irrevocably; part of my intention is to add nuance to the discussion of broad trends in German literary history with reference to individual careers.[21] By continuing their reflections on artistic professionalism within the novels themselves, moreover, these writers challenge the familiar notion that "real" artists live only for their art, while only hacks toil for monetary gain. In fact, I would argue that it is precisely the willingness to allow the concerns of life to impinge on their works of art that distinguishes these novels from the broad spectrum of popular literature, where all traces of the labor of literary production have been carefully concealed to ensure effortless consumption.

In reflecting on their difficulties with the public, these artists take part in the familiar romantic critique of Philistine society. Life as a misunderstood genius may be hard, but at least one can find solace in the conviction that one leads a more authentic existence than the average *Spießbürger.* At the same time, however, these texts work to

---

21. Here I am in agreement with Darnton, who insists that the seemingly old-fashioned investigation of individual careers provides "a needed corrective to the more abstract study of ideas and ideologies" (*The Literary Underground,* 70).

undermine the distinction between the artist and society by revealing that both participate in the same intersubjective culture of the public sphere. The reading experiences of characters within the texts provides a good example of the way in which public discourses imprint themselves on individual consciousness. Like Don Quixote before them, the protagonists of these novels set off to realize the adventures they encounter in fictional texts. The German novels are said to differ from the picaresque tradition in their greater focus on the inner development of the protagonist; as Thomas Mann put it, the *Bildungsroman* involves "the rendering inward and sublimation of the adventure novel."[22] However, when a reader in one text appropriates the desires of fictional models, it becomes difficult to determine where "ownership" lies.[23] What Mann refers to as the internalization of the picaresque novel can be described more accurately as the rendering *self-conscious* of the same tradition. Literary quotations inspire actions, and characters develop self-awareness through identification with fictional heroes.[24]

Like the characters in their literary works, the authors themselves have been molded by their reading experiences. Writing involves both reflection on the fictions that have shaped the self and the active construction of new identities. As such the authors of the *Bildungsroman* are engaged in a form of what Steven Greenblatt describes as the project of self-fashioning:

> Self-fashioning derives its interest precisely from the fact that it functions without regard for a sharp distinction between literature and social life. It invariably crosses the boundaries between the creation of literary characters, the shaping of one's own identity, the experience of being molded by forces outside one's control, the attempt to fashion other selves. Such boundaries may, to be sure, be strictly observed in criticism, just as we may distinguish between literary and behavioral styles, but in doing

22. Mann, "Die Kunst des Romans," 2:357. See also Swales, *Bildungsroman,* 19, and my discussion of Miles, "Picaro's Journey to the Confessional," in Chapter 4.

23. See Girard's discussion of "'triangular' desire" in the opening chapter of *Deceit, Desire, and the Novel.* Smith develops a stimulating analysis of alienated desire in the *Bildungsroman* with reference to Hegel and Lacan ("Sexual Difference, *Bildung,* and the *Bildungsroman*").

24. "Einerseits wiederholt der sich einfühlende Leser die in der Literatur vorgezeichneten privaten Beziehungen.... Anderseits ist die von Anfang an literarisch vermittelte Intimität, ist die literaturfähige Subjektivität tatsächlich zur Literatur eines breiten Lesepublikums geworden; die zum Publikum zusammentretenden Privatleute räsonieren auch öffentlichlich über das Gelesene und bringen es in den gemeinsam vorangetriebenen Prozeß der Aufklärung ein" (Habermas, *Strukturwandel,* 68-69).

so we pay a high price, for we begin to lose a sense of the complex interactions of meaning in a given culture.[25]

Although Greenblatt discusses writers of the English Renaissance, his understanding of the fluid boundaries between traditionally distinct categories applies equally well to the work of these German writers, whose texts hover on the border between confession and re-creation. Seen from a positive perspective, self-fashioning allows for a sort of Nietzschean freedom to reinvent the self in fiction. The negative component of this same freedom lies in the troubling awareness that the created identity is not one's own.

This is not to say that romantic artists lead a more authentic existence than their Philistine counterparts, but that they are more self-conscious about their inauthenticity. Such awareness becomes particularly acute in the works of Jean Paul and Hoffmann. Just as serious writers are not immune to the financial pressures that trouble the literary drudge, so too they are not immune to the increasing sense of alienation in the modern world. Here again the distinction between popular and serious fiction still obtains, but in a different sense than commonly assumed. Rather than creating a pristine aesthetic world defined in opposition to lower literary forms and everyday language, both authors work through parody, by dismembering and reassembling existing discourses into their own idiosyncratic fictional constructs.

Thus the period that marks the beginning of autonomy aesthetics already contains the seeds of its own critique. Peter Bürger's attempt to rewrite the history of art in terms of its institutions helps situate this phenomenon in a broader context. In his *Theory of the Avant-Garde*, Bürger calls attention to the fact that "works of art are not received as single entities, but within institutional frameworks and conditions that largely determine the function of the works."[26] He distinguishes between three broad phases in the history of the institution of art in Western society: the sacral art of the Middle Ages, the courtly art of the sort found in seventeenth-century France, and the bourgeois art that emerged in the course of the eighteenth century. Whereas in the first two periods

---

25. Greenblatt, *Renaissance Self-Fashioning*, 3.
26. Bürger, *Theory of the Avant-Garde*, 12. See Christa Bürger, *Der Ursprung der bürgerlichen Institution Kunst*, for specific discussion of literature in its institutional context in Germany during the late eighteenth century. See also the essays included in *Aufklärung und literarische Öffentlichkeit*, ed. C. Bürger, P. Bürger, and J. Schulte-Sasse. All of these critics are indebted to Habermas's earlier study of the *Strukturwandel der Öffentlichkeit*. Hohendahl helps situate these writers in the history of German literary criticism (*The Institution of Criticism*, esp. 35-36).

art is subordinate to either the church or the state, only bourgeois art is produced by individuals for individual consumption. Rather than giving glory to God or the king, "this art is the objectification of the self-understanding of the bourgeois class. Production and reception of the self-understanding as articulated in art are no longer tied to the praxis of life."[27]

Within any given epoch we can of course trace the development of a particular artist or specify differences between successive schools. At moments of crisis, however, the framing institutional context itself becomes visible. Bürger identifies one such moment in the historical avant-garde of the early twentieth century. In their attempt to "reintegrate art into the praxis of life," Dadaists went beyond the critique of individual artistic works or movements to challenge the concept of aesthetic autonomy itself.[28] By employing such unconventional materials as bottle driers and urinals in his Ready-mades, for example, Marcel Duchamp did more than modify a particular sculptural tradition: he exposed the cultural conventions that create the seemingly self-evident category of the aesthetic. He insisted, that is, that there is nothing intrinsically artistic about the work of art; rather, art *is* whatever is viewed *as art*.

Dadaism was restricted to a relatively small number of intellectuals and lasted less than a decade. Since the 1960s, however, the questions first raised by the members of the avant-garde have returned on a large scale as a symptom of the cultural condition François Lyotard has diagnosed as postmodern. As the term indicates, postmodernism has been viewed as either a reaction against or a development within high modernism. The postmodern work of art crosses boundaries and reverses hierarchies sacred to modernism, in particular the boundary between art and life and the hierarchy of serious over popular or mass culture.[29] However, these divisions do not originate in twentieth-century modernism, but rather in the autonomy aesthetics that emerged toward the end of the eighteenth century. Thus from our current perspective the eighteenth century takes on particular interest, for it marks an earlier period of crisis in the institutional history of art in which writers struggled to establish the aesthetic principles that are once again being called into question today.

If the historical avant-garde anticipates questions raised by today's postmodernists, then the parodic fiction of the German romantic novelists anticipates the insights of the avant-garde. Of course, the differences

27. Bürger, *Theory of the Avant-Garde*, 47.
28. Bürger, *Theory of the Avant-Garde*, 22.
29. Huyssen argues convincingly that American postmodernism of the 1960s can be viewed as a continuation, with variations, of the European avant-garde of the 1920s ("Mapping the Postmodern," in *After the Great Divide*, 178-221).

between the various periods are considerable and should not be obscured. Whereas today's postmodernism is international, multimedia, and open to the voices of women and minorities, these romantic *Bildungsromane* remain the literary product of a patriarchal and provincial national culture. With these reservations in mind, we could nevertheless go so far as to view romantic fiction as itself a form of the postmodern in the sense suggested by Lyotard: "Postmodernism thus understood is not modernism at its end but in the nascent state, and this state is constant."[30]

To sum up: in the following pages I will examine moments of literary self-consciousness in the *Bildungsroman* as reflections on the rapid transformation of the German literary institution.[31] In doing so I view the novels as examples of what Patricia Waugh has called "metafiction," that is, "fictional writing which self-consciously and systematically draws attention to its status as an artifact in order to pose questions about the relationship between fiction and reality."[32] By concentrating on the interaction between literary form and institutional context in these novels, it becomes possible to mediate between the extremes of those who would view literature as a mere reflection of historical conditions and those who would maintain the purity of the aesthetic object. Literature in this view neither repeats reality nor does it escape reality; instead, it *transforms* reality, and the *Bildungsroman* is the genre that examines this transformation.

In defining the *Bildungsroman* as metafiction I have deliberately sidestepped the question of genre. Even a cursory reading of studies devoted to the German novel reveals that the term *Bildungsroman* is as problematic as it is ubiquitous. At first we are liable to be struck by the frequency with which the label is applied to texts. Critics not only introduce the term to discuss novels ranging from Grimmelshausen's *Simplicissimus* (1669) to Botho Strauß's *Der junge Mann* (1984), but also to analyze such less likely candidates as Wolfram's *Parzival* (1200-1210) or even Schiller's *Über die ästhetische Erziehung des Menschen*. More often than not, however, we discover upon further reading that the text originally designated as a *Bildungsroman* turns out not to be an example of the genre after all. Critics repeatedly invoke the generic category

30. Lyotard, *The Postmodern Condition*, 79.
31. Voßkamp, in "Gattungen als literarisch-soziale Institutionen," suggests that the German *Bildungsroman* offers a good example for the study of literary types. In his brief comments he particularly emphasizes the link between the emergence of the *Bildungsroman* and the dichotomization of the literary institution during the last decades of the eighteenth century (36).
32. Waugh, *Metafiction*, 2.

only to deny its appropriateness for the discussion of a particular text: whatever this work may be, it is most certainly *not* a *Bildungsroman!* This puzzling situation leads to two related questions: (1) instead of asking what a *Bildungsroman* "is," we ask why it is that previous definitions of the genre have proven so unsatisfactory, and (2) given that critics seem so dissatisfied with the term *Bildungsroman,* why do they continue to use it?

The key to answering the first question lies in the temporal gap between the historical context of the novels themselves and that in which their genre was defined, and in the gap between those contexts and our current perspective: we in the late twentieth century are reading eighteenth-century texts through the lens of a nineteenth-century definition. Although Karl Morgenstern gets credit for having invented the term *Bildungsroman,* Wilhelm Dilthey introduced it into common usage. In such works as Goethe's *Wilhelm Meisters Lehrjahre* and Hölderlin's *Hyperion,* writes Dilthey, we see "how he [the youth] enters life in a blissful daze, searches for kindred souls, encounters friendship and love, but then how he comes into conflict with the hard realities of the world and thus matures in the course of manifold life-experiences, finds himself, and becomes certain of his task in the world."[33] The hero of the classical *Bildungsroman,* as Dilthey defines it, engages in the double task of self-integration and integration into society. Under ideal conditions, the first implies the second: the mature hero becomes a useful and satisfied citizen. Viewed in this way, the *Bildungsroman* is a fundamentally affirmative, conservative genre, confident in the validity of the society it depicts, and anxious to lead both hero and reader toward a productive place within that world.[34]

With this definition of the genre firmly in hand, Jeffrey Sammons set out a few years ago to solve "The Mystery of the Missing *Bildungsroman,*"

---

33. Cited from Selbmann, ed., *Zur Geschichte des deutschen Bildungsromans,* 120. This volume contains a useful anthology of major articles on the genre. Martini was the first to recognize that Karl Morgenstern had used the term before Dilthey ("Der Bildungsroman"). Although the genre's existence has been questioned frequently in recent years, there is no shortage of secondary literature on the *Bildungsroman.* See Köhn, *Entwicklungs- und Bildungsroman* (1968), Jacobs, *Wilhelm Meister und seine Brüder* (1972), Selbmann, *Der deutsche Bildungsroman* (1984), Mahoney, *Der Roman der Goethezeit* (1988), and Jacobs and Krause, eds., *Der deutsche Bildungsroman* (1989), for the history of the genre and extensive bibliography.

34. "*Bildungsroman* wird er heißen dürfen, erstens und vorzüglich wegen seines Stoffs, weil er des Helden Bildung in ihrem Anfang und Fortgang bis zu einer gewissen Stufe der Vollendung darstellt; zweytens aber auch, weil er gerade durch diese Darstellung des Lesers Bildung, in weiterm Umfange als jede andere Art des Romans, fördert" (Morgenstern, "Ueber das Wesen des Bildungsromans," 64).

only to discover that one nineteenth-century German novel after the next failed to fit into the pattern allegedly established by Goethe. If we were to continue Sammons's search into the twentieth century, we would also be hard put to find a novel that fits Dilthey's description of the genre. In both cases we might well argue that we are dealing with late, ironic variants of a literary tradition with close ties to the *Humanitätsideal* of late eighteenth-century Germany.[35] Yet matters seem little better even in the supposed heyday of the genre. In novel after novel protagonists fail to mature into self-confident, autonomous individuals; the expected integration into an affirmed society yields to alienation from an unacceptable reality. A number of critics have questioned whether even *Wilhelm Meister* really fits Dilthey's definition of the *Bildungsroman,* emphasizing both the degree of resignation involved in Wilhelm's maturation and the oppressive nature of the Tower Society. With the exception of Jung-Stilling, who grows increasingly self-congratulatory in the course of his *Lebensgeschichte,* we are left with Hoffmann's cat as the only character who measures up to Dilthey's standard, and even he dies before he can complete his autobiography.

Dilthey, it would seem, got it all wrong. Or to state the point more judiciously, Dilthey approached these novels with certain presuppositions that we no longer share. It is not that we now can see the novels for what they really are, although we may formulate our arguments as if that were the case. Rather, we have changed the way we read. Literature worth its salt is problematic, we have been told by critics on both sides of the Atlantic, whether in terms of the author's unwillingness to convey a single, unequivocal meaning, or in terms of the text's critical commentary on its contemporary society. From today's perspective, Dilthey's understanding of the *Bildungsroman* seems better suited to the large number of popular "novels of education" published in the second half of the eighteenth century.[36] Hegel in fact already satirizes the genre in his *Ästhetik:* however many vicissitudes the hero may

---

35. Swales, *The German Bildungsroman,* 14. "Die meisten Autoren stimmen wenigstens darin überein, daß der (deutsche) 'Bildungsroman' eine Leistung Goethes und seiner Zeitgenossen ist, daß man auf jeden Fall vorher keine nach Gehalt und Gestalt präzis vergleichbaren Romane finden wird. Es scheint deshalb sinnvoll, den Begriff historisch zu verstehen" (Köhn, *Entwicklungs- und Bildungsroman,* 303). See also Martini, "Der Bildungsroman," 263, and Jacobs, *Wilhelm Meister und seine Brüder,* 14.

36. "Indem der Bildungsroman zur historischen Gattung wird, gleiten die Definitionsversuche an ihm ab und beschreiben Erzählstrukturen, wie sie nur mehr für den Trivialroman der jeweiligen Zeit Gültigkeit haben!" (Selbmann, *Der deutsche Bildungsroman,* 17). As Stanitzek has argued, Morgenstern's earlier definition of the *Bildungsroman* coincides with common assessments of the novel in general around 1800 ("Bildung und Roman als Momente bürgerlicher Kultur," 418). He goes on to investigate depictions of *Bildung* in a

face, "in the end he usually gets his girl and some sort of job, gets married and becomes a Philistine just like the others."[37] Measured against this standard, it is hardly surprising that critics hesitate to label a particular text a *Bildungsroman,* since to do so would be tantamount to stamping the novel with a seal of mediocrity. While Horatio Alger stories may interest the cultural historian, they are unlikely to attract the sustained attention of readers trained to look for socially critical or self-deconstructing literary texts.

Twentieth-century German history adds particular urgency to the dissatisfaction with the *Bildungsroman.* The affirmative understanding of art that seems merely quaint in the work of Morgenstern and Dilthey takes on sinister connotations during the period of National Socialist rule. It was all too easy to transfer the ideology of *Bildung* from the individual to the state. Thus in 1941 Hans Heinrich Borcherdt praises Hans Grimm's *Volk ohne Raum* as a novel in which "all of Germany [appears] as the hero of the work" and speaks of the protagonist of another Grimm novel as the personification of "the struggle of the German soul for a new peculiarly German knowledge of nature and the world" ["das Ringen der deutschen Seele um eine neue arteigene Natur- und Welterkenntnis"].[38] Karl Schlechta's bitter rejection of the authority figures of the Tower Society in his 1948 study of *Wilhelm Meister* becomes understandable in the light of this blatant abuse of literature as propaganda. While German critics of the 1950s and early 1960s tend to concentrate on formal textual analysis, the reception theory born in the politically charged climate of 1968 has encouraged a new generation of critics to subject Germany's "spiritual heroes" to renewed critical scrutiny.[39] As a result, the *Bildungsroman,* with its apparent faith in the self and society, referentiality and poetic closure, seems to be both poetically and ideologically outdated.

Or rather: certain forms of discourse *about* the *Bildungsroman* seem poetically and ideologically outdated. For, as Adena Rosmarin points out, genres do not function as preexistent categories in search of suitable

---

wide variety of often-neglected late eighteenth-century novels. See also Germer's *The German Novel of Education from 1764 to 1792,* which contains an extensive bibliography.

37. Hegel, *Ästhetik,* 568.

38. Cited from Selbmann, ed., *Zur Geschichte des deutschen Bildungsromans,* 209, 212. See also Selbmann's introduction to this volume on the appropriation of the *Bildung* by German nationalists around the turn of the century (24). He notes that Borcherdt fills the above-cited essay "mit den zu erwartenden Tributen an den Zeitgeist" (27).

39. I refer to the title of Anselm Kiefer's monumental painting, "Deutschlands Geisteshelden" (1973); reproduced in Rosenthal, *Anselm Kiefer,* 28-29, plate 10. See Holub's opening chapter (*Reception Theory*) for an excellent discussion of the historical roots of German reception theory.

objects already "out there" in the world, but rather as "the critic's heuristic tool, his chosen or defined way of persuading his audience to see the literary text in all its previously inexplicable and 'literary' fullness and then to relate this text to those that are similar or, more precisely, to those that may be similarly explained."[40] Martin Swales's introduction to his study of the *Bildungsroman* provides a good example of how the genre can be redefined to produce more satisfying interpretations of individual works. Rather than seeking novels that rigidly adhere to a specific pattern, he claims that "as long as the model of the genre is intimated as a sustained and sustaining presence in the work in question, then the genre retains its validity as a structuring principle within the palpable stuff of an individual literary creation."[41] For Swales, the essential characteristic of the various *Bildungsromane* is their "pervasive tentativeness," "obliqueness," and "consistently sustained irresolution."[42]

Swales's pragmatic understanding of the genre allows us to move away from the question of whether or not a particular novel fits into a prefabricated mold, and I am willing to follow his lead and speak of the novels examined here as *Bildungsromane*. This does not mean that I am satisfied with his concentration on ambiguity as the salient feature of the novels, as it threatens to reduce historical differences between the works to a problem shared by each protagonist.[43] In order to specify differences between texts, we have to view them in historical, biographical, and institutional context. Nevertheless, Swales does manage to redefine the genre in a way that renders it more palatable to contemporary critical taste. As a result, we can discard the awkward category of the *Antibildungsroman,* a term that says little more than that a given novel fails to conform to a simplistic understanding of *Wilhelm Meisters Lehrjahre.* [44]

40. Rosmarin, *The Power of Genre,* 25.
41. Swales, *Bildungsroman,* 12.
42. Swales, *Bildungsroman,* 30, 34, 35. Sorg also stresses the lack of narrative closure in the *Bildungsroman:* "Dadurch entsteht in den Bildungsromanen eine Spannung, ans Ziel kommen zu wollen, gleichwohl aber ständige Belege anführen zu müssen, weshalb dies nicht überzeugend gelingen kann, die nur um den Preis der Ideologie aufzulösen ist" (*Gebrochene Teleologie,* 46).
43. According to Swales, all are caught "between the *Nebeneinander* (the 'one-alongside-another') of possible selves within the hero and the *Nacheinander* (the 'one-after-the other') of linear time and practical activity, that is, between potentiality and actuality" (*Bildungsroman,* 29).
44. In making this comment I in no way mean to belittle Gerhart Mayer's excellent analysis of four novels under the rubric of the *Antibildungsroman.* I do question the unproblematic understanding of Goethe's novel that functions as the starting point for his analysis. His introduction of the term *Antibildungsroman* into the discussion of the genre typifies a number of recent attempts to circumvent interpretive difficulties by inventing new terminology. Thus Selbmann attempts to distinguish between *Bildungsstruktur,*

As Swales views the genre, any *Bildungsroman* worth reading, including *Wilhelm Meister,* is always an *Antibildungsroman.*[45]

Why then continue to use the term at all? If, to quote Rosmarin again, "there are precisely as many genres as we need,"[46] why do we still need the *Bildungsroman?* In one rather apologetic view, we should acknowledge that the genre is an "embarrassment," but one that serves a limited purpose as "a place-holder at best."[47] I would argue that there is a more compelling reason why critics continue to invoke the genre, if only to dispute its existence: it legitimates the interpretive act. For reasons we have seen, contemporary readers are liable to suspect the *Bildungsroman* on both poetical and political grounds. At the same time, however, they are also well aware that literary histories of "important" German novels around 1800 tend to be roughly identical to histories of the *Bildungsroman.* Different genres have always had different cultural status; among German novels, the *Bildungsroman* has traditionally enjoyed the most prestige.

The critic confronts a dilemma: on the one hand, to label the object of interpretation something other than a *Bildungsroman* —for example, an epistolary novel, a Gothic novel, or a *Familienroman* —is to signal that the work is perhaps of historical interest, but probably second-rate as a work of literature. Again, I refer not to the inherent quality of a given text, but to perceptions generated by critical tradition. On the other hand, to declare the novel a *Bildungsroman* outright is to risk ridicule as a hopelessly conservative, mystified reader. The solution lies in denial: by first raising the question as to whether or not the text is a *Bildungsroman,* the critic establishes its importance; by then concluding that the novel is not a *Bildungsroman* after all, the critic suggests that it is profoundly problematic, and hence not to be confused with either *Trivialliteratur* or trivializing readings of serious fiction. The interpretive digression through the category of the *Bildungsroman* is thus doubly reassuring: we can enjoy a work of art that has the appropriate cultural cachet and still appease our critical conscience in the conviction that we are devoting our time to a sufficiently sophisticated narrative.

Bildungsgeschichte, and *Bildungsroman* in his introduction to the genre (*Der deutsche Bildungsroman,* 38-41), while Ratz adds the term *Identitätsroman* to the clutter of *Erziehungsroman* and *Entwicklungsroman,* after dispensing with other recent suggestions such as *Individualroman, Sozialroman, Sozialisationsroman,* and *symbolischer Roman* (*Der Identitätsroman,* 3).

45. See also Janz: "Die Tradition des Bildungsromans zwischen 1795/96 und 1815 stellen Romane her, die jeweils vor Augen führen, daß sie keine Bildungsromane sind—jedenfalls dann nicht, wenn man die Gattung über den intendierten Ausgleich zwischen Individuum und empirischer Wirklichkeit definiert" ("Bildungsroman," 162).

46. Rosmarin, *The Power of Genre,* 25.

47. Amrine, "Rethinking the *Bildungsroman,*" 136.

This argument has played an important role in enabling the reassessment of several all-too-prestigious texts, particularly in postwar Germany. Yet it has outlived its usefulness. If we accept Swales's notion of an inherently self-critical genre, then there is no need to reintroduce the phantom of the affirmative *Bildungsroman* into the discussion of what are now generally acknowledged to be aesthetically complex and socially critical novels. Thus I will not rehearse the tired debate as to whether or not particular texts examined here "count" as *Bildungsromane*. Obviously I think they do, even if they provide an ironic commentary on the process of *Bildung* they portray. In the final analysis, however, I am less interested in what one calls the novels than in their function as metafictional commentaries on the changing public sphere. The critical detour through denial has been taken often enough; by now the term *Bildungsroman* is sufficiently familiar and problematic to justify its continued use, which enables us to avoid further arguments about terminology and get on with the interpretation.

Private Life in the Public Sphere: Heinrich Jung-Stilling's *Lebensgeschichte* (1777-1804)

2

Pietist autobiographies hold a pivotal position in the history of the German *Bildungsroman*. In many ways they look back to the long tradition of what M. H. Abrams has termed "Christian Psycho-Biography," which can be traced through the writings of medieval mystics and St. Augustine's *Confessions* to the story of Paul's conversion on the road to Damascus. In recounting the often dramatic events that led to the conversion of the former sinner, the writers in this tradition "internalize apocalypse by transferring the theater of events from the outer earth and heaven to the spirit of the single believer, in which there enacts itself, metaphorically, the entire eschatological drama of the destruction of the old creation, the union with Christ, and the emergence of a new creation—not *in illud tempus* but here and now, in this life."[1] For example, the Pietist Johann Henrich Reitz introduces his popular anthology of religious autobiographies, the *Historie der Wiedergebohrnen* (History of the Reborn) (1691-1701), with the following assertion: "Thus one can see how heaven with its secrets, indeed, how all of scripture *is in us:* hell, heaven, Adam, Christ, Cain, Abel, sin, justice, judgment, death, life, darkness and light."[2]

Precisely this stress on the individual's internalization of the Christian paradigm of salvation history makes the Pietist autobiography

---

1. Abrams, *Natural Supernaturalism,* 47.
2. Quoted from Reitz's unpaginated preface to the first volume of his collection.

important for the development of the secular *Bildungsroman.* Because the presence of God's grace in one's life could only be determined by the individual's concentration on his or her feelings, the Pietist autobiographers developed a sensitivity to their psychology and a language to express these inner states that prepared the way for the typically passive, introspective protagonists of the *Bildungsromane* to come.[3] Here again, Reitz's anthology provides interesting examples. His first volume consists primarily of short autobiographies of English women. Almost all follow the same formula: oppressed by an awareness of her sinfulness, each woman undergoes a conversion experience and concludes her narrative with a list of her newly won Christian beliefs. While this pattern remains constant, individual differences reveal themselves in the various events that precede conversion. The religious crises experienced by these women usually result from acute suffering brought on by life-threatening illness or accident, unwanted pregnancy, or the death of a husband or child. No less than five of the thirty-three women included in this volume seriously contemplate suicide before they are saved. Thus these religious autobiographies not only document the common faith of the believers, but also provide insight into the particular psychological states that precipitated the conversions.

Jung-Stilling's relation to the German Pietists is complex.[4] He was remembered by Goethe and his circle of friends in Straßburg as a man with "an unshakable faith in God," a traditional Pietist amidst a group of radical free-thinkers.[5] When Friedrich Nicolai published *Sebaldus Nothanker* (1773-76), which contained a critical portrait of the Pietists, Jung-Stilling was quick to publish an angry response, "since he believed that errors in religion should be lamented and mourned, but not ridiculed, for that would make a mockery of religion itself."[6] However, he almost

3. This type of hero, exemplified by Wieland's *Agathon,* was first described by Blanckenburg in his *Versuch über den Roman.* Lämmert's afterword to the facsimile edition of Blanckenburg's essay provides a good review of the general disrespect in which the novel was held in the 1770s, a prejudice that affected the initial reception of Jung-Stilling's fictional autobiography. Both Stahl ("Entstehung," 127-47) and Jacobs (*Wilhelm Meister,* 39-42) stress the importance of the Pietist autobiography for the development of the *Bildungsroman* as a genre.

4. Both Cunz ("Nachwort") and Gutzen ("Jung-Stilling") provide solid introductions to Jung-Stilling's biography. Pfeiffer-Belli's afterword is also informative, although both less detailed and less critical than Cunz and Gutzen. Vinke provides an extremely detailed account of Jung-Stilling's life between 1740 and 1775 (*Jung-Stilling und die Aufklärung,* 27-135).

5. *Dichtung und Wahrheit,* in *Goethes Werke: Hamburger Ausgabe* 9:370.

6. Jung-Stilling, *Lebensgeschichte* ("life history" or "autobiography"), in his *Sämmtliche Schriften* 1:342. All further references to the *Lebensgeschichte* will be cited in the text; translations are my own. Vinke closely examines the exchange between Jung-Stilling and Nicolai (*Jung-Stilling und die Aufklärung*).

immediately regretted the harsh tenor of his rash polemic. Elsewhere in the *Lebensgeschichte* he clearly distances himself from the Pietists, repeatedly chastising them for their intolerance. Jung-Stilling sums up his ambivalent relation to the Pietists in an ironic comment on the suspicion that greeted him when he arrived to assume a professorship in Mannheim. Here he had acquired the reputation of being a Pietist through his publications, and he was warned that in this Catholic region he must be very careful to avoid excessive discussions of religious matters: "Stilling agreed to all this and gave his sacred vow to observe everything very carefully. At the same time he had to laugh, for in Schönenthal he was [considered] a free-thinker, and now here a Pietist: so little truth lies in human judgment" (369).

The basic difference between Jung-Stilling's life and those of the *Stillen im Lande* (Pietists) is that he actively pursued a variety of careers that led him out of the privacy of an introspective rural existence into the public professions of doctor, professor, and writer. His decision to exchange the simple clothing of the Pietist for the attire of the educated professional man was enough to arouse the suspicions of both the local townspeople and his own grandmother. But this distrust of his outer appearance was symptomatic of a more deep-seated suspicion: "It was more than the newly won ruff and wig that distanced the Pietists from him. They sensed vaguely that here, for the first time, a representative of a secularized Pietist way of life had appeared who differed from such Pietists of the old school as Spener, Francke, and Spangenberg."[7]

This new type of public life, combined with a traditional belief in God and His providence, has a decisive effect on the form of the *Lebensgeschichte*.[8] While the plot of the autobiography recounts the

---

7. Cunz, "Nachwort," 375-76. Similar comments by Ritschl, *Geschichte des Pietismus* 1:524, and Günther, *Jung-Stilling*, 51. Hahn opens his study of Jung-Stilling's novels with a detailed and polemical survey of the critical literature, which culminates in the rather predictable assertion that Jung-Stilling was neither Pietist nor rationalist. Instead, he sought a "Mittelweg zwischen Pietismus und Aufklärung" ("Jung Stilling—Ein Pietist?" in his *Jung-Stilling*, 1-36, 30). In contrast, Vinke argues that Jung-Stilling remained "sein ganzes Leben hindurch ein seiner reformierten Kirche treu verbundener Pietist" (*Jung-Stilling und die Aufklärung*, 326). While Vinke presents a strong case for the consistency of Jung-Stilling's beliefs, the fact remains that his active life exposed him to new experiences and ideas that challenged this faith (see further comments below on Jung-Stilling's philosophical crisis). The ambivalence with which others perceived him indicates his distance from an earlier generation of believers.

8. Jung-Stilling published five separate volumes of his *Lebensgeschichte*. *Heinrich Stillings Jugend: Eine wahrhafte Geschichte* appeared in 1777; it describes Heinrich's childhood and introduces his parents and grandfather. *Heinrich Stillings Jünglings-Jahre* was published along with *Heinrich Stillings Wanderschaft* in 1778. Together these volumes trace his life up to his departure from Straßburg in 1772. *Heinrich Stillings*

events in Jung-Stilling's life that led him away from the strict religious upbringing of his father, these events themselves are constantly being interpreted by Jung-Stilling as evidence of God's ongoing presence in his life. The rhythm of the novel as a whole is marked by the constant attempt to recapture the external movement of the plot through religious interpretation, thereby sanctifying the otherwise secular course of his life. Thus the *Lebensgeschichte* becomes a key transitional text in the movement from the Pietist autobiography toward the secular *Bildungsroman*, as Jung-Stilling struggles to maintain the traditional form of the religious genre in constructing a narrative of a life that no longer conforms to the pattern of previous generations. The tension is precipitated by the young man's active engagement with the secular fiction of the emerging public sphere in Germany, and further complicated by the place of the opening segments of the fictionalized autobiography within that sphere. As a result, the book is no longer merely a passive reflection of the content of his life, but rather an exercise in "self-fashioning" that recalls the pattern Greenblatt has traced in the work of Thomas More, where the deliberate attempt to construct a public image eventually compels the author to conform to his own fiction.[9]

Jung-Stilling's ambivalence toward Pietism may well have had its roots in his highly unusual childhood. He was born into a pious, hardworking Protestant family that could trace its roots back to the Reformation. But when Heinrich's mother Dorothea died in his father Wilhelm's arms, the shaken man seized upon the teachings of the Pietists with a fervor that bordered on religious hysteria. Wilhelm decided to cut himself and his child off from any meaningful contact with the external world, and to devote what time his profession as a tailor left him to protracted grieving over the loss of his first wife, the study of Pietist texts, and the strict upbringing of his only child. Awakened

---

häusliches Leben (1789) documents Jung-Stilling's life up to about 1787, and *Heinrich Stillings Lehrjahre* (1804) continues the autobiography through 1803, when Jung-Stilling would have been 63 years old. He died in 1817, and that year Wilhelm Schwarz edited the fragmentary continuation of the autobiography that reaches only into 1805 (*Heinrich Stillings Alter*). Schwarz also included his own description of Jung-Stilling's final year and death, "Vater Stillings Lebensende." The Winkler edition (ed. Pfeiffer-Belli) gives publication details on p. 553.

9. Greenblatt examines "the complex interplay in More's life and writings of self-fashioning and self-cancellation, the crafting of a public role and the profound desire to escape from the identity so crafted" (*Renaissance Self-Fashioning*, 12-13). While most critics who have written on the *Lebensgeschichte* are aware of the limitations of Jung-Stilling's work, the tendency is to ascribe the gradual impoverishment of the text to personal flaws on the part of the author, rather than to tensions caused by the fictional autobiography's reaction to and participation within the changing public sphere.

regularly by his father's tearful prayers, and isolated from other children, it is not surprising that the young Heinrich grasped at any form of reading material as a means of escape from the narrow confines of his world. "Wilhelm never allowed the boy to play with other children. He kept him so isolated that in the seventh year of his life he still did not know any of the neighboring children—but he did know a whole series of beautiful books" (66).

As one might expect, Heinrich's early reading centers on the Bible, as well as some of the major writings of Protestant reformers like Luther and Calvin. He also reads Reitz's autobiographies and Gottfried Arnold's *Leben der Altväter* (Lives of the Patriarchs), a popular collection of stories about early Christian hermits in Egypt. This reading material encourages the sort of "intensive" reading described earlier, involving the repeated study of a limited number of religious texts for the purpose of centering the child in the traditional faith of his ancestors. At the same time, Heinrich is introduced to a wide variety of secular literature that encourages a different approach: that of "extensive" reading. Certainly Arnold's *Vitae Patrum* would have appealed to the boy at least as much for its exotic stories of mythological creatures and miracles, its graphic accounts of struggles in the desert with devils and wild beasts, as for its explicit Christian message. Heinrich also reads fairy tales and romances, and eventually becomes familiar with the major works of philosophy and literature of the century. For an individual like Karl Philipp Moritz, this sort of extensive reading will lead to a series of frustrating attempts to turn his life into the type of adventure encountered in works of fiction. Jung-Stilling responds as a member of an earlier generation. While his imagination is stimulated by works of fiction, he is satisfied by his vicarious participation in the adventures. Thus, when a cousin accuses him of developing unrealistic expectations in his life by reading too many novels, he emphatically denies the charge: "No! with the novels I only feel—it's as if everything that I read about were happening to me, but I have no desire at all to experience such things myself" (168). Instead of attempting to model his life on the adventurous world of the novel, Jung-Stilling judges the characters of secular stories according to his own Christian standards of morality. "Since he constantly heard people talking about God and pious people, he, without noticing it, adopted a perspective from which he viewed everything. The first thing he asked, when he read or heard about someone, concerned the person's attitude toward God and Christ" (67). As a result, Heinrich avoids open conflict between his religious and his secular reading experiences, for the extensive movement of the latter is recovered by interpreting it in light of the values dictated by the former.

We see this process in action in the opening two books of the autobiography. While they focus on Heinrich's youth, they also include a wide variety of ballads, fairy tales, and anecdotes that are often only loosely related to the main narrative. The inclusion of these novelistic (*romanhafte*) elements in the text reflects the influence of the Storm and Stress (*Sturm und Drang*) movement, inspired in part by Herder's appreciation of folk poetry (*Volkspoesie*). They undoubtedly contributed to the initial popularity of the work, and continue to make the opening books of the autobiography much more attractive than those lengthy portions written in Jung-Stilling's old age.[10] Yet just as Jung-Stilling managed to filter his perception of secular fiction through the values of his Christian education, these incidental stories often serve to reinforce implicitly the social and religious views adopted by the growing boy.

For example, a number of the anecdotes convey a strong message of political conservatism.[11] The calmly pious mood established in the opening pages of the work is disrupted by the news that Dortchen's father, Moritz, is being brutally beaten by three of the Junker's henchmen for having allegedly poached a snipe. The townspeople gather and threaten revolt, as we learn that the Junker had in fact granted Moritz permission to hunt. One might expect the scene to culminate in an indictment of the tyrannical petty aristocrats, such as one finds in Schiller's *Kabale und Liebe* (Intrigue and Love) and other works of the Storm and Stress. Instead, old Stilling and his sons quiet the rabble, and when the Junker returns home he punishes the offending servants and grants Moritz a generous sum of money. Order is restored by the benevolent father figure, who rewards his hardworking and loyal subjects. This tale of the just punishment of those who abuse their authority is repeated in the story of Johann Hübner, a hard-drinking cattle poacher who is finally slain by a Prince Christian, and again in the story of the evil knights of the Kindelsberg, who die of the plague after squandering the wealth of their silver mines and wasting food while others went hungry.

The second major theme of the poetic interludes in the text involves the fate of young virgins threatened with seduction. While these inserts clearly condemn the male aggressors, they also reveal a disturbing tendency to extend blame to their victims as well. The first ballad

---

10. Thus the editors of the popular Reclam edition of the work only reprinted the first half of the entire autobiography. Further comments on the degenerating quality of Jung-Stilling's work will follow.

11. Gutzen points out that Jung-Stilling later become a vehement opponent of the French Revolution ("Jung-Stilling," 457). Vinke suggests that this opposition was one factor that led him to become a novelist in the 1790s (351).

included in the autobiography tells the story of a knight who leaves his sister to travel to a foreign country. Left alone, the girl succumbs to the advances of the "Knight with the Black Horse," who entices her into his castle. Here she realizes that she is only one of many victimized maidens and promptly poisons herself and her would-be seducer. Like Emilia Galotti, the realization that she is susceptible to seduction is apparently enough to justify her death, although she does go one step further than Lessing's heroine by murdering the knight. A later ballad recounts the tale of a shepherdess raped by an impassioned young shepherd, who then comes to his senses and falls sobbing to the side of his unconscious victim, where he remains until both are dead. Once again, it is not merely the seducer who must suffer death for his actions, but also the raped woman. Another woman resists the advances of a murderous knight until he stabs her to death in a fit of rage. While Jung-Stilling provides no explicit evaluation of these incidents, his family's horrified rejection of a fallen woman who stops briefly at their house suggests strongly that the sin of illicit passion, whatever the circumstances, is unforgivable.

By the beginning of the third section of the *Lebensgeschichte, Heinrich Stillings Wanderschaft* (Travels), the various inserted tales fall away, as the narrative begins to focus exclusively on the life of the hero. Instead of interpreting secular fiction from a Christian perspective, Jung-Stilling now sets about interpreting the events of his own life. The logic that structures the autobiography from this point on is made explicit in the penultimate section of the completed work, entitled *Rückblick auf Stillings bisherige Lebensgeschichte* (A Backward Glance at Stilling's Previous Life-History), published in 1804. Here he sets out his two fundamental beliefs: first, that God exists as a guiding force in our lives, and second, that we have free will. When summarizing the major events of his life, Jung-Stilling concludes that each major turning point was not the result of his own decision, but rather revealed the active presence of God in his life. His repeated assertion that he was "merely passive material in the molding hand of the artist [God], clay in the hand of the potter" (599) typifies the passivity of previous generations of believers. For example, Reitz includes the following passage from John Bunyan's autobiography in the third volume of the *Historie der Wiedergebohrnen:* "Finally, I too discover a powerful submission of my will to God's will.... Let Him do with me as He wills! May my own desires die and make room for the will of Jesus!"[12]

However, Jung-Stilling's traditional faith is complicated by his knowl-

---

12. Reitz, *Historie der Wiedergebohrnen,* 198.

edge of contemporary intellectual developments. He has long been aware that belief in divine providence poses a problem for his contention that he has free will, a concern that has been intensified through his study of the philosophies of Leibniz and Wolff. The basic problem is the following: if it is true that each new event in the universe arises inevitably out of the events that preceded it, then appeals to God in prayer to alter this inexorable pattern are futile.[13] While Jung-Stilling expresses his confidence in being able to refute this heresy in the *Rückblick*, he prefers not to enter into a proof at this point. He has alluded to the solution previously in the *Lebensgeschichte*, however, where he claims that his understanding of the new Kantian philosophy helped solve this problem for him.[14] After reading the *Kritik der reinen Vernunft* Jung-Stilling feels that Kant has proven irrefutably "that human reason knows absolutely nothing beyond the boundaries of the sensory world — that whenever it judges according to its own principles it always runs into contradictions concerning spiritual matters, i.e., contradicts itself" (445). While Kant's proof of the limits of human knowledge will fling both Moritz and Kleist into an epistemological crisis, Jung-Stilling finds in Kantian philosophy indirect proof of the revelatory truth of scripture: "He found the source of spiritual truths in God's revelation to humanity, in the Bible, and the source of all truths that belong to this earthly life in nature and reason" (445). Jung-Stilling does not consider the possibility that the Bible may be a product of human imagination, and thus subject to potential error, or that human beings may not be able to perceive its message correctly. Instead, he feels that it reveals the metaphysical truth that human beings cannot discover on their own; it takes on the status of the *Ding an sich* that Kant insists cannot be perceived directly.

Jung-Stilling pursues a different argument in the *Rückblick*. Here he defends his belief in free will with a peculiar use of the contemporary concept of genius. There are many individuals who from the time of their birth are driven by their innate genius to excel in certain professions or as artists: "In every discipline one finds such aspiring individuals;

13. See Willert's detailed exposition of this philosophical problem in his *Religiöse Existenz*, esp. 62-70, 75-80.
14. Vinke argues that Jung-Stilling exaggerated the extent of his philosophical crisis in his missionary zeal to save others from similar doubts: "Die Kant-Lektüre bedeutet daher keinen Bruch in der geistigen Entwicklung Jung-Stillings, bietet sie ihm doch gerade die Bestätigung für seine schon immer vertretene Position.... In beiden Fällen übertreibt er. Die Verunsicherungen waren nicht so stark, und die Errettung aus ihnen war nicht so nachhaltig, wie er es darstellt" (*Jung-Stilling und die Aufklärung*, 319-20). While it is possible to reconstruct a more nuanced account of the historical Jung-Stilling today with reference to his private correspondence and notebooks, my concern is with the logic presented to the public in the *Lebensgeschichte* itself.

one calls them great men, great spirits, geniuses, etc." (586). Could it be Jung-Stilling's particular genius to devote all his energies to the Christian religion? Not at all, he concludes; his own basic impulse (*Grundtrieb*) pulls him toward the "extremely frivolous enjoyment of physical and intellectual sensual pleasure [*geistiger sinnlicher Vergnügen*]" (586-87). It is God who has instilled in him the opposing impulse that directs him toward Christianity. Thus while Goethe and his contemporaries use the concept of genius to assert their Promethean ability to rival the creative activity of God, Jung-Stilling uses the same concept to claim that his particular genius lies in the fact that God has chosen him to be a vehicle for His own ends.

The immediate problem, then, in recounting each major decision of his life, is to determine whether he chose to follow the will of God or was misled by his own sinful desires. A good case in point involves his impulsive decision to marry his first wife Christine. Jung-Stilling has agreed to spend the night sitting with the sickly young woman. At about two in the morning she wakes up from a brief slumber to tell Stilling that she has received "a very lively impression in her soul" (257), which, however, she feels she ought not articulate. Correctly suspecting what she has in mind, Jung-Stilling grasps her hand and proclaims that God has spoken and that they will be eternally joined in marriage. What follows is a very difficult marriage plagued by constant debts and Christine's ill health, until she finally dies some ten years later. The pressure of the small children left him from this marriage convinces Jung-Stilling that he must remarry, which leads him to rethink the series of events that led to his rash decision to propose to a woman he barely knew and who, as it now appeared to him, would have been better suited to a different sort of husband. Could it really have been God's will that guided him to his first marriage? He concludes that he was mistaken, "for it is the Christian's highest duty (while under the guidance of providence) to examine every step, and particularly the choice of a spouse, according to the rules of healthy reason and propriety, and when this has been properly observed, to await God's blessing" (393-94). Nevertheless, he concludes, the whole difficult experience has been good for him: "God had used his own corruption to cleanse him, to make him more and more pure, and his dear transfigured Christine had also withstood the test of fire, and was in this way perfected. Thus Stilling burst out in loud thanks to God, who had accomplished everything so well" (394).

I have recounted this episode in detail because it typifies the decision-making process in Jung-Stilling's life, and reveals the somewhat slippery logic he uses to convince himself of his belief in God and the presence of His guidance in his life. The most obvious problem is raised by his final prayer of thanks to God, cited above. Jung-Stilling begins the analysis of his first marriage by concluding that he has made a mistake, namely that he chose to follow his own sinful impulses rather than God's will. As he later concludes, what he really should have done was to think the matter through clearly, make a decision, and then wait for God's blessing. Nevertheless, within two paragraphs we find him bursting into praise of the God who used this mistake to cleanse him of his errors. In retrospect, the very deed that marked his deviation from God's will becomes God's method of purging his soul for future purity. In other words, Jung-Stilling would like to have things both ways: he proves his free will by admitting a mistake, and he simultaneously uses the exact same event to argue that God had his best interest in mind after all. In this way Jung-Stilling attempts to combine the Enlightenment's respect for human rationality with his faith in divine providence, but ends up caught within a hermeneutic circle, in which he first thinks the problem through logically, and then sanctifies his secular logic by proclaiming it the will of God.

Jung-Stilling's reflections on his first marriage provide a pattern for the various career decisions he makes in his life. At different times he feels himself destined to be a teacher, tailor, eye doctor, and professor. In each case, the decision to accept the new occupation suddenly reveals that the seemingly random events of his life are in fact stages on a path whose goal had been previously unknown to him, but which was in fact part of God's plan. From a purely logical standpoint, he often becomes entangled in the sort of contradictions detailed above. Yet the fascination his autobiography continues to exert lies less with the rigor of its logic than with its relentless depiction of the extreme hardship endured by Jung-Stilling and the resulting psychological trauma he suffered. At one point the father who beat him daily as a child actually attacks the exhausted young man as he returns home from a grueling day of physical labor on the farm (177). The extreme poverty, isolation, and mistrust he suffers as a tutor in Stollbein's family results in a drastic change in his appearance. "He had become so pale and haggard that he could no longer cover his teeth with his lips; his features were horribly distorted by grief.... everyone who saw him stared and then looked away in embarrassment" (219). As in the case of the poetic inserts examined above, however, Jung-Stilling minimizes the socially critical potential of such incidents by pressing them into a religious mold. In the final analysis suffering is never due solely to social or psychological causes for Jung-Stilling; rather, adversity is God's way of both punishing the sinner and indirectly guiding the believer to a new chapter of his life.

The act of writing the autobiography itself takes on particular significance in Jung-Stilling's search for the meaning of his suffering. By reflecting on the events of his life and organizing them into a coherent narrative, Jung-Stilling can perceive his past mistakes as evidence of divine providence. The autobiography also has public significance. As he tells us in the *Rückblick,* before his autobiography he had written a few religious books that enjoyed no real success. His autobiography, in contrast, won him sudden popularity and became his forum for disseminating his ideas to a wide public. For this reason he can claim that the autobiography itself is the single most important step in devoting his life to God: "Thus Stilling's *Lebensgeschichte* laid the first important foundation to my true destiny and to the pursuit of my basic religious impulse" (596).

However, the public reception of the *Lebensgeschichte* was not without a certain ambivalence. The *Lebensgeschichte* was first conceived in Straßburg as an attempt to justify Jung-Stilling's own beliefs amidst those of Goethe and his group of liberal friends. However, Goethe's unsolicited help in the publication of the manuscript had the opposite effect of what Jung-Stilling had intended, in that it aroused the suspicions of his native townspeople: "For while the publication of the story of his youth brought him great fame outside of Elberfeld, there it associated him with precisely that circle he had hoped to convert."[15] From the opposite perspective, Goethe in later years would have nothing to do with Jung-Stilling's increasingly self-righteous defense of traditional religious views. Thus the conflicting feelings that marked Jung-Stilling's relationship with the Pietists from the beginning were only intensified by the publication of his autobiography.

From this point on Jung-Stilling leads a double existence. On the one hand, he is the *Hofrat* Jung, an extroverted Pietist who periodically continues work on his autobiography in the attempt to discover evidence of God's plan for his life and for the purpose of solidifying the faith of his readers. On the other hand, he is Heinrich Stilling, hero of a popular book whose initial appeal was due at least in part to its incorporation of preromantic inserts that extended the boundaries of the religious autobiography. Of course, anonymity in publishing was an accepted eighteenth-century convention, and the initiated knew that the fictional Stilling was actually Jung. Yet this transformation of a private life into public fiction reinforces the impression that Jung-Stilling straddled two distinct phases in the development of the public sphere in Germany, just as a child he had engaged in both the "intensive" reading of one generation and the "extensive" reading of another.

15. Gutzen, "Jung-Stilling," 449.

As the second half of the work continues, his disguised autobiography becomes both his calling card and his character reference. It precedes him on his journeys, winning him both sympathy and suspicion. It even gets him a second wife. His marriage to Selma is arranged by Sophie de la Roche before the two ever meet. Yet when Jung-Stilling proposes to her he is able to claim that his "character is just like I described it in my *Lebensgeschichte*... (for she had read his story)" (400). Thus the religious autobiography of the unorthodox Pietist helps to establish his reputation as it becomes part of the public sphere, even as the work itself is conceived in reaction to the more liberal values that sphere helped develop. The private search of the Christian autobiographer for God becomes the letter of introduction for the extroverted Pietist Jung-Stilling.

Toward the end of the work he finally sheds his pseudonym to reveal what had long since become an open secret, namely that the *Hofrat* Jung and Heinrich Stilling are in fact one and the same person (583). This revelation leads Jung-Stilling to pose the rhetorical question "whether my entire story, as I have told it in *Heinrich Stilling's Youth, Adolescence, Travels, Life at Home,* and *Apprenticeship,* is indeed really true" (584). The answer, of course, is yes; there are certain embellishments (*Verzierungen*) in the opening chapters, disguised names of persons and places in later sections, until in the final pages he simply records the unadorned facts. In this way Jung-Stilling seeks to counter the ambivalent response evoked by the earliest segments of the work to make it seem more like a conventional religious autobiography. He succeeds only too well.[16] The appeal of the first chapters is enhanced by Goethe's editing; he added little or nothing to the manuscript, but he did delete a substantial number of religious passages he felt detracted from the poetic nature of the text.[17] Midway through the work Jung-Stilling holds our attention with the distressing account of his financial, psychological, and marital difficulties, as well as with his firsthand accounts of Goethe's life in Straßburg. Nevertheless, it is hard to imagine that even Goethe's editing could have salvaged some of the final segments of the work. It gradually degenerates into a dreary list of names and places encountered by the aging Jung-Stilling, interspersed with the

16. Boeschenstein refers to Jung-Stilling's work as "Traktätchen-literatur... in riesigem Masse" (*Deutsche Gefühlskultur* 1:76). Stecher speaks of the conclusion as "schier unerträglich und der Bankerott seiner Autobiographie" (*Jung-Stilling als Schriftsteller,* 36). Other critics cited in this discussion are similarly critical of the concluding sections of the work.

17. Gutzen, "Jung-Stilling," 449.

repeated assertion that his life has an exemplary status as proof of his religious convictions.

It is quite plausible to suggest that Jung-Stilling's seemingly exaggerated sense of self-importance in the concluding pages of his autobiography barely conceals an inferiority complex,[18] or a sense of repressed religious crisis.[19] Jung-Stilling repeatedly develops penetrating social and psychological analyses that are abruptly cut off with reassertions of traditional religious faith. But the most obvious motivation for the increasingly didactic and self-congratulatory tenor of the text lies in the author's awareness of himself as a self-created public figure. The book itself takes on a public life that exerts pressure on its author to live up to the expectations created by his fiction.[20] If the self-analysis involved in the act of writing his autobiography enables him to discover evidence of God's providence in his past, then his life must continue to bear witness to His guidance in the present. When writing about his youth Jung-Stilling has the benefit of hindsight, which enables him to produce a positive interpretation of troublesome episodes, such as his first marriage, that seem to contradict his initial conviction that his actions are in accordance with God's will. When writing the last volumes of the autobiography, however, Jung-Stilling has no such advantage. Ignorant of the future, he cannot afford to admit a mistake in the present. He has outlived his autobiography, and his last years are merely a postscript to a life already concluded in public.[21]

---

18. Cunz, "Nachwort," 402.

19. Gutzen, "Jung-Stilling," 453.

20. Vinke points out that the older Jung-Stilling kept a private diary in secret script in which he confessed doubts that he excluded from the *Lebensgeschichte* (*Jung-Stilling und die Aufklärung*, 363).

21. In a literal sense, Schwarz's description of Jung-Stilling's death provides the public epitaph to his life. For all its gruesome detail in describing Jung-Stilling's gradual asphyxiation, however, the "Lebensende" seeks to confirm Jung-Stilling's own self-created image as a man of exceptional Christian faith. Thus the interpretive struggles of the earlier segments of the autobiography are as absent from the "Lebensende" as they are from the last volumes written by Jung-Stilling himself.

Creative Destruction: Karl Philipp Moritz's *Anton Reiser* (1785-90)

3

Jung-Stilling begins his fictional autobiography with a reverent depiction of his pious grandfather that sets the tone for the rest of the work. Some eight years later, Karl Philipp Moritz opened his *Anton Reiser* with a sketch of his father's religion similar in content to that of the *Lebensgeschichte,* but sharply different in tone. Moritz's father, Johann Gottlieb Moritz, was a regular participant in the meetings of a group of Quietists or Separatists led by Johann Friedrich von Fleischbein. Fleischbein had encountered the writings of the Quietist Jeanne Marie Bouvier de la Motte-Guyon (1648-1717) while travelling in France and devoted his life to their translation and to the dissemination in Germany of her brand of what Moritz derides as "dry, metaphysical fanaticism."[1] While Jung-Stilling had grown up in the devout atmosphere of a family whose faith had been nurtured in one small region for generations, Moritz's father became a sudden convert to an imported sect only after the death of his first wife. Moritz describes his conversion as the case history of a neurotic man, not as the record of one man's discovery of an incontrovertible truth.[2]

---

1. *Anton Reiser,* 2:13. Quotations of *Anton Reiser* are taken from the second volume of his works in the *Aufbau Verlag.* Unless otherwise noted, all subsequent references to Moritz's work will be cited from this edition with volume and page number included in the text.
2. As Minder explains in his analysis of Moritz's life and work, Quietists differed from the more common Pietists in their even greater stress on passive introspection in the

As Moritz recalls in *Anton Reiser,* his father's newfound religion had the primary effect of ruining his second marriage. Dorothee Henriette König was a strong believer in the adage that "faith without works is dead" (2:14) and thus had little patience for the utter passivity encouraged by Madame Guyon's mysticism. While she read her Bible regularly, she resisted her husband's attempts to read to her from Madame Guyon's numerous publications. "Thus the domestic tranquility as well as the peace and welfare of a family was disturbed for years by these unfortunate books, which one person probably understood just as little as the next" (2:15). The constant quarreling between Reiser's parents caused them to neglect their son, who later declared with bitter sarcasm that the only benefit of his father's religion was that it made him into a complete hypochondriac. The boy who had been "oppressed from the cradle" (2:15) felt by his thirteenth year that he had been "disgracefully cheated out of the pleasures of youth" (2:82).

This unhappy childhood sets the pattern for the remainder of the fictional biography, where Reiser's fortunes oscillate in a monotonous rhythm of despair followed by hope crushed by further disappointment.[3] The narrator repeatedly cites the circumstances of Reiser's youth as the decisive factor that prohibits him from attaining any sense of personal maturity or social utility before the novel breaks off. The very dissonance of this fragmentary conclusion reveals what Jung-Stilling's increasingly self-righteous autobiography seeks to conceal, namely that harsh social conditions prohibit satisfying personal development. "At bottom it was the feeling of humanity oppressed by middle-class circumstances that overwhelmed him and made his life hateful to him" (2:324). Lacking any sense of self-esteem as an adolescent, he is all too willing to blame himself for poor study habits, his excessive reading, and his debts:

---

mystic tradition: "Hier [Quietismus]: stille Selbstversenkung, schauerndes Aufsichnehmen einer Wanderung im Dunkeln, mit der Intuition als alleiniger Stütze. Dort [Pietismus]: nach außen aktive 'praxis pietatis' und in ihrem Dienst stets strenge Selbstprüfung, d.h. also Reflexion, und zielbewußter Wille" (*Glaube, Skepsis und Rationalismus,* 124). He argues that Moritz's "neurotic" father took the passivity of the Quietists one step further, using it as an excuse to sink into a completely inactive life after his first wife's death (57). *Anton Reiser* as a whole has close ties to Moritz's pioneering work in psychological studies; in fact, parts of the text were originally published in his *Magazin zur Erfahrungsseelenkunde* (Boulby, *Moritz,* 21). Stemme's "Die Säkularisation des Pietismus zur Erfahrungsseelenkunde" sketches Moritz's influence. Lothar Müller uses *Anton Reiser* as a starting point for his monumental history of psychology in the eighteenth century (*Die kranke Seele*).

3. Schrimpf emphasizes Reiser's lack of development in this novel: "Diesem immerwährenden Antagonismus entspricht der ständige Wechsel von Aufschwüngen und Niederbrüchen, von Weltüberhebung und realen Demütigungen, der den monotonen Rhythmus des Romans ausmacht" ("Moritz: Anton Reiser," 118).

"... for at that time he was unable to explain all these things as a natural result of his extremely restricted circumstances" (2:186).

Moritz carries through his self-analysis with an unflinching openness that is all the more effective for its understated presentation of the environment that made his early years so unhappy. Yet Jung-Stilling's childhood and youth seem hardly less unhappy by comparison. What distinguishes *Anton Reiser* from the *Lebensgeschichte* is not that the protagonist suffers more, but that Moritz is no longer willing to justify his suffering as part of a divine plan.[4] While his introspective work has its roots in the tradition of the Pietist autobiography, it lacks the conversion experience that would place the events of his life into a meaningful perspective. Nor can he give his fictional autobiography the type of closure he describes in secular terms in his essays on aesthetics. Anton Reiser remains suspended between two worlds, between a religious worldview he can no longer accept and an aesthetic ideal that he cannot yet attain.[5] As a result, Moritz's writing becomes the paradoxical sort of creative destruction he describes in his *Fragmente aus dem Tagebuche eines Geistersehers* (Fragments from the Diary of a Ghost-Seer) (1787): "Since we were unable to become God-like creators, we became destroyers; we created backwards, since we could not create forwards. We created a world of destruction, and then considered our work in history, tragedy, and poetry with pleasure."[6] In writing *Anton Reiser* Moritz first constructs and then contemplates the ruins of his own life.

The unhappiness that Moritz later attributes to the detrimental effects of a bad environment is experienced as a religious crisis by the young Anton Reiser. As a boy Anton is eager to have the sort of personal

---

4. "Der Wert des 'Reiser' als eines psychologischen und soziologischen Dokumentes liegt gerade darin, daß er es verschmäht, zu harmonisieren. In *dieser* Hinsicht ist er sogar Goethes 'Wilhelm Meister' überlegen" (Schrimpf, "Moritz: Anton Reiser," 119).

5. As Kestenholz has suggested, the process of secularization engenders the constitution of the (problematic) self in German Idealism: "So kann an Moritz besser als an den großen Männern der deutschen Klassik und des Deutschen Idealismus aufgezeigt werden, inwiefern die Hypostasierung des Subjekts in der Subjektivitätstheorie der Zeit nicht nur begleitet wird von Ich-Verlust, Sinn-Verlust und Agnostizismus, sondern sich in einem komplexen Wechselspiel Erfahrungen diesen Zuschnitts geradezu verdankt. Die Höhe und Reinheit des auf Hypostase beruhenden Ideals spiegelt das Elend mangelnder Identitätsfindung in reziproker Umkehrung; die überbordenden Sinn-Konstrukte leben von intellektueller Orientierungslosigkeit — zunehmende Säkularisierung und zunehmende Sinn-Absicherung im klassischen Menschenbild laufen parallel" (*Die Sicht der Dinge*, 8).

6. Moritz, *Andreas Hartknopf*, 376. Further references to this edition are included in the text with page number and the abbreviation AH.

religious experience expected among members of his father's sect. However, he is soon troubled by images of God, the universe, and the self that render such experiences impossible. Madam Guyon encouraged her followers to efface their personal identity in the hope of achieving a mystical union with God: "The entire household down to the lowest servant consisted exclusively of people who strove—or seemed to strive—only to return to their Nothingness (as Madame Guyon put it), to kill all passion and to eradicate all individuality" (2:11). Identity involves separation from God; thus the retreat into nothingness involves losing one's particular identity to merge with the primal unity of God, which contains everything.[7]

Instead of experiencing an *unio mystico,* Anton Reiser is disturbed by his conception of the universe as an infinitely receding structure, in which this world is encased in another world encased by yet another world in a never-ending progression: "Often when the skies were clouded over and the horizon narrowed he was afraid that the whole world was covered with the same sort of ceiling that covered the room where he lived, and when he thought beyond the vaulted ceiling the world itself appeared much too small, and it seemed to him as if it too must be confined in another world, and so on forever" (2:37). The same is true of his image of God. In a passage that seems to anticipate Kafka's parable of the doorkeeper, Reiser sees God not as one presence, but as an endless series of ever more remote figures: "He imagined God above the heavens, but every one, even the highest God his thoughts created, seemed too small and had to have an even higher God above him, in whom he completely disappeared, and so on into infinity" (2:38).[8]

Given these images of God and the universe, the very concept of an *unio mystico* becomes impossible, for there *is* no primal unity with which to merge. Nor is Anton Reiser convinced of the unity of his own self. Because all human beings live in time, he reasons, how can we say that we are the same person from one moment to the next? "At the end of his investigations his own existence seemed a mere deception, an abstract idea—a combining of the similarities that each successive moment in his life had with the ones that faded away" (2:239-40). Uncertain of his ability to know himself, Reiser also doubts his ability to perceive the world around him. The very words that enable him to conceive of space and time may only entrap him within his own consciousness: "Language

---

7. See Abrams on the roots of this thought in pagan and Christian Neoplatonism and the esoteric tradition (*Natural Supernaturalism,* 146-63).

8. I realize that Kafka's text need not be interpreted as a religious allegory. Nevertheless, the infinitely receding *structure* of his parable is strikingly similar to Anton Reiser's concept of God.

seemed to get in his way when thinking, but on the other hand, he was unable to think without language" (2:227).

Moritz pursues this thought at some length in the first volume of his allegorical novel *Andreas Hartknopf* (1786), written concurrently with the opening sections of *Anton Reiser*. Here he takes up the problem of the subjectivity of human perception posed by Kant's *Critique of Pure Reason* that had inspired Jung-Stilling to a renewed assertion of his religious faith. Hartknopf is unable to share in Jung-Stilling's confidence. Although he disdainfully refers to what he terms philosophical egoism as "the most tasteless [system] in the world," a "subtle madness" (AH, 140), Hartknopf is forced to entertain the possibility of "the most horrifying and terrible" idea (AH, 141), "that all beings outside of him were really only dream images within himself, and that he was the single solitary creature in this vast and desolate world, a world that had blown up like a bubble with him and that together with him would sink back into nothingness again" (AH, 140). Instead of renewing his faith in the revelatory powers of the Bible, Hartknopf trembles at the thought that reality may only be the fleeting hallucination of a creature who has emerged for a moment from the void.

This sense of self-entrapment also torments Anton Reiser: "The fact that he always had to be himself and could never be anyone else, that he was confined and imprisoned in himself, gradually brought him to a degree of despair that led him to the banks of the river that flowed through part of the city, to a place where there was no protective railing" (2:235). Suicide becomes the desperate alternative to mystical loss of the self in God: "Even the thought of his own destruction not only seemed pleasant, but even caused him a sort of titillating sensation when, at night, before falling asleep, he often vividly imagined the dissolution and the collapse of his body" (2:30). If not directed against himself, Reiser turns his violent impulses against his environment. Fascinated by the "animal dismemberability [tierische[r] Zerstückbarkeit]" (2:233) of his own body, he invents games in which he is the source of a randomly destructive power, smashing cherry pits when blindfolded, ceremoniously executing flies, and burning down cardboard cities (2:29).

These violent games become Moritz's nihilistic response to his lost faith in divine providence. As Abrams reminds us, the Christian paradigm of history is finite and "constitutes a sharply defined plot with a beginning, a middle, and an end, and a strongly accented sequence of critical events."[9] God created the world, man sinned, Christ was sent as the Redeemer, and on Judgment Day the believers will be saved and

9. Abrams, *Natural Supernaturalism*, 35.

everyone else will be damned for eternity. In contrast, Moritz entertains the possibility that time may be infinite and history a series of pointless repetitions. "The sand in the hourglass ran incessantly and the goal was there, nothing was between it but the monotonous recurrence of what was already present. The abyss yawned terribly close to the feet of the wanderer" (AH, 281). The sense of dread that Moritz expresses in this passage of *Andreas Hartknopf* carries over into Anton Reiser's morbid fascination with images of destruction. When a house burns down in his native city, Reiser finds himself hoping that the fire will not be extinguished, not, as the narrator explains, out of *Schadenfreude,* but rather "out of a dark premonition of great changes, migrations, and revolutions, where all things would take on a completely different shape and the previous uniformity would cease" (2:29-30).

This particular passage sounds like a presentiment of the apocalypse after all. But Reiser's vision of the transformation of this uniform world into something radically different stops short of affirming his belief in either personal salvation or the end of history. Rather, he delights in images of destruction because they negate a reality he finds unbearable. Nor can he expect to find solace in the sort of mystical experience advocated by Madam Guyon. His vision of an infinitely regressing series of gods renders union with one God impossible. One divinely planned universe yields to an infinite series of universes, each containing the next; a finite plot of history becomes eternal recurrence, and the self becomes a form of entrapment that is prevented from attaining certain knowledge of God, external reality, or even itself.

The thought of suicide represents Anton's most extreme response to the childhood depression that religion cannot cure. More frequently, however, he seeks escape through reading: "Reading had suddenly opened up for him a new world, whose pleasure could compensate to a certain degree for all of the unpleasant things in his real world. Whenever he was surrounded by nothing but noise and quarreling and domestic discord, or when he could not find a playmate, he then rushed off to his book" (2:18-19).[10] Reading enables him to compensate in his imagination for indignities suffered in reality: "Whenever his soul was degraded by a thousand humiliations in the real world, he practiced the noble qualities

---

10. Wuthenow stresses this compensatory function of reading in *Anton Reiser* in his brief look at the work. He also provides a detailed list of the various works that Reiser reads (*Im Buch die Bücher,* 87-95). Müller examines Reiser's *Lesesucht* in the broad context of the history of reading in the eighteenth century ("Symptome der kranken Seele," in *Die kranke Seele,* 322-75).

of magnanimity, determination, selflessness, and steadfastness each time he read or thought about a novel or a heroic drama" (2:174).

Sometimes Anton can even find the escape he seeks by focusing his thoughts on a single, misunderstood word. His pastor in Hannover is in the habit of punctuating his sermons with the slurred Low German phrase " 'You will get to *Heben* [heaven]' " (2:87). "The last word, which was always garbled, sounded like *Heben* to him, and this word or sound moved him to tears whenever he thought of it" (2:87). Somewhat later Anton becomes fascinated with a hymn that he mistakenly believes begins with the words "*Hylo* beautiful sun / Your rays' rapture [*Hylo schöne Sonne / Deiner Strahlen Wonne*]" (2:174). He discovers later to his great disappointment that he had merely misunderstood the pastor's Thuringian accent; the hymn really began with the words "Hide, o beautiful sun... [*Hüll o schöne Sonne*...]" (2:175). Why should Anton have been so attracted to the word *Hylo?* Not, as one might expect, because it had a particularly delightful meaning for him. Quite the contrary, the word attracts him precisely because it means nothing at all to him, which is to say that in his mind it could come to mean anything: "The word 'Hylo' itself transported him into higher realms and gave an extraordinary boost to his imagination, since he thought it was some sort of oriental expression that he did not understand, and into which for just that reason he could insert whatever sublime meaning he wanted" (2:174).

In these moments Reiser manages to escape himself and his surroundings in a way that compensates for the mystical experience he has been encouraged to seek. As such, his reading takes on a function that contrasts sharply with earlier tradition. Jung-Stilling reads religious texts to reaffirm his faith and measures the characters he encounters in secular fiction against the yardstick of his religious beliefs. Reiser's reading either obscures or transforms a world that lacks a unifying masterplot. In his most negative moments, Reiser refers to reading as a drug, an opiate that dulls the pain of daily life. More often, however, he delights in literature's ability to turn his perception of reality into something more pleasant.[11] This tendency begins during his apprenticeship in

---

11. Minder was the first to point out that Anton Reiser fluctuates between flight from the world and a desire to take part in it: "Die erste Reaktion von Moritz-Reiser besteht immer darin, sich vor den Gefahren der Welt in ein schützendes—anheimelndes, nicht unheimliches—*Dunkel* zu flüchten; die zweite Reaktion aber ist der immer heftigere Wunsch, dennoch am *Glanz* des Lebens teilzuhaben—ohne aber die eigene Sicherheit preiszugeben" (*Glaube, Skepsis und Rationalismus,* 41). See also Catholy, ch. 2, "Die Grundspannung des Moritzschen Lebensgefühls zwischen 'Ausbreitung' und 'Einschränkung' " (*Karl Philipp Moritz,* 29-40). This oscillation between extroversion and introspection has its roots in the Pietist tradition. In Reiser's case, however, this rhythm has been

Braunschweig. As long as he is not too cold, hot, or exhausted, he can occasionally pretend that his dull chores are part of a holy ritual of the sort he had encountered in stories of the Homeric world. When he returns home he plays with his younger brothers outside the city in a similar fashion. "He lost himself and wandered aimlessly with them in the forests, climbed high cliffs, and came upon uninhabited islands—in short, he realized his entire idealistic novel-world (*Romanenwelt*) with them, as best he could" (2:97).

As the novel progresses, Anton is no longer willing to restrict his amusements to such childish games. Rather, he seeks to realize to some degree the adventures and freedom of the novel-world in his adult life.[12] He initially wants to become a preacher, holding the townspeople in the sway of his rhetoric. Later, he embraces acting as an ideal profession, because it provides him with the opportunity to assume a series of new identities on stage. He also enjoys travelling, as he can see some of the sights he has previously only read about and because as a traveller he is free of his own past, able to adopt new roles among strangers. While engaged in the pursuit of an acting career, Reiser occasionally flirts with the idea of taking up other professions, only to discover that here too he is more interested in role-playing than reality: "Now suddenly the extremes of becoming a peasant or a soldier arose, and suddenly the poetic and theatrical was there again, for his ideas about peasants and soldiers again turned into a theatrical role that he acted out in his imagination" (2:351). Later he is attracted to the profession of a common laborer, until he notices "that his imagination deceived him again and that he once again was playing a role in his mind" (2:377). While wandering in delirium after having eaten practically nothing for days, he decides that the truth, namely that he is in search of a theater troupe, is "not novelistic enough" (2:383), so he invents the story that he is fleeing from a duel in which he wounded a young nobleman, just as he had pretended that his abject poverty upon arrival in Bremen was due to his having been led astray by gamblers (2:299).

---

transferred to his secular reading habits. See comments below on Reiser's intensive reading of Goethe and Shakespeare.

12. Boulby notes suggestively that "Anton Reiser as a figure in European literature owes no little of his importance to the fact that he is one of the very first characters in a novel who tries to live out his life as if it itself *were* a novel" (*Moritz*, 115). He attributes this tendency to "the final shattering of the cosmos of Christian society in the eighteenth century, the crumbling of the authoritarian aristocracy and the arrival on the scene of the autonomous radical" (115). To these general trends we can add the growth of fiction and the transformation of middle-class reading habits. Reiser typifies the extensive readers of the decade, both in his enthusiasm for current fiction and in the disappointment that resulted from the attempt to transform fiction into reality.

These last examples point to another characteristic of Anton Reiser that goes along with his gift for role-playing: he is a good liar. As a child he had learned that he could attract adult attention by faking religious experiences (2:60). After having been expelled briefly from school, Anton writes a letter begging forgiveness, in which he describes himself as one of the worst sinners in history, but he is aware that even this bold confession is itself a lie (2:213). He realizes later that he could never have been a good preacher for the same reason: "... for if he were to become a preacher, he would probably become a big hypocrite—despite the greatest heat of passion and the power of his declamation, he would only be playing a role" (2:307). But the alternative career of a poet provides no guarantee of sincerity. Incapable of even imagining what it would be like to be in love, he nevertheless constructs love poems by copying the appropriate sentiments from novels and his friend (2:292). He even works himself up into a state of grief that enables him to begin an elegy for a boy who actually died eight days later. "This time poetry really turned him into a hypocrite" (2:253).

In the final section of the novel, Reiser's combined interest in reading, travel, and the theater sends him out looking for a troupe of actors, but one thing after the next goes wrong: he runs out of money, narrowly avoids conscription into the army, and discovers that he is going bald. His desire to become an actor is also frustrated; one troupe rejects him, he exhausts himself in pursuit of a second company, and the fictional autobiography breaks off as Reiser learns that the next troupe he had hoped to join has just disbanded. It would be hard to imagine a greater contrast to Jung-Stilling's depiction of himself in the final chapters of the *Lebensgeschichte* as a devout old man secure in the faith of his forefathers. From the beginning Jung-Stilling has been convinced that the outward movement of his life has been contained within the benevolent embrace of providence, and his extensive reading habits pose no serious threat to his religious convictions. Anton Reiser reads with a desperation nurtured by the fear that his existence and the universe are hollow at the core.

Thus viewed in the context of the *Lebensgeschichte, Anton Reiser* appears at the end of a tradition. Whereas Jung-Stilling still tried to fit the extensive movement of his life into the pattern of previous religious autobiographies, Moritz is too sensitive to the destructive effect of his father's religious fanaticism on his family life to embrace this faith for himself. The cracks in the mold that Jung-Stilling tried to smooth over can no longer be concealed. Yet the work conceived within—and ultimately against—the tradition maintained by Jung-Stilling also contains the seeds of a more positive understanding of the individual, a reappraisal that points the way toward the aesthetics of German Classicism.

Already in the preface to the first volume of *Anton Reiser,* Moritz justifies his work in terms that directly contradict the emphasis on self-abnegation in Madame Guyon's writings. Here he argues that the seemingly trivial details of the following narrative are justifiable not for their own sake, but because of the light they shed on the inner development of the protagonist. "Granted, this is not so easy that every attempt of the sort must necessarily succeed—but at least the effort to direct the attention of people more toward themselves and to make their individual existence more important will never be completely useless, particularly from a pedagogical point of view" (2:9).

Humanism replaces mysticism, as individuals are deemed interesting in their own right, rather than sinful deviations from God's unity. Yet Moritz's new stress on the innate value of the individual represents not so much a complete break with past tradition as it does a transformation of religious beliefs into aesthetic concepts grounded in secular humanism.[13] In his essay "Über die bildende Nachahmung des Schönen" ("On the Imitation of the Beautiful in the Plastic Arts") (1788), Moritz transfers the self-sufficiency traditionally attributed to God to the autonomous individual: "The noble individual attracts our complete attention and admiration, without any consideration for anything else or for any advantage we might obtain for ourselves through his existence" (1:248).[14] The autonomous individual, in turn, becomes the model for the autonomous work of art. In the same year in which the opening book of *Anton Reiser* was published, Moritz wrote a short essay entitled "Über den Begriff des in sich selbst Vollendeten" ("On the Concept of That Which is Perfect in Itself") in which he was already developing the concept of aesthetic autonomy that only subsequently became important in the work of Kant, Schiller, and Goethe.[15] Here Moritz distinguishes between objects used for a specific purpose and works of art, which are said to be sufficient unto themselves: "In the consideration of the beautiful I shift the purpose from myself to the object: I view it not as something

13. See Minder, "Die religiöse Verwurzelung der Moritzschen Kunstlehre," in *Glaube, Skepsis und Rationalismus,* 246-56; Todorov, *Theories of the Symbol,* 156; and Woodmansee, "The Interests in Disinterestedness," 33.

14. "God is an end in himself, perfectly self-sufficient. To love him selfishly—as a source of private gains—would be to make of him a mere instrument or means of pleasure. An analogous relationship is established between the work of art and the 'aesthetic' attitude.... In its origins, the theory of the autonomy of art is clearly a displaced theology" (Woodmansee, "The Interests in Disinterestedness," 33).

15. The date of this essay (1785) disproves the common assumption that Moritz derived his ideas from Goethe in Rome. On Moritz's originality see Minder (*Glaube, Skepsis und Rationalismus,* 250), Szondi ("Antike and Moderne," 95), and Todorov (*Theories of the Symbol,* 149-50).

perfected in me, but rather in itself" (1:196). Just as Moritz finds the "noble individual" superior to the merely useful person, he also rates the autonomous work of art above the simple tool: "Now, since I am fond of the beautiful for its own sake, and of the useful merely for my own sake, the beautiful grants me a higher and less self-interested pleasure than the merely useful" (1:196).

The emergence of the concept of autonomous art in Moritz's essays signals a significant change in the understanding of the work's relation to reality. "The key event in this development was the replacement of the metaphor of the poem as imitation, a 'mirror of nature,' by that of the poem as heterocosm, 'a second nature,' created by the poet in an act analogous to God's creation of the world."[16] As Goethe will express it, the completed work of art is both part of nature, since it is a product of man, but also more than nature, nature refined to its essence through human consciousness.[17] Instead of reflecting external reality, the work now exhibits internal coherence that reproduces in miniature the order of the macrocosm. In spatial terms, Moritz argues that each work should be organized around a central point that he alternately terms a "focal point" (*Brennpunkt*) (1:260) or a "point of perfection" (*Vollendungspunkt*) (1:263). In this spirit Goethe will praise the centripetal pull of the artist's composition in the sculpture of "Myron's Cow"[18] and admire the delicate balance of disparate elements in "Laokoon."[19] The visual harmony of the "Laokoon" sculpture is matched by the artist's shrewd selection of the proper "pregnant moment" for the simultaneous representation of the incident narrated sequentially by Virgil.[20] Thus a diachronic progression is sublated into a single moment that implicitly contains both past and future. That is, the autonomous work of art is self-reflexive, "mirroring itself in all its parts," and thus self-sufficient, "complete in itself," having "the final purpose and the intention of its existence in itself" (1:270).

16. Abrams, *The Mirror and the Lamp*, 272.
17. "Aber indem die zerstreuten Gegenstände in eins gefaßt und selbst die gemeinsten in ihrer Bedeutung und Würde aufgenommen werden, so ist es über die Natur" (*Hamburger Ausgabe* 12:72). Goethe's understanding of art as a reflection of the essence of nature surfaces again in his definition of *Stil:* "Wie die einfache Nachahmung auf dem ruhigen Dasein und einer liebevollen Gegenwart beruhet, die Manier eine Erscheinung mit einem leichten, fähigen Gemüt ergreift, so ruht der *Stil* auf den tiefsten Grundfesten der Erkenntnis, auf dem Wesen der Dinge, insofern uns erlaubt ist, es in sichtbaren und greiflichen Gestalten zu erkennen" (*Hamburger Ausgabe* 12:32). See also "Maximen und Reflexionen," #722: "Kunst: eine andere Natur, auch geheimnisvoll, aber verständlicher; denn sie entspringt aus dem Verstande" (*Hamburger Ausgabe* 12:467).
18. *Hamburger Ausgabe* 12:133.
19. *Hamburger Ausgabe* 12:58.
20. *Hamburger Ausgabe* 12:59, 64.

While the balanced composition of a Greek sculpture may delight its viewers, these same individuals are liable to experience their own lives as a disconnected series of confusing events. In this case order must be created in the act of self-reflection. This insight has great significance in the development of the *Bildungsroman* as a self-conscious genre. The life of the autonomous individual has to be transformed into an autonomous work of art, or rather, the self-sufficiency of the individual only first becomes apparent after this transformation has taken place. Thus the narrator in *Anton Reiser* sets out to create a harmonious totality out of the seemingly random events of the protagonist's life: "Whoever becomes attentive to his past life often seems to see nothing but purposelessness, torn threads, confusion, night and darkness; but the more one gazes into the past, the more the darkness clears, the purposelessness gradually disappears, the torn threads are reconnected, the jumbled confusion orders itself — and the discord resolves unnoticed into harmony and euphony" (2:111). The same act of retrospection also plays a crucial role in the composition of Jung-Stilling's *Lebensgeschichte*. However, for him there is still only one masterplot that contains all narratives within it, namely God's plan of universal history revealed in the Bible; Jung-Stilling's activity as autobiographer centers on the effort to discover his place within that scheme. In contrast, Moritz seeks to discover the logic of his personal development for its own sake.

There are a few moments in the text when he begins to understand his life as a coherent whole. Reiser's two most important reading experiences in the second part of the work help expand his nascent self-awareness while compensating for his crushing sense of alienation. In Shakespeare, Reiser finds "more than he had ever thought, read, and felt" (2:236), which drives him to share this experience with his friend Philipp Reiser. Their "Shakespeare Nights" not only provide him with the direct personal contact so often lacking in his life, they also give him a sense of belonging to the community of all those who have read Shakespeare before him: "He no longer lived so isolated and meaninglessly that he was lost among the crowd — for he had shared the experiences of thousands while reading Shakespeare" (2:237). For the first time reading promises him more than escape from suicidal depression, as it offers him both heightened self-awareness and the comforting assurance that his personal sufferings are part of "the common lot of humanity" (2:238). Again, in Goethe's *Werther* Reiser finds a work with which he can identify intensely, and which provides him with a rare sense of self-esteem. "The intensified feeling of his isolated existence — in that he thought of himself as a creature in which heaven and earth reflected themselves as in a mirror — allowed him to be proud of his humanity, to be no longer the meaningless, disposable creature he seemed in the eyes of others. No wonder, then, that his entire soul clung to a book that gave him back himself every time he savored it" (2:262).

Reiser's passionate identification with Goethe's Werther and Shakespeare's Hamlet represents an important stage in the transformation of the reading habits of a new generation. As mentioned above, the general trend among the compulsive *Vielleser* of the 1770s and 1780s was to seek stimulation and novelty through the rapid consumption of fiction in a way that was directly opposed to the reverent and repetitious study of religious texts that characterized earlier readers. Very quickly, however, a few authors like Shakespeare, Goethe, and Klopstock were granted a canonical authority that substituted for that of the Bible in their perceived ability to enable self-understanding and to establish community. While Reiser is willing to read himself into debt to satisfy his voracious appetite for new fiction, he reserves special treatment for Shakespeare and Goethe, whose works he reads and rereads with an intensity formerly reserved for sacred texts.

The sense of finding himself in Shakespeare's works leads Reiser to take up his diary for a second time. His first attempt had contributed nothing toward his self-understanding, as he had recorded only external events, not internal developments: "At that time Reiser did not yet understand how to observe the influence of real, external events on his inner disposition; his attention to himself had not yet been properly directed" (2:220). However, a second attempt proves more promising, as he now records "the inner history of his spirit" (2:238). This exercise in articulating his self-observations "made Anton Reiser into a writer for the first time" (2:238). Later, as a student in Erfurt, he further develops his insights to discover for the first time in his life the sort of harmonious order described by the narrator in the preface to the second volume of the work: "And these were the happiest moments of his life, when his own existence began to interest him for the first time, because he viewed it in a certain context and not isolated and fragmented" (2:398).

However, such moments remain rare incidents in a life dominated by a series of abrupt swings in mood and fortune that break off before any sense of personal maturity or social utility has been attained. Far from helping him to achieve a lasting sense of identity, the very process of stringing together disparate memories into a coherent narrative leads him to question whether his identity is not itself a fiction: "His own existence seemed to disappear out of his very hands, to have no purpose, to be torn and cut into little pieces" (2:240). His intensive rereading of *Werther* has the insidious effect of destabilizing the identity it seems to offer, as it influences his thinking and writing so strongly that for years he cannot tell whether a particular idea or phrase is his own or a quotation from Goethe's novel (2:262). His personal experiences become doubly mediated by literature: already as a child Reiser had pretended that he was living in the world of Homer; now when he sets out on his travels in search of a theater company, he cannot be sure whether his renewed sense of being "the image of the Homeric wanderer" (2:350) is his own idea or itself due to "a leftover idea from *Werther's Sufferings*" (2:345).

As noted above, the narrator attributes Anton Reiser's inability to maintain a consistent sense of personal identity to the unfavorable social conditions in which the boy was raised. These socially induced personal problems have a direct effect on his attempts to transform his life into the purposeful, coherent narrative set forth as an ideal. In order to produce a superior work of art, as Moritz writes in "On the Imitation of the Beautiful in the Plastic Arts," the artist must be a noble individual: "Incidentally, this also explains the concept of the noble style in artworks of every sort, which is no other than that style which is characterized by the inner dignity of the producing genius's soul" (1:249). If this is true for the production of art in general, then it becomes crucial for the most important task of the artist, namely the transformation of his or her life into an ordered form that can be contemplated with disinterested pleasure. As circumstances have prevented Anton Reiser from attaining the necessary personal dignity, art for him can only substitute for an empty life. "Because he had had too little existence since childhood, every destiny other than his own attracted him all the more; this led very naturally to his furious desire to read and see comedies during his school years. Attracted by every foreign fate, he felt simultaneously torn away from his own while finding only in others the spark of life that external pressures had nearly extinguished in himself" (2:367).

Reiser's mistake, as the narrator sees it, lies in his passionate interest in literature and the theater as a source of adventure and fulfillment that could provide him with the life he was denied. "He wanted to have everything for himself that art demands as a sacrifice" (2:367). Instead of subordinating his life to the production of art, Reiser wants to *use* art to compensate for the emptiness in his life. He errs again in his role as theater director by valuing the effect on the viewers over the intrinsic value of the play. "For the true poet and artist does not expect and find his reward in the effect that his work will have, but rather he finds pleasure in the work itself and would not consider the work lost even if no one else were ever to see it" (2:422). Thus the narrator has become the spokesman for ideas developed by Moritz in the 1780s, measuring

Reiser's shortcomings in terms of his "improper" aesthetic attitudes. As a result, the text does not practice the aesthetics its narrator preaches. Instead of creating a 'second nature' whose harmony rivals that of God's creation, Moritz produces a work of art that remains as discordant as the life of the character it portrays. Unable to transform his life into coherent whole, he becomes the author of his own destruction in a demonic parody of divine creation.

The gap between the aesthetic principles espoused by the narrator and Anton Reiser's inability to understand his life in accordance with these principles invites reflection on the unusual generic status of the work. Although Moritz, like Jung-Stilling, writes an essentially accurate account of his youth, he never drops the pseudonym to identify himself with Anton Reiser. Why does Moritz stop short of the revelation that Jung-Stilling makes in his autobiography? Is *Anton Reiser* an autobiography or a novel? Apparently something between the two, for Moritz subtitles his work "a psychological novel," while maintaining in the preface to the first volume that it could also be called a biography. A contemporary critic viewed this psychological novel's distance from the typical novel of the day as a virtue. Readers who had given up fiction as a waste of time could make an exception with this work, as it contained "neither a web of adventurous or sordid intrigues, nor a dull love story, nor a terrible tale of heroism [*eine schreckliche Heldengeschichte*]" (2:455). Yet the same critic goes on to complain about the low social position Moritz chose for the protagonist of his work and his inclusion of too many trivial details that could hardly interest the sort of individual who would read the text: "Since Herr Moritz writes for people who read, that is, not for craftsmen, etc., he should have avoided scenes whose details are certain to provoke boredom, not sympathy, among the readers" (2:455). It seems that Moritz is guilty of excessive virtue: the work is *too* prosaic, the characters *too* common, the study *too* psychological to qualify as a novel.[21]

Then why not avoid the misleading term altogether and call the work "Confessions" in the tradition of Rousseau?[22] Why does Moritz insist on analyzing his own life as if it were the biography of someone else? Part of the reason lies in the purpose of his work, which is fundamen-

---

21. This critic's objections provide an interesting example of the persistence of the common prejudice against the novel as a picaresque form even after increasingly introspective works like Wieland's *Agathon* and Goethe's *Werther* began to emerge. Moritz's sober account of his unhappy childhood in provincial Germany clearly broke with the "horizon of expectations" of its contemporary readers.

22. The same anonymous critic made this suggestion, claiming that the term "novel" had created misleading expectations (2:455).

tally different from that of Jung-Stilling. Like Augustine before him, Jung-Stilling records his life in the hope that it will provide encouragement for other Christians. He insists on the veracity of his account so that others may believe in the same providence that he feels has guided his life. Moritz also intends *Anton Reiser* to be an example, but an example to be avoided, not emulated. "This part contains an accurate representation of scenes from his youth, which may serve as a lesson and warning to those for whom this precious time has not yet slipped away" (2:211). Like the sketch of Anton's father that begins the work, the portrayal of Anton Reiser himself stands in close proximity to the sort of case history Moritz published in his *Magazin zur Erfahrungsseelenkunde;* it is not conceived as the inspirational account of a sinner's search for God.[23]

Thus the act of writing *Anton Reiser* has been described as a type of therapy: "The writing of 'Anton Reiser' had a calming effect on him, for now he was able to identify in complete clarity the imaginary guidelines of his childhood and youth. In their place he demanded the dismantling of false assurances and a courageous affirmation of life."[24] Yet it is hard to imagine how Anton Reiser is to progress toward this "courageous affirmation of life," since we leave him no better off than we found him in the first place.[25] Nor does Moritz ever seem to have discovered the sense of personal fulfillment denied him in his youth.[26] While his

23. Both Kestenholz and Müller stress this aspect of *Anton Reiser:* "der 'psychologische Roman' ist eher eine wissenschaftliche Abhandlung in Romanform zu nennen" (Kestenholz, *Die Sicht der Dinge,* 110). "Der psychologische Roman ist in diesem Sinne kein Roman" (Müller, *Die kranke Seele,* 39).

24. Minder, *Glaube, Skepsis und Rationalismus,* 44.

25. Boulby implies that Reiser at least has the potential to attain the insights of the narrator: "That is to say, until Anton becomes mature enough to write his 'history,' he cannot avoid living out his 'novel.'" (*Moritz,* 39). Jacobs questions whether Reiser will ever attain this maturity. While the narrator is said to have overcome the problems facing Anton Reiser, "der Weg zu solcher Überlegenheit wird nicht dargestellt. Daher steht die Position des Erzählers dem Schicksal seines Helden eigentümlich vermittlungslos gegenüber. Er hat die Distanz des Diagnostikers, der eine Anamnese erheben und kausale Zusammenhänge feststellen kann, der aber einen Ausweg aus dem Dilemma nicht anzugeben weiß" (*Wilhelm Meister und seine Brüder,* 52). Fürnkäs provides a still more pessimistic— and in my opinion more accurate—assessment of the novel by claiming that the narrator's apparent superiority to Anton Reiser is only "die Aufhebung der Melancholie Anton Reisers und darin deren in sich reflektierte Form: sie ist erzählende Melancholie" (*Der Ursprung des psychologischen Romans,* 127). As Müller writes, "Der Erzähler ist Diagnostiker, Heilender kann er nicht sein" (*Die kranke Seele,* 388).

26. See Boulby's biography for a compelling account of Moritz's troubled life. Numerous anecdotes hover between the pathetic and the bizarre. Given Moritz's persistently unhappy life, Catholy has questioned whether his entire aesthetic theory should not be considered "doch nur eine großartige Ideologie der Einheit" (*Karl Philipp Moritz,* 130). While there is an element of truth in this assertion in terms of the relation between the

aesthetic and anthropological ideals provide him with a standard against which he can measure his personal shortcomings in the figure of Anton Reiser, they cannot show him how to overcome these problems. The writing of *Anton Reiser* does not heal Moritz of his psychological wounds; instead, he compiles a merciless depiction of the circumstances that make it impossible to find a cure.

For all its affinity to a clinical analysis, however, he still publishes *Anton Reiser* as a (admittedly unconventional) novel. If we treat the text as a case history, then we have to assume that the lines are clearly drawn between reality and fiction. As Müller writes, "the narrator of *Anton Reiser* is a strict border guard between the prosaic facticity of life and the poetic illusions of his hero."[27] Yet the narrator does not necessarily speak for Moritz. If we take those passages seriously in which Reiser questions our ability to know God, reality, or ourselves, then we can also question whether the firm ground from which the narrator claims to speak may not itself be an unstable fiction. Moritz's work as a whole reveals a fascinating combination of two conflicting tendencies: on the one hand, he often anticipates Marx and Freud as he traces the social causes of personal neurosis; on the other hand, his work also reveals nihilistic tendencies that mark him as a troubled heir to Kant and as a precursor of Kleist, Grabbe, and Büchner. The reality that oppresses the analysand crumbles beneath the feet of the analyst. By placing *Anton Reiser* on the border between fiction and autobiography Moritz finds the appropriate form in which to express this ambivalence. The fiction that is to lend a greater sense of truth to the autobiography simultaneously raises the possibility that the truth itself is a fiction. Anton Reiser's abortive attempts to stabilize his identity through the act of self-reflection yield to Moritz's struggles to resurrect the fragmented self in fiction. In this sense his work anticipates the modern concept of authorship offered by Foucault: "Where a work had the duty of creating immortality, it now attains the right to kill, to become the murderer of its author."[28] Moritz's fictional autobiography substitutes for the suicide he considered as a child. In *Anton Reiser* he re-creates the prison he cannot escape.

---

theory and its author, we need not dismiss Moritz's pioneering work in aesthetics altogether as an exercise in compensation for an unhappy life. More important in this context is Moritz's refusal to impose this "ideology of unity" onto *Anton Reiser*.

27. Müller, *Die kranke Seele*, 322.
28. Foucault, "What Is an Author?" In *Language, Counter-Memory, Practice,* 117.

The Aesthetic Alienation of Wilhelm Meister (1795-97)

4

About a third of the way into his essay on *Wilhelm Meisters Lehrjahre*, Friedrich Schlegel interrupts himself to ponder the difficulties of subjecting Goethe's novel to an academic analysis. "Maybe it should be judged and at the same time not judged," he concludes, "which does not seem to be an easy task." Yet the novel itself comes to his rescue: "Fortunately it is one of those books that judge themselves, thus sparing the critic the effort. Indeed, it not only judges itself, it also describes itself."[1] Having asserted that *Wilhelm Meister* anticipates its own critique, Schlegel nevertheless goes on to complete his essay. As he points out several pages later, the novel's self-awareness is only partial; like any superior work of art, *Wilhelm Meister* "knows [more] than it says, and [intends] more than it knows."[2] The partial blindness that Schlegel identifies here as inevitable appears as a deliberate strategy from Goethe's point of view. In a polite but firm response to Schiller's repeated demands that he express the philosophical idea behind his novel more clearly, Goethe conceded his "mistake," but went on to point out that this mistake came out of his innermost nature, "from a certain realistic whim, through which I find it agreeable to make my existence, my actions, and my writing inscrutable to others."[3]

---

1. Schlegel, *Kritische Ausgabe* 2:133-34.
2. Schlegel, *Kritische Ausgabe* 2:140.
3. Goethe to Schiller, 9 July 1796, *Briefwechsel Schiller Goethe* 1:242.

If Goethe enjoyed cultivating an aura of mystery around himself and his works, there has been no dearth of those who step forward to propose solutions to his riddles. In the case of *Wilhelm Meister,* critical attention has been focused primarily on the character of the protagonist and the nature of his development. Many have regarded *Wilhelm Meister* as the prototypical *Bildungsroman* that traces the successful growth of the hero toward personal maturity and integration into cultivated society. In a particularly influential early interpretation of the novel, Christian Gottfried Körner argued that the work's unity lay in the "representation of a beautiful human nature, which gradually develops through the collaboration of inner predispositions and external circumstances. The goal of this development is a perfect equilibrium, harmony with freedom."[4] Others have protested the notion that Wilhelm Meister develops positively at all. Like Novalis before him, Schlechta argues that Meister's fortunes take a consistent turn for the worse after the opening chapter, and Schlaffer goes so far as to term the work a "novel of destruction" (*Zerstörungsroman*).[5]

Despite their diametrically opposed conclusions about the novel, members of both critical camps focus their attention on the novel's protagonist. Yet Schiller had already cautioned against this approach to the novel in a letter to Goethe of 28 November 1796:

4. Cited from Goethe, *Hamburger Ausgabe* 8:552. Unless noted otherwise, further references to Goethe's works are cited from this edition in the text with volume and page number. Gille provides an excellent account of the novel's early reception; see his pp. 41-42 for comments on the lasting influence of Körner's interpretation (*'Wilhelm Meister' im Urteil der Zeitgenossen*). Older studies of the *Bildungsroman* tend to echo Körner's language while identifying *Wilhelm Meisters Lehrjahre* as the best example of the genre. See for example Stahl, "Entstehung," 163-81, and Gerhard, *Entwicklungsroman,* 134-60. Beddow and Schings provide two of the more recent versions of this frequently recurring understanding of the novel. Beddow somewhat apologetically concedes his awareness of certain problematic aspects of the text, but insists that Goethe's belief in the possibility of natural growth for the individual is never radically shaken (*Fiction of Humanity*). Schings promises a revision of this critical tradition when he claims that therapy rather than *Bildung* characterizes the development of the modern subject in the *Bildungsroman* ("Zur Pathologie des modernen Subjekts," 45), but his conclusion reproduces the affirmative interpretation of the novel in clinical terminology: "Mit einem Wort: er [Wilhelm Meister] wird geheilt" (55).

5. Schlechta, *Goethes Wilhelm Meister;* Schlaffer, "Exoterik und Esoterik," 222. More moderate critics like Bollnow ("Vorbetrachtungen") and May (" 'Wilhelm Meisters Lehrjahre': ein Bildungsroman?") argue for a qualified success based on lowered expectations. Meister's ideal is not to become a *uomo universale;* rather, he achieves the more limited goal of practical activity involving a degree of personal resignation. Eichner presents a somewhat more critical perspective: he argues that Meister not only fails to become a *uomo universale,* but that he also never takes up any practical activity. Instead, he sets off on another journey at the end of the novel: "Meisterschaft ist nicht bloß Entfaltung, sie ist auch Verkümmerung" ("Zur Deutung von 'Wilhelm Meisters Lehrjahre,' " 191).

Körner exaggerated the importance of this character as the actual hero of the novel; the title and the old custom that every novel has to have a hero mislead him. Wilhelm Meister is certainly the most necessary, but not the most important character; it is just this that is peculiar about your novel, namely that it has no such most important character, nor does it need one. Everything happens *to* him and *around* him but not really *for his sake;* precisely because the things around him represent and express energies (*Energien*), and he the capacity for improvement, he has a completely different relationship to his fellow characters than the hero has in other novels.[6]

By asserting that there *is* no single most important character in the novel, Schiller directs attention away from Meister himself and toward his function within the structure of the work as a whole. It was precisely this concentration on the work's *Kunstcharakter* that won Goethe's praise for Friedrich Schlegel's essay on the novel. According to Caroline Schlegel, Goethe was particularly pleased by the fact that Friedrich Schlegel had concentrated on the "construction of the whole," rather than focusing on the "pathological analysis of individual characters."[7]

These comments by Schiller and Schlegel anticipate David Miles's contemporary study of the novel. He emphasizes the surprising lack of psychological depth in Goethe's protagonist. As he puts it, the novel "may not be a Bildungsroman at all, for one of the most curious facts about the work is that for a book purportedly describing a leisurely odyssey to self-awareness, it is strangely *un*psychological."[8] Wilhelm Meister is better understood, according to Miles, if we view him in the tradition of the picaresque novel. He views Wilhelm Meister as a hero

---

6. Schiller to Goethe, 28 November 1796, *Briefwechsel Schiller Goethe* 1:319.
7. Cited from Gerhard, "'Geprägte Form,'" 65. Nevertheless, Gerhard goes on to argue that Schlegel's stress on form over content causes him to misunderstand Goethe's novel, which allegedly portrays "ein organisches, nach eingeborener Notwendigkeit vor sich gehendes Wachstum" (77). Immerwahr also downplays the self-conscious aspects of *Wilhelm Meister,* pointing out that it "does not allude to the circumstances of its own creation, much less play upon them like the 'grotesques' and 'arabesques' of Sterne, Jean Paul, and Diderot" ("Friedrich Schlegel's Essay," 14). Finally, Behler claims that Schlegel overemphasizes "the poetic character of Goethe's work" ("Poetic Unity of the Novel," 113), thus ignoring Goethe's stress on willful limitation toward the end of the novel. In other words, all three critics argue against Schlegel's reading of the work as *Poesie der Poesie* in order to reproduce familiar content-oriented analyses of the text.
8. Miles, "Picaro's Journey to the Confessional," 981.

essentially lacking in interiority who bounces from one episode to the next without deep character development. One might well argue that Miles overstates his case for the purpose of his argument;[9] my particular concern stems from the fact that he bases his analysis of Goethe's "picaro" on Erich Auerbach's reading of Homer's *Odyssey*. Like Don Quixote, and most unlike Odysseus, Wilhelm Meister is a modern hero who lives after the invention of the printing press, or more specifically, in the period of the rapid transformation of the German public sphere toward the end of the eighteenth century. The course of Odysseus's wanderings is determined by the gods; Wilhelm Meister is a typical bourgeois reader who seeks to escape the narrow confines of his home by joining the theater. Like Don Quixote before him, Meister's adventures have "the character of a quotation" (*Zitatcharakter*),[10] and the novel itself is metafictional, a self-conscious reflection on the relation between fiction and reality.

Goethe had already addressed this relation in his first novel, *Die Leiden des Jungen Werther* (The Sufferings of Young Werther) (1774). For years readers have responded to Werther's passion, which drives him toward the immediate experience of nature, love, and ultimately suicide. However, critics in recent years have pointed out that a good many of Werther's seemingly direct experiences are in fact inspired by literature. From the passages in Homer that accompany his enjoyment of spring to those in Ossian that intensify his sense of impending despair in the fall, from the love nurtured by a mutual enthusiasm for Klopstock to the carefully staged death with *Emilia Galotti* left open on the table, Werther moves in a world shaped by his half-conscious appropriation of moods and events from works of literature.[11] Schiller had addressed just this aspect of the novel already in 1795 when commenting on

   9. While critics from Novalis to Schlechta and Schlaffer have quite correctly pointed out that Meister's development is *problematic,* Miles goes too far when he claims that Meister never develops at all. His encounter with Werner at the beginning of the eighth book alone provides clear evidence that he has at least made some progress. Miles's further claim that the narrator is the real hero of the novel is equally troubling. In aligning the narrator with "the humanists of the Tower" ("Picaro's Journey to the Confessional," 984) Miles conveniently ignores their often exploitative and manipulative behavior toward others, particularly Wilhelm Meister. Moreover, he exaggerates the narrator's alleged development: as Friedrich Schlegel observed and Hass underscores ("Wilhelm Meisters Lehrjahre"), Goethe's narrator maintains an ironic distance from his protagonist *throughout* the novel.
   10. Mandelkow, "Roman der Klassik und Romantik," 400.
   11. While Alewyn wrote that the communicative power of the mere name "Klopstock" between Werther and Lotte signaled a new intimacy in the relation of reading to the life of the reader ("'Klopstock!'"), Pütz has pointed out that Werther's intimacy with literature also involves a degree of alienation from reality: "Werther also, der ein Ohr für den

Werther's "sentimental" relation to the "naive" Homer: "It was without doubt a completely different feeling that filled Homer's soul, when he had his divine swineherd entertain Ulysses, than that which moved the soul of young Werther when he read this song after an annoying social gathering. Our feeling for nature is like the feeling of the sick man for health."[12]

If Werther's identification with literature was ultimately to prove fatal, the fragmentary first version of Goethe's next novel ends with the triumphant merger of fiction with reality, as Wilhelm Meister fulfills his "theatrical mission" by becoming an official member of Serlo's theater troupe. Like Anton Reiser, the theater attracts Wilhelm Meister as an adventurous, mysterious realm that promises to tear him "out of stagnant, tedious, middle-class life" (7:35).[13] While Reiser exhausts himself in the futile pursuit of his ambitions, Meister actually succeeds in becoming involved with a great variety of the types of theater that existed in Germany in the eighteenth century, ranging from juggling and acrobatics, through commissioned performances for the nobility, to Serlo's professional company. The gradual turn away from the Bible and toward secular fiction we have traced in the development of the German *Bildungsroman* seems complete. The extensive reader and theatergoer no longer tries to fit his unorthodox life into the pattern of previous religious autobiographies, as did Jung-Stilling, but rather, embraces new experiences in the rapidly changing public sphere.

We will never know whether Goethe intended to conclude the *Sendung* with the apotheosis of his hero and the glorification of the German theater; as Eric Blackall pointed out, Goethe probably did not know himself.[14] We do know that Meister's involvement with the theater has been reduced to a temporary stage in his development in the *Lehrjahre* and that he must abandon it to join the Society of the Tower. With the decrease in the importance of the theater in the new novel comes an increase in the number of directly self-reflexive moments in the text. In the place of a linear narrative that traces the protagonist's movement

---

Herzschlag der Natur zu haben vorgibt und sogar selbst zum Maienkäfer werden möchte, um alle Nahrung im Wohlgeruch der Blüten aufzuspüren, nährt sich in Wirklichkeit von seinen Lesefrüchten" ("Werthers Leiden an der Literatur," 60). See also similar comments in Vaget, "Werther," 37-44, and Waniek, "*Werther* lesen und Werther als Leser."

12. Schiller, *Werke* 5:711.

13. Schrimpf emphasizes the similar role played by the theater in both *Anton Reiser* and *Wilhelm Meister* as a means of escape from the oppressively narrow bourgeois world ("Moritz: Anton Reiser," in *Der deutsche Roman*, 95-98).

14. *Goethe and the Novel*, 67.

away from home and out into the world, *Wilhelm Meisters Lehrjahre* circles back on itself, with the protagonist as its point of origin. Now he narrates the story of his youth that had been presented by the narrator in book one of the *Sendung*. Lengthy comments on Shakespeare's *Hamlet* toward the middle of the work serve indirectly to characterize Wilhelm and the novel itself. Finally, Wilhelm Meister now reads the Tower Society's (*Turmgesellschafts*) version of his own biography in the final book of the novel. The process marks a further stage in the development of German aesthetics, which move forward to a new stress on aesthetic autonomy by adapting elements of a previously discarded religious tradition. The extensive movement of the plot is now contained within a new, secular version of the closure that typified the religious autobiography.

As I mentioned in Chapter 1, it was Friedrich Schiller who developed the theoretical justification for the social function of aesthetic autonomy in his letters *Über die ästhetische Erziehung des Menschen*. Rejecting any sort of didacticism, he argued that the contemplation of autonomous works of art provides humanity with a foretaste of that God-like harmony denied us in the modern state, where we live in a condition of fragmentation and alienation. Although Schiller has since been charged with encouraging aesthetic escapism, *he* claimed that the proper form of aesthetic experience could solve the political problems that had led to revolution in France. He defended this proposition abstractly in the twenty-seven letters of his *Ästhetische Erziehung;* of equal practical importance was their prominent place in his new literary journal, *Die Horen*, which was to be the central cultural institution that would begin to realize the program of aesthetic education it set forth. Thus Schiller's ambitions for his journal were far from modest; in fact, he expressed the hope at one point that it would become so dominant as to drive all other journals out of business.[15]

If Schiller's plan were to succeed, he had to enlist the cooperation of Goethe, Germany's most famous writer. It is within this context that we must view their sudden rapprochement in the summer of 1794. One month *before* the "fortunate occurrence" that brought them together after a meeting of a "Naturalists' Society" in Jena, Schiller had already

---

15. Thus when writing of his plans for the journal to his publisher, Cotta, Schiller expressed the hope "daß der [deutsche] Merkur nach dem ersten Jahr der Horen von selbst fallen soll, so wie alle Journale, die das Unglück haben, von ähnlichem Innhalt mit den Horen zu seyn" (10 July 1794, *National Ausgabe* 27:21). As Böhler writes, "man müßte sein Vorgehen als einen erstaunlich geschäftstüchtigen Versuch zur Durchsetzung eines Monopols bezeichnen" ("Freundschaft von Schiller und Goethe," 50). Schulz's *Schillers Horen* is an informative history.

written to Goethe in request of contributions to *Die Horen*. Thus the encounter Goethe later described as accidental may well have been a carefully premeditated ambush on Schiller's part. Goethe himself hints as much in his description of their discussion: "Schiller, who had much more worldly wisdom and good breeding than I, and who was more interested in attracting than repelling me on account of the *Horen* that he was about to edit, responded as a good Kantian" (10:541). The flattering portrait of Goethe that Schiller developed one month after this meeting leads up to another request that Goethe publish *Wilhelm Meisters Lehrjahre* in his journal. The conclusion is unavoidable: Goethe and Schiller's sudden collaboration in the summer of 1794 was the result of a tactical move on Schiller's part to enlist Goethe's cooperation for his new literary journal *despite* their clear and lasting differences.[16]

Unfortunately for Schiller, Goethe had already agreed to publish his novel with Unger, and was in the process of correcting the proofs of the first volume. If Schiller was disappointed in his failure to capture the *Lehrjahre*, he must have been incensed at Goethe's first contribution to *Die Horen*, two sarcastic poems that seem to ridicule Schiller's grandiose plan to circumvent the chaos of political revolution through the aesthetic education of humanity. "Noble friend," writes Goethe in his first "Epistle,"

you long for the well-being of the human race,
Of our Germans in particular, and still more of the nearest
Citizen, and you fear the consequences of dangerous books; we have,
Alas, seen them often. What should one, or what could
Worthy men united, what could the rulers achieve?
The question seems serious and important, but just now it finds me
In a good mood....
Should I say what I think? It seems to me that
Only life shapes the man and words mean little.[17]

16. "Nichts wäre falscher als die Vorstellung, hier hätten sich zwei füreinander bestimmte Naturen gefunden. Nein, gegensätzlicher als Goethe und Schiller können zwei Persönlichkeiten nicht gedacht werden.... wir müssen Abschied nehmen von der Freundschaftslegende" (Pyritz, "Der Bund zwischen Goethe und Schiller," 40). While Pyritz provides a necessary correction to the "harmlos-idylischen Begriff der klassischen Zwillinge" (40), his dismissal of the friendship between the two men as a "legend" goes too far. More balanced assessments of the limited, but genuinely cordial relations between the two men are presented by Staiger, primarily in personal terms ("Einleitung," *Briefwechsel Schiller Goethe*), and more recently by Böhler, who places their friendship in socio-historical context ("Die Freundschaft von Schiller und Goethe").
17. Goethe, *Gedichte: 1756-99*, 479-80.

How could Schiller tolerate Goethe's contribution, and why would he publish this poem together with the first letters of the *Aesthetic Education* in the opening volume of *Die Horen?* Practically speaking, he had little choice: even the cooperation of a satirical Goethe was better than no Goethe at all. But on a deeper level, Schiller shared much of Goethe's low regard for the public. While Schiller tended to express his hostility in terms of imposing enlightenment with an almost dictatorial will on a recalcitrant public, Goethe tended toward ironic detachment. Before long both men were to collaborate on scores of hostile *Xenien* in response to the failure of the *Horen* to unite the public: "Horen, first issue: 'Some stride too solemnly, the others step boldly / Few walk the pace of the public' " ("Horen, erster Jahrgang: 'Einige wandeln zu ernst, die andern schreiten verwegen, / Wenige gehen den Schritt, wie ihn das Publikum hält' ") (1:217).[18]

To characterize Goethe's relation to the public in the late 1790s as merely hostile would be an oversimplification, however. Despite the dominant tone of skeptical distance that marks his assessment of the public during this period, Goethe never retreated into self-imposed isolation. If most of his works did not inspire the enthusiastic response of *Werther,* he was nevertheless quite aware of his market value and knew how to charge accordingly.[19] His most popular work of the late 1790s, *Hermann und Dorothea,* was also a commercial success. Goethe not only received the enormous sum of one thousand taler from his publisher, Vieweg, but the most costly editions of the work were shrewdly packaged in such a way as to appeal to the materialism of its bourgeois readers.[20] Although Goethe adopts an ironic attitude toward the dream of "aesthetic education" in the "Epistles" and a sarcastic tone toward just

18. Böhler argues convincingly that the *Horen* project together with the "Xenien" constitutes a two-stage process in the construction of the poets' public identity and also the development of their friendship ("Die Freundschaft von Schiller und Goethe," 56-57). As Brandt summarizes the problematic cultural politics of Weimar Classicism, Goethe and Schiller addressed their "Botschaft, an ein Publikum, das noch nicht da war, und gegen ein Publikum, das da war" ("Die 'hochgesinnte' Verschwörung gegen das Publikum," 25). Reed reminds us that the very concept of Weimar Classicism as the apex of German literary history is a myth created in the nineteenth century: "Die Weimarer Klassik war im wesentlichen immer eine Opposition und hat sich auch als solche empfunden" ("Ecclesia militans," 46).

19. Goethe was paid forty taler per sheet for his contributions to the *Horen,* considerably more than anyone else (Bruford, *Die gesellschaftlichen Grundlagen der Goethezeit,* 280).

20. "When the poem appeared in print, it was available in several formats, among them a deluxe edition bound in silk, and with a little knife *and* a pair of scissors attached to the binding as a convenience for the cutting of the pages. The poem itself was thus sent into the world as one of the lovely amenities of the middle-class life it ostensibly praised"

about everyone in the *Xenien,* we should hesitate to identify these stylized literary forms with a heartfelt confession of his deepest feelings. In the slightly later "Prelude in the Theater" in *Faust,* the director's disparaging remarks about the public are countered by the harlequin's insistence on his right to be entertained. Finally, Goethe's essay "Literary Sansculottism," published in *Die Horen* in the spring of 1795, contains another mixed assessment of the current literary scene. Although Goethe spends much of the essay explaining why Germany has not developed a classical literature, including the fact that writers are deterred "by a large public without taste that devours the bad after the good with the same pleasure" (12:242), he concludes the essay with a defense of the public's ability to appreciate the considerable achievements of recent German writers despite the objections of certain reactionary critics.

Thus Schiller's move to solicit Goethe's contributions to his new literary journal touched off repeated efforts by both men to define the function of literature in its institutional context. If the tone adopted is generally hostile, the very existence of the dialogue indicates a willingness to address their own and other writers' difficult but essential relation to the public. Schiller's *Ästhetische Erziehung* marked the most sustained theoretical attempt to formulate the cultural ambitions of classical German aesthetics in this period. Although Goethe enjoyed reading at least the beginning of Schiller's theory, he had no interest in producing a similar work himself.[21] Instead, he addressed the same problems in his most important literary work of the period, *Wilhelm Meisters Lehrjahre.* While the passages in the novel that focus on the theater provide him with the most obvious forum for the examination of the social function of art, the new, self-reflexive moments in the text have equal significance, as they exemplify the autonomous aesthetics developed

---

(Weisinger, *The Classical Façade,* 177). See Conrady's biography for a general overview of Goethe's dealings with the financial aspects of publication ("Von Editionen und Verlegern," in *Goethe: Leben und Werk,* 133-41.)

21. Goethe responded enthusiastically to the letters Schiller published in the first edition of *Die Horen:* "Das mir übersandte Manuskript habe sogleich mit großem Vergnügen gelesen, ich schlurfte es auf Einen Zug hinunter" (to Schiller, 26 October 1794, *Briefwechsel Schiller Goethe* 1:59). If one examines the comments by each man about the other, before and after their rapprochement in the summer of 1794, however, one finds that despite the increasing cordiality, each continues to view the other as the representative of an alien way of looking at the world. Thus Barner concludes that the correspondence between Goethe and Schiller concerning *Wilhelm Meister* reveals less a productive interchange than the gradual emergence of fundamental, irreconcilable differences between the two men in their assessment of both the novel and the public (" 'Die Verschiedenheit unserer Naturen,' " 404).

theoretically in Schiller's treatise. It is in Wilhelm Meister's attempts to translate aesthetic contemplation into meaningful action that the novel provides its most critical commentary on the idealistic program of aesthetic education.

The disillusionment that ultimately drives Wilhelm Meister away from the theater is anticipated in the opening book of the novel, where his earliest attempts to combine reality and fiction are repeatedly undercut by irony. He disrupts his first staging of a puppet play by reaching down to pick up a fallen puppet, "an accident which destroyed the illusion, provoked much laughter, and upset [him] greatly" {9} (7:22).[22] He is embarrassed again when he decides to perform Tasso's *Gerusalemme Liberata* with his friends without bothering to rehearse: "They imagined that all they had to do was to present themselves as heroes and that it would be easy to act and speak like the characters in the world I had told them about" {13} (7:29), which they of course are unable to do. While Wilhelm Meister longs to join the exciting world of the theater, he encounters the actor Melena and his bride, who are forced to defend themselves before a hostile court in a scene that becomes living theater for Meister. "For what usually happens only in plays and novels, was now played out before his very eyes in this wretched courtroom" {27} (7:52). As it turns out, Milena wants nothing more than to return to the security of a normal bourgeois profession, but is instead compelled to head off once again in search of some sort of acting company.

While Milena longs to escape the theater, Meister has found the fulfillment of his dreams in his love for the actress Mariane. Meister's interest in the theater has been accompanied since childhood by his interest in the opposite sex.[23] The narrator of the *Sendung* associates his exploration of the puppets' bodies with the child's first interest in sexual differentiation.[24] As he later recalls in the *Lehrjahre*, the disappearance of the enchanting puppet theater affected him like the loss of a beloved woman (7:17). Later performances of comedies often result in affairs between the budding actors and actresses Meister directs: " 'It

22. For the reader's convenience, I include references to the English edition in brackets and to the German edition in parentheses.
23. Both Kittler and Roberts point out "the unconscious sexual roots" of Wilhelm's interest in the theater (Roberts, *The Indirections of Desire*, 56; Kittler, "Über die Sozialisation Wilhelm Meisters," 14-44). See further discussion of Kittler that follows.
24. *Wilhelm Meisters theatralische Sendung, Gedenkausgabe* 8:532. Further references to the *Sendung* will be included in the text with the abbreviation TS and page number.

was not long before natural instincts began to stir in boys and girls, and the company divided up into little love affairs—plays within plays" {14} (7:31). Although Meister is also attracted to the opposite sex, he carefully avoids infatuation with any of the young actresses, thus keeping his love for the theater "pure": "His love for the theater remained completely pure, and he was able to look on without rivalry when each of the others wanted to put his princess on the throne" (TS, 546). Finally, however, Meister permits his erotic interest in the theater to be incorporated in the figure of Mariane. "She had first appeared in the flattering light of a theatrical performance, and his own passion for the stage was closely connected with his first love for a woman" {4} (7:14).

Goethe intensifies the association between the theater and sexuality in the *Lehrjahre* by incorporating Meister's memories of the puppets into the sexual foreplay of the two lovers. The boy who had once secretly stolen away to examine the bodies of his puppets now brings the same puppets to Mariane's bedside. "Not much is needed to amuse two lovers; they had a wonderful evening" {5} (7:15). While Wilhelm reminisces, Mariane examines each character, finally settling on Jonathan as her favorite. She playfully manipulates the wires that control him, making him bow and declare his love in a game that soon carries over to her real lover: "Him she treated with particular delicacy, and in the end transferred her cherishing embraces from the puppet to Wilhelm. And so, once again, a little game became the preliminary for hours of bliss" {5} (7:16). Werther and Lotte were brought to the brink of passion while reading Ossian; now the puppets that Wilhelm had once explored lasciviously in secret precipitate the consummation of desire.

Upon awakening, Wilhelm Meister launches into a long narrative about his childhood love for the theater that soon puts Mariane back to sleep. Blithely unaware of her inattentiveness, Wilhelm talks on, revealing a rather smug sense of self-satisfaction: " 'It is pleasant and satisfying to remember the obstacles that we sadly thought were insurmountable, and then compare what we, as mature persons, have now developed into, with what we were then, in our immaturity' " {6} (7:17). The act of reflection creates a sense of order and mastery over the seemingly random and difficult events of his life. The perception of purposeful development in the past inspires hope for a happy future with Mariane: " 'I cannot tell you how happy I am now that I can talk to you about the past—now that I gaze out towards the joyous landscape that we shall travel hand in hand' " {6} (7:17). Not surprisingly, he encourages Mariane to narrate her own personal history, attempting to extend their current union back into the past and forward into the future: " 'Tell me all about it and I will tell you about mine. Let's use our imagination as much as possible, and try to recover those past times that were lost to our love' " {11} (7:25).

The structural parallel between this episode and similar moments in religious autobiographies ranging from Augustine's *Confessions* to Jung-Stilling's *Lebensgeschichte* should be clear. Like these earlier figures, Meister also reaches an important turning point that enables him to perceive a previously obscured teleology in the random events of his life. However, Meister no longer strives to discover the place of his particular life within God's plan of universal history. Instead, he strives to combine the narrative of his past with Mariane's own life history to form a self-sufficient whole. Secularization of the religious paradigm proceeds through the sexualization of the private narrative. The "pregnant moment" in which their son Felix is conceived becomes the focal point of a self-centered narrative that is to transform the transience of life into the permanence of autonomous art.

The sexual dimension of classical aesthetics is already evident in the closing pages of Moritz's essay "Über die bildende Nachahmung des Schönen," where he writes of the perennial rejuvenation of nature despite the inevitable death of individuals. The pan-eroticism that empowers the eternal cycle of "formation, transformation" (*Gestaltung, Umgestaltung*) (3:193) finds two of its most original poetic representations in the Earth Spirit of *Faust I* and the Mothers of *Faust II*. The classical world can only appear in the third act of *Faust II* after the ejaculation of Homunculus out of his test tube and into the water has brought about the harmony of the elements. The gradual union of the two civilizations represented by Faust and Helena culminates when they conceive the child Euphorion; after his death primordial chaos returns.[25] Moreover, Goethe conceived of human creativity in the arts as a higher form of the same reproductive drive and repeatedly explored the metaphor of writing as a form of sexual reproduction in his poetry of the classical period. The most famous image linking the act of writing and the sex act occurs in the fifth Roman Elegy, where the happy poet/lover

---

25. Goethe frequently uses the image of a ring to express the notion of the permanence of the species despite the transience of the individual, as in the following passage from the poem "Die Metamorphose der Pflanzen": "Und hier schließt die Natur den Ring der ewigen Kräfte; / Doch ein neuer sogleich fasset den vorigen an, / Daß die Kette sich fort durch alle Zeiten verlänge / Und das Ganze belebt, so wie das Einzelne, sei" (1:200, lines 59-63). The same image occurs in "Grenzen der Menschheit": "Ein kleiner Ring / Begrenzt unser Leben, / Und viele Geschlechter / Reihen sie dauernd / An ihres Daseins / Unendliche Kette" (1:147, lines 37-42).

taps out hexameters on the back of his slumbering partner. The poet's love for Faustina not only breathes life into the dutiful tourist's pilgrimage to the sights of Rome, but also inspires modern verse that reawakens the erotic poetry of antiquity. The elegies represent the first fruit of Goethe's renewed creativity upon his return from Rome, and their subsequent publication in *Die Horen* came at the time of his most productive association with Schiller.[26] Five years after Schiller's death Goethe returned to a troubled variation on the theme in his poem "Das Tagebuch" ("The Diary"), where an aging man's sexual impotence and his inability to write go hand in hand.[27]

The link between sex and writing occurs once again in *Wilhelm Meister,* although the theme has been transposed from the classical soil of Rome to the mundane circumstances of life in Germany. As Kittler has pointed out in his pioneering "discourse analysis" of the novel, Goethe thereby situates Meister's eroticized narrative in the context of the emergence of the nuclear family toward the end of the eighteenth century. Crucial in this movement from the *Großfamilie* to the *Kleinfamilie* was the increased intimacy of the bond between mother and son. In the *Sendung* Meister receives the puppets from his grandmother via his father; in the *Lehrjahre,* however, his mother awakens his interest in the theater. She gives him what she would have enjoyed receiving herself.[28] While Wilhelm's animated account of his childhood interest in the puppets falls on deaf ears with Mariane, his mother remembers the events fondly and eagerly supplements her son's narrative.[29] However, the contrast Kittler draws between the mother and Mariane obscures an underlying similarity. The bond established between the mother and son through the present of the puppets is simultaneously displaced into the theatrical world the puppets represent. In an analogous way, when

---

26. Here again Goethe's contribution of these poems to *Die Horen* aroused mixed feelings in Schiller: "Er [Goethe] las mir seine Elegien, die zwar schlüpfrig und nicht sehr decent sind, aber zu den beßten Sachen gehören, die er gemacht hat" (to Charlotte Schiller, 20 September 1794, *National Ausgabe* 27:49). When the elegies were published in the following spring, Schiller agreed with Goethe that the "Schamhaftigkeit, die von einem Journal gefordert wird" required the suppression of some of the more scandalous elegies (to Goethe, 15 May 1795, *Briefwechsel Schiller Goethe* 1:103).

27. See Vaget for an excellent discussion of the link between male sexuality and writing in this poem ("Der Schreibakt und der Liebesakt").

28. "Die Mutter, statt an Wunsch und Vergnügen des Kindes anzuknüpfen und sein Erzähltalent zu belohnen, schenkt, was sie selbst liebt: Ihr Bezug zum Sohn ist Identifikation" (Kittler, "Sozialisation," 23).

29. "Die Sexualisierung der Kindheit *und* der Reden, die sie erinnern, hat indessen—wie könnte es anders sein—unterschiedliche Effekte auf die zwei Hörerinnen Wilhelm Meisters" (Kittler, "Sozialisation," 30).

Meister introduces the puppets to Mariane, he both creates and destroys intimacy: on the one hand, the puppets symbolize the shift of his affections away from his mother and toward his lover; on the other hand, his desire remains constant, namely for the theater and neither his mother nor his lover. Mariane seems to understand this, as she arouses Wilhelm's desire by playing with his puppets. In her role as Meister's living doll she stays in costume for their tryst, and when he arrives it is not her so much as her uniform that he embraces: "How eagerly she rushed towards him! And how passionately he embraced that red uniform and the white satin vest" {2} (7:11).

The irony that marks this particular passage typifies the structure of the opening book as a whole. We as readers are aware from its first page of what Meister only discovers on its last, namely that his rival, Norbert, is on his way to shatter Meister's illusory sense of self-mastery. Self-satisfied contemplation of the past is disrupted by an unexpected event in the present. The desire to unite his life with the beloved through mutual narration of the past is also ironically undercut, as Mariane falls asleep in the midst of Meister's story and assiduously avoids telling him her own. The result is not union with Mariane but, instead, self-absorbed narcissism. "Happy youth," comments the narrator dryly, "when we converse readily with ourselves, delighting in echoes of our own conversation and satisfied when our invisible partner merely repeats the last syllables of what we have just uttered!" {30} (7:57). Union with Mariane is revealed as narcissism; narration as the extension of sexual intercourse becomes merely verbal masturbation.[30]

When we encounter Wilhelm Meister again at the beginning of book two, several years have passed, and he is beginning to pull himself out of the depression caused by his unexpected disappointment. The narcissism that characterized his autobiographical narrative in book one has not changed, however. Rather than asking Mariane to explain her version of the affair with Norbert, he listens to Werner's brutally insensitive tirades against the folly of such a relationship, to the point that he becomes physically sick. Upon recovery, however, Meister continues the

---

30. That such an analogy is warranted is confirmed by Kittler's identification of an indirect reference to the biblical Onan in the description of Meister's deluded conviction that "kein Wort seiner Geschichte auf die Erde gefallen [sei]" (7:25). "And Onan knew that the seed should not be his; and it came to pass, when he went in unto his brother's wife that he spilled it on the ground, lest that he should give seed to his brother" (Gen. 38:9). Wilhelm Meister is not the only Goethean character who tends toward "masturbatory inwardness" (Bennett, *Faust,* 88). See Bennett's extended discussion of "tragedy and masturbation" in his recent book on Goethe's *Faust,* 83-111.

punishment in a masochistic game that consists of torturing himself with memories of past happiness, a game that leads to renewed despair. "And so he tore himself to pieces in repeated accesses of savagery" {42} (7:78). The story of his childhood enthusiasm for the theater, which culminated in his love for Mariane, has now turned into a source of often-repeated, self-inflicted suffering.

Eventually Meister moves to distance himself from the past. Having grown critical of his affair with Mariane and the theatrical world she represents, he also becomes critical of his own talents as an actor and a poet, which only intensifies his sense of despair: "Hard as it is to abandon one's love of a woman, it is equally painful to desert the company of the muses" {43} (7:79). In the opening book, Wilhelm's love for Mariane had functioned as a turning point in his life that enabled him to grasp his entire past as part of a coherent narrative. Now when he opens the packet of his own writing that he had planned to bring along with him on his elopement with Mariane, he is overcome instead by a sense of alienation from himself that the narrator likens to opening a piece of one's own returned mail: "We have a strange feeling as we break the seal, our own seal, and converse with our different self as with a third person" {44} (7:81). In a symbolic act of renunciation of both Mariane and the theater, Meister seizes his old manuscripts and flings them into the oven.

But not quite *all* of his old productions; as we learn somewhat later, some of his plays were saved "by chance" {88} (7:153), and Meister has even brought these remnants of past creativity along with him on his business trip! Even if he had managed to destroy all of his old manuscripts, he still remembers his own poetry enough to recite passages "with particular satisfaction" {47} (7:87) as he sets out on his journey. On the evening after he makes his first successful collection of outstanding debt for his father, Meister attends an amateur theater performance by local factory workers, and before long he has drifted into an association with a group of itinerant actors and neglected his duties completely.

He justifies this resurgence of interest in the theater primarily in terms of its benefits for society. Already in the opening book Meister had been exposed to the actors' discussions about not only practical considerations of the reception of their work but also "the influence of the theater on the cultural level of the nation, indeed of the world" {32} (7:60). Now after observing a performance by a group of miners, he holds forth on the edifying function of comedy for members of all social classes (7:95). A variety show reawakens "his passionate desire to incorporate into drama all that was great, noble and good" {59} (7:106). Meister supplements this faith in the theater's ability to improve society with the idea that the theater troupe itself anticipates the sort of democratic society it hopes to inspire. "They considered it a foregone conclusion that a republican administration would be the most suitable for good people like themselves, and insisted that the office of director should rotate amongst them. The director should be elected by the whole company, and he should be assisted by a kind of small senate" {127} (7:215). The actors choose Wilhelm as their first director.

Thus as Wilhelm's engagement with the theater moves ever further away from its initial association with his mother and into the public sphere, it begins to assume a position analogous to that of the "aesthetic condition" in Schiller's *Ästhetische Erziehung*.[31] For Schiller, aesthetic experience functions both as a means of guiding current society toward a future aesthetic state and as a miniature, anticipatory version of the aesthetic state itself. However, just as Schiller is always ready to anticipate pragmatic objections to his idealistic theory within the theory itself, so too Goethe creates ironic distance between his protagonist's dreams and reality.[32]

One example of this tendency occurs when the actors decide to read a German chivalric drama (*Ritterstück*) together. As the narrator explains, these plays were new and popular at the time. The particular play chosen by the group awakens patriotic sentiments among the actors: "Everyone was enflamed by national fervor. Being Germans they were delighted to indulge poetically in a piece that expressed their own national character and played on their native soil" {70} (7:125). But they accompany their reading of the play with steady drinking, until the distinction between fiction and reality becomes blurred: "Since there was a great deal of toasting and drinking in the play, what could be more natural than that the audience each time joined the heroes in clinking their glasses and singing the praises of the most favored personages in the play" {70} (7:125). Predictably, the group members awaken with hangovers the next morning, and an annoyed Wilhelm pays for the damages; such are "the sad results which a stimulating, spirited and well-intentioned work of literature had produced" {71} (7:126).

---

31. The increasing stress on the social function of the theater in the *Lehrjahre* contrasts with its primarily private function in *Anton Reiser*: "Weder als Podium bürgerlicher Öffentlichkeit noch als ästhetische Verkleidung politischer Aktion oder Kompensation ihrer Unmöglichkeit tritt das Theater im psychologischen Roman auf, sondern als Projektionsraum höchst privater Obsessionen" (Müller, *Die kranke Seele*, 349).

32. See Kontje on Schiller's consistent tendency to introduce possible objections to his theory of aesthetic education into his own text (*Constructing Reality*, 75-79, 98-115).

A similar episode in the fourth book of the *Lehrjahre* also deserves attention in this regard, particularly because it differs significantly from the *Sendung* in terms of how Goethe assesses Meister's tendency to identify with fictional characters. In book five, chapter seven of the *Sendung*, Meister becomes acquainted with Shakespeare's Prince Hal. Immediately sensing an affinity between the dissolute prince and himself, Meister begins to imitate Hal's manner of dress and action. Later in the same book Meister sets off at the head of the colorful band of actors, whom the narrator describes as follows: "Their peculiar clothing gave them an exotic appearance, and the weapons that they carried with them made them look even stranger.... Wilhelm was delighted at the sight" (TS, 819). Meister's momentary confusion of fiction with reality is soon interrupted by an ambush that scatters the troupe and leaves him seriously wounded. The lesson seems clear: Wilhelm has been guilty of the same sort of passionate identification with literature displayed by Werther and some of the readers of Goethe's first novel, though now the narrator maintains an ironic distance from his protagonist that prevents the readers from making the same mistake.

However, Goethe adds a fascinating narrative aside to the *Sendung* at this point that qualifies the critique of his protagonist: "We cannot conceal from our readers that this was the original scene that we have seen imitated and reproduced ad nauseum on the German stage of late. The notion of gallant vagabonds, noble robbers, magnanimous gypsies, and all sorts of other idealized rabble owes its true origin to this resting place which we have just depicted with a sort of reluctance, for it can only be extremely annoying not to be able to acquaint the public with the original before the copies have already robbed the theme of its charm and novelty" (TS, 819). The narrator is annoyed that this poetic scene has since become a hackneyed cliché on the German stage. He depicts this "original" scene with some reluctance, because the subsequent proliferation of copies has made it difficult for the audience to appreciate its novelty. The original looks like a copy to those who have been inundated with copies of it, yet it is quite clear that the "original" is itself a self-conscious copy of Shakespeare.

The ambivalence with which this episode is portrayed in the *Sendung* can be seen as Goethe's indirect comment on the reception of *Werther.* While Werther is willing to identify with works of literature to the point of arranging his suicide as a literary quotation, Goethe signals his distance from his protagonist by introducing an impartial "editor" of Werther's final letters. However, many of the novel's first readers, like Anton Reiser, tended to emulate Werther's own form of reading, rather than assuming a posture of critical detachment toward the text.[33] These readers identified with the novel to the extent that they began to dress like Werther, think like Werther, and even kill themselves like Werther. In the *Sendung* Goethe has increased the distance between the narrator and Wilhelm Meister to the extent that such naive identification is impossible. Nevertheless, he still offers a qualified defense of his protagonist based on the claim that he is at least one step closer to the source than those who merely imitate his imitations. Seen in terms of a commentary on *Werther* and *Wertherwirkung,* the passage suggests Goethe is aware that his heroes' seemingly spontaneous emotions and actions are derivative, and it also includes a disclaimer to the effect that Goethe cannot be held responsible for the literary parodies and personal tragedies his novel provoked. Like Werther, Wilhelm Meister is a fool to get carried away with the charade to the extent that he does; still, it is better to set a trend than to copy a copy.

In the revised version of this episode in the *Lehrjahre,* Goethe has removed the ambivalence. The argument for the relative originality of Meister's imitation has been deleted, and the stance of the narrator toward his actions has grown more distant and critical. Neutral statements of fact by the narrator in the first version are now identified as the thoughts of individual characters. For example, he writes in the *Sendung* that the fresh air and beautiful scenery has had a positive effect on the group, "since the wide-open sky and the beauty of the landscape put everyone into high spirits [*jedes Gemüt höher stimmte*]" (TS, 818). The same passage in the *Lehrjahre* suggests that the scenery merely contributes to the troupe's general willingness to have a "romantic" adventure: "... they were all much more alive and alert when ... the wide-open sky and the beauty of the landscape [*seemed* to cleanse everyone's spirits] (*jedes Gemüt zu reinigen* schien)" {131} (7:223; emphasis added, translation modified). In the *Sendung* the narrator simply reports that Wilhelm Meister imagines himself to be the director of the shared illusion: "He could see himself as the leader of the group. He talked about this idea to each and every one, building it up into a thing of color and poetry" (TS, 819). In the revised account of Meister's role as

---

33. See Scherpe for analysis of the contemporary reception of the novel and reprints of some of the literary responses it inspired (*Werther und Wertherwirkung*). While Scherpe claims that Goethe's work broke with the expectations of the public (15), Mandelkow asserts "daß der 'Werther' den Erwartungen des bürgerlichen Publikums in einer geradezu idealen Weise entsprach" ("Einleitung," xl). Waniek takes a middle position, asserting that *Werther* only partially broke through its contemporary horizon of expectations ("*Werther* lesen und Werther als Leser"). Whatever the reason, all agree that *Werther* enjoyed a degree of popularity unmatched by Goethe's later fiction.

self-appointed leader of a foolish enterprise, the tone has become sharply critical: "Wilhelm was in a state of unusual delight, seeing himself as the leader of a nomadic tribe, and, with this in mind, talking to each and every one and building up *this illusion of the moment* [*den Wahn des Moments*] into a thing of color and poetry" (7:223; emphasis added).

The revision of this particular episode characterizes the transformation of Meister's "theatrical mission" into an important but limited episode in his overall development. The model society that promised to improve the German public disintegrates into a quarreling group of selfish ragamuffins after the bandits puncture their common illusion. But even as Wilhelm Meister's patriotic hopes for the theater are being ironically undercut, he periodically resumes the autobiographical project he had begun so enthusiastically in the first book with his mother and Mariane. His reassessment of his youthful literary productions at the beginning of book two stands as a negative counterpart to the attempt to overcome temporality by uniting his life with Mariane's in a common narrative in book one. However, as he takes up his engagement with the theater again, he also makes tentative efforts toward reflecting on the events of his own life. After neglecting his business duties entirely for some time, Wilhelm sits down with a guilty conscience to write a letter to his family. He makes good progress on the letter—although he realizes that he has drifted away from the true story more than once—until he discovers to his frustration that he has written his letter on the back of a page with some verses he had copied for Madame Melina (7:110). These verses foil his effort to construct a fictional narrative that he had planned to pass off as autobiography. Irritated, he tears up the letter and postpones writing another.

When he finally does manage to complete his second letter, the product is no more accurate than the first fragment. "He avoided giving a factual account. Instead he merely hinted, in significant and mystical terms, at what it was that might have happened to him" {121} (7:206). The narcissistic tendency of the "fantastic castle in the air" {121} (7:207) he has created—not so much an attempt at honest communication as an exercise in fictional self-aggrandizement—is underscored by the fact that as soon as he seals the letter he begins to recite its contents to himself, "an extensive monologue, recapitulating the contents of the letter and picturing for himself an active and distinguished future" {121} (7:207). Both Werner and Wilhelm's father respond generously to this strange narrative, and Wilhelm foolishly promises them a more factual account of his travels in a forthcoming letter. Here he is caught in his own trap, for he realizes that he has paid no attention to the world around him during his self-absorbed journey. He solves the problem by constructing a diary with the assistance of Laertes by plagiarizing various travelogues. Paradoxically enough, the fake diary that inspires Werner's admiration actually begins to make Wilhelm pay attention to the world around him.

While the diary helps direct Meister's attention away from himself and toward his surroundings, his prolonged study of Shakespeare's *Hamlet* enables a continuation of his autobiographical concerns in displaced form. From the moment Wilhelm begins to read Shakespeare's works he realizes that they have a significance that transcends all other literature he has encountered. " 'They are not fictions!' " he exclaims to Jarno, " 'One seems to be standing before the huge open folios of Fate in which the storm winds of life in all their turbulence are raging, blowing the pages back and forth' " {112} (7:192). Shakespeare does not write works of fiction that provide a temporary escape from reality; rather, his *oeuvre* constitutes *the* book that contains all reality. Like the Bible, then, Shakespeare's works must be read intensively, and Wilhelm's first reaction to Jarno's present is to retreat into an isolated room, where "he lived and moved in the world of Shakespeare, entirely oblivious of all that was going on outside" {108} (7:185).

In other words, Meister's encounter with Shakespeare precipitates a second secularized conversion experience. The combination of Meister's love for the theater with his love for Mariane placed his childhood into a new perspective in book one and inspired him to reconstruct his own self-contained world in the act of narration. Now he loses himself in the larger world offered him in Shakespeare. At first he simply surrenders his identity to that of Prince Hal, with the disastrous results noted above. In the case of Hamlet, however, Wilhelm Meister substitutes analysis for identification. His version of literary criticism consists of constructing a psychological portrait of Hamlet that aims to make his behavior in the play plausible. This project parallels his attempts to discover a personal teleology through the narration of the events that brought him to Mariane's bed in book one, except that he has substituted Hamlet's childhood for his own.

That is, Wilhelm Meister constructs another version of his autobiography by developing a biography of Hamlet. As David Roberts has pointed out in meticulous detail, the structure of the *Lehrjahre* mirrors the structure of *Hamlet,* and Wilhelm's oedipal crisis mirrors that of Hamlet. In first analyzing Hamlet, Meister objectifies his own psychological problems; by then enacting the role on stage, he is said to play through "the oedipal conflict, which... releases him from the spell of the tragedy."[34] Now, it is certainly true that Meister avoids the tragedy that overcomes Hamlet, but the avoidance of tragedy is not due to any conscious application of lessons learned by analyzing Shakespeare's work. On the contrary, Meister's insights into Hamlet remain alienated from insights into himself—*we* can perceive the mirroring, but he does not. As Aurelia says, he may be remarkably insightful when it comes to understanding Hamlet, but he remains ignorant about himself and the people around him: " 'When I hear you explaining Shakespeare, it seems as if you have just come from a council of the gods and heard them discussing how to make humans; but when you are associating with real people, you seem like some first child of creation' " {153} (7:257).

Here again we encounter the relative *lack* of psychological depth in Goethe's protagonist. Hamlet requests the performance of "The Murder of Gonzago" or "The Mousetrap" to awaken Claudius's repressed guilt: "The play's the thing / Wherein I'll catch the conscience of the king" (act II, scene 2, lines 611-12). By contrast, Wilhelm Meister's insight into Hamlet's character remains alienated from any potential insight into himself. Like Faust beholding the sign of the macrocosm, Wilhelm Meister's study of Shakespeare's "folios of Fate" grants him an image of ultimate truth—"But alas! only a spectacle (*Aber ach! ein Schauspiel nur!*)" (3:22)—that resists his attempts to incorporate it into his life. Moreover, the public success of the *Hamlet* performance is short-lived, and Wilhelm soon discovers that the theater troupe can get along quite nicely without him.

When Aurelie becomes increasingly disturbed toward the end of the fifth book, the same doctor who claims to have cured the harpist by having him read the daily newspaper suggests that Wilhelm Meister read to her from the manuscript he has entitled *Bekenntnisse einer schönen Seele* (*Confessions of a Beautiful Soul*) {212} (7:350). Wilhelm follows the advice, and his reading does seem to have a comforting effect on Aurelie in the few days left before she dies. Soon after her death Meister takes his leave of the theater troupe and sets off to chastize her unfaithful lover, Lothario. But before the reader is allowed to discover what happens next, Goethe interrupts the novel for a full sixty pages to provide us with the apparently unrelated text Meister has just read to Aurelie. This "unmotivated" interruption seems calculated to disorient the uninitiated reader. While Schiller tactfully asserted that he found the *Bekenntnisse* intrinsically interesting, he also pointed out that other

---

34. *The Indirections of Desire,* 29.

readers might be impatient to get on with the rest of the novel, a point Goethe readily conceded.[35]

By the end of the novel we realize that the *Bekenntnisse* do in fact introduce us to an earlier generation of the family and friends that we meet in the final two books of the novel, and who, as it turns out, have been fleetingly present already in the opening books. As in the restructured version of the novel's opening book, Goethe has disrupted the chronological order of events to produce a self-contained narrative that, as he indicates in a letter to Schiller, points simultaneously in two different directions. "This book, which I plan to complete before Palm Sunday, has very unexpectedly proven to be a great stimulus to my work, as it points both forward and backward, and while it limits, it simultaneously leads and guides."[36] Once again, the extensive movement of the picaro has been sublated, *aufgehoben,* in the circular form of a self-contained narrative. In the process, however, Meister grows increasingly passive and distanced from the mirroring text. In the opening book of the novel he had been the author of his own self-analysis. In books four and five this analysis was displaced onto the figure of Hamlet. Now he becomes the passive consumer of an autobiographical narrative that would seem to have nothing to do with himself.

As it turns out, Wilhelm unexpectedly encounters figures already present in his past and who are soon to play an important role in his future. Rather than being a foreign body in an otherwise unified text, the *Bekenntnisse einer schönen Seele* introduces a pattern that dominates the final two books of the novel. While the forward progress of the narrative slows to a near halt, Wilhelm listens to one story after the next about events in the lives of others. Theresa tells him of her love for Lothario, Barbara informs him of Mariane's cruel fate, and the Marchesa clarifies the identity of Mignon and the harpist. If only by implication, these seeming digressions do have some bearing on Wilhelm's life: the *Bekenntnisse* not only introduce him to the members of the Tower Society, but also present him with the autobiography of a person whose apparent strength of character contrasts with his own tendency toward vacillation.[37] Theresa's story inspires sympathy and indirectly leads

---

35. "Jedermann findet das Sechste Buch an sich selbst sehr interessant, wahr und schön, aber man fühlt sich dadurch im Fortschritt aufgehalten" (to Goethe, 20 November 1795, *Briefwechsel Schiller Goethe,* 1:155). Similar comments in the earlier letter of 17 August 1795, 1:126. To this first letter Goethe acknowledged that the "Effekt aufs große Publikum" would be "etwas geschwächt" (to Schiller, 18 August 1795, 1:129); the second provoked a polemic against the public's insatiable desire for more of the same from its well-known writers (to Schiller, 23 November 1795, 1:159).

36. 18 March 1795, *Briefwechsel Schiller Goethe,* 1:96.

37. Wilhelm praises the " 'Selbständigkeit ihrer Natur und die Unmöglichkeit, etwas in

him back to Natalie; Barbara reawakens repressed guilt; and the Harpist's suicide, caused as it is by his reading of the Marchesa's family history, provides a negative contrast to Meister's unexpected good fortune at the end of the novel. But what has happened to Wilhelm Meister's own attempts to understand the purpose of his life? For an answer, we must turn to his discovery of the *Lehrjahre* manuscript written by the members of the Tower Society.

As in the opening book of the novel, Wilhelm's impulse toward autobiographical reflection is motivated by his love for a woman, in this case Theresa. In a reversal of the Mariane episode in the opening book, Theresa tells Wilhelm her story at great length when he first meets her, while he resists her request to narrate his own: "'Unfortunately, ... I have nothing to relate except one mistake after another, one false step after the other, and I cannot think of anybody I would rather not tell about the constant confusion I was and still am in, than you'" (273) (7:446). Soon after the Tower Society has declared that his apprenticeship is over, however, Meister realizes that he must find a wife to take proper care of his young son Felix. Theresa seems the logical choice. Now he decides that he has to include an account of his own life along with his proposal of marriage. "She should get to know him as well as he knew her, and he began to work over his own life story; but it seemed so totally lacking in events of any significance, and anything he would have to report was so little to his advantage that more than once he was tempted to give up the whole idea" (309) (7:504). In the opening book Wilhelm looked back over his life with the self-satisfaction of a deluded young man; now, after years of experience, he has learned only to despair at the pointlessness of his existence. "Finally he decided to ask Jarno for the scroll of his apprenticeship from the tower, and Jarno said this was just the right time. So Wilhelm got possession of it" (309) (7:504).

It may seem slightly surprising to discover that the Tower Society

---

sich aufzunehmen, was mit der edlen, liebevollen Stimmung nicht harmonisch war'" (7:518). As such, she provides a marked contrast to the man who, as Lydia puts it, has "'wenigstens keinen Charakter!'" (7:462). As various readers have pointed out, however, Wilhelm overlooks a number of factors that qualify the exemplary character of Natalie's aunt: her "natural" aversion to sex may well be attributable to her own sickness, or, as Zantop has argued, to her victimization by a society in which the female sex drive cannot be fulfilled without the renunciation of her *Bildungstrieb* ("Eignes Selbst und fremde Formen," 78-79). Her Pietism also marks her as a member of an earlier generation whose religious faith is no longer accessible to Wilhelm Meister. See Strack's article and the reproduction of the discussion that followed the original presentation of his paper for a balanced account of the positive and negative aspects of this character in her relation to Goethe's protagonist ("Selbst-Erfahrung oder Selbst-Entsagung?").

members have not only been secretly observing Wilhelm Meister throughout the novel, but have also been writing their own version of his life. Jarno explains the logic behind their actions in a later conversation with Wilhelm. Originally, he says, the members of the Tower Society tended to look down on those not in their ranks with a sense of superiority; the Abbé, however, convinced them that they should also be interested in encouraging the education of others, while continuing to pursue self-observation in the midst of purposeful activity. "That is how the various confessions arose, written sometimes by ourselves and sometimes by others, from which the records of apprenticeship were subsequently put together" {336} (7:549).

After the bitter self-critique cited above, Meister opens the *Lehrjahre* with understandable trepidation, yet is soon pleased to find the precise, objective, yet sympathetic record of his life that he was unable to compose himself: "He saw a picture of himself, not like a second self in a mirror, but a different self, one outside of him, as in a painting. One never approves of everything in a portrait, but one is always glad that a thoughtful mind has seen us thus and a superior talent enjoyed portraying us in such a way that a picture survives of what we were, and will survive longer than we will" {309} (7:505). Satisfied with this portrait, he sits down again to write the autobiographical letter to Theresa, which he accomplishes by paraphrasing the contents of the text he has just read. He then sends this sizable manuscript along with a brief, decisive letter of proposal to Theresa.

As so often in the past, this attempt to gain control over his life fails. Although Theresa accepts the proposal, Lothario soon steps in to block the marriage. Matters only grow worse as the novel moves toward its conclusion, until its hero begins to despair of any attempt to improve himself. "'Does the world take such trouble to educate us,'" he questions bitterly, "'merely to show us that it cannot educate itself?'" {344} (7:562). He finally surrenders altogether and submits passively to the authority of the Tower Society. "'I consign myself entirely to my friends and their direction,' said Wilhelm, 'for it is useless trying to act according to one's own will in this world'" {364} (7:594). By the end of the novel he has become a complete cynic: "'There is no sense in blaming either fate, or ourselves. We are all miserable creatures, destined for misery; and is it not a matter of complete indifference whether it is our own fault or the workings of some higher force, or chance, virtue or vice, wisdom or madness, that plunges us into destruction?'" {371} (7:607). Of course, the novel ends on a positive note, as Lothario decides that Wilhelm can marry his sister Natalie instead of Theresa, but Wilhelm is merely the passive recipient of an unexpected reward at this point, hardly the shaper of his own destiny.

In this particular instance the Tower Society's plans for Wilhelm Meister happen to coincide with his desires. Earlier, however, the secret society's members were only too happy to use him in their devious plans to manipulate the lives of others. Instead of delivering his well-rehearsed tirade against Lothario, Wilhelm reluctantly agrees to lead the distraught Lydia on a wild-goose chase. When he returns bubbling with the news of his decision to leave the theater, the members of the Tower Society greet his confessions with utter indifference {301} (7:492). The superior degree of self-awareness allegedly possessed by this society's members has no noticeable effect on the way they choose to treat others. To cite only the most glaring example, Lothario is indirectly responsible for Aurelie's death, has abandoned Theresa after having slept with the woman he thinks is her mother, and still finds time for a sentimental visit to another old lover while recovering from wounds incurred during a duel in which he had seriously wounded the estranged husband of yet another of his sexual conquests.[38]

Caught in the web of characters like this, Meister deludes himself to think that he can assume direct control over his life. How could the character Goethe once described as "a poor dog" (8:519) hope to assert his will against that of the amoral, manipulative, and hypocritical group of aristocrats who comprise the Tower Society? The futility of his most important, decisive action, namely the proposal to Theresa, is already indicated in the method of his proposal itself. Unable to write his autobiography, he paraphrases the account of the Tower Society and tries to pass it off as his own, just as he had forged a diary from various publications to please his father {159} (7:267). Subsequent events reveal that he is merely a passive participant in *their* version of his life. In other words, his characterization of Hamlet as a purposeless character caught up in the machinery of a purposeful play applies equally well to himself. Unable to author his own existence in book one successfully, he now sees an alienated vision of attained harmony in the creation of the Tower Society and mistakes it for his own.[39]

38. See Schlaffer for a biting critique of Lothario and other members of the *Turmgesellschaft* ("Exoterik und Esoterik," esp. 220-21).

39. For Kittler, Meister's confrontation with his own *Lehrjahre* within the *Lehrjahre* marks the point at which his individuality is subsumed into the "discourse machine" of the *Turmgesellschaft* and becomes literature: "Er hört auf, ein Held von Begebenheiten zu sein, und wird zum Kettenglied einer Maschine, die Diskurse produziert, distribuiert und konsumiert. So wird die Literatur, in den *Lehrjahren* auf einen autoreferenziellen Punkt beschränkt, zum Element, darin der Held verschwindet" ("Sozialisation," 107). While Kittler's conclusion is correct, his formulation obscures a crucial point, namely that the dispersal of Meister's own identity into the discourse of the *Turmgesellschaft* occurs at precisely the moment when he thinks he has achieved this identity for himself. This sets

In the autobiographical poem "Dauer im Wechsel" ("Permanence in Change") and in his essay on Winckelmann, Goethe describes in positive terms the creative process that transforms the transience of life into the permanence of art, and Wilhelm Meister also takes pleasure in the fact that the Tower Society's portrait will continue to exist after he is gone. From another perspective, however, the triumph of art over time is a hollow one for the individual, for it does nothing to stop one's inevitable progress toward death. Thus when Meister contemplates the aesthetic order of the "Hall of the Past," he realizes that he is excluded from the timeless world he perceives. " 'What life there is,' " he exclaims, " 'in this Hall of the Past!... One could just as well call it the Hall of the Present, and of the Future. This is how everything was, and this is how everything will be. Nothing perishes *except him who observes and enjoys*' " {331} (7:541; emphasis added). Pleasurable contemplation of the symbolic transcendence of time in art flip-flops into increased awareness of his own mortality.

Wilhelm Meister's more pressing concern lies in making the transition from passive contemplation of an aesthetic order to renewed meaningful activity in the world around him. This problem is central to the cultural aspirations of German Classicism. Schiller contends in his *Aesthetic Education* that the autonomous work of art presents us with an image of the God-like freedom we deserve to experience as human beings. However, after having celebrated "the aesthetic mood" (*die ästhetische Stimmung*) as "the highest of all gifts, as the gift of humanity" in his twenty-first letter, he concedes that in actuality one loses the harmonious plenitude of this mood "with every particular condition [one] enters into" (*Werke* 5:636). If aesthetic education is going to solve real political problems while rendering revolution unnecessary, as Schiller contends at the end of his second letter, then this later admission constitutes a major threat to the efficacy of his entire project.[40]

While Schiller highlights the irreconcilable conflict between his idealistic hopes and his awareness that they stand only a slim chance of being realized, Goethe tends to accept the conflict with a shrug that recalls his "Epistles," with their dismissive attitude toward the notion of aesthetic education. Pithy axioms replace idealistic polemics tortured by self-questioning. "The one who acts is always without conscience," writes Goethe in one of his late "Maxims and Reflections." "The only person with a conscience is the one who observes" (#251; 12:399). This calm

---

up the tension that will govern the novel until its conclusion, as Meister gradually discovers his mistake. The very bitterness of this process constitutes the novel's strongest commentary on the negativity inherent in the concept of aesthetic education.

40. Kontje, *Constructing Reality*, 110.

acceptance of the irreconcilability of action and ethics recalls the basic premises of Goethe's *Faust*. God identifies error as inevitable in the "Prologue in Heaven," but the striving that results in error paradoxically guarantees Faust's salvation. Human tragedy takes place within the benevolent embrace of a divine comedy. Goethe suggests a similar interpretation of *Wilhelm Meister* in a later conversation with Eckermann: " 'For after all the whole thing seems to imply nothing more than that the individual who is guided by a higher hand, despite all stupid mistakes and embarrassments, still reaches a happy ending' " (8:520).[41]

The parallel is imperfect, however. The ever-striving Faust may be led by the higher hand of God through the intermediary of Gretchen, but the ever-passive Wilhelm Meister is pressed into a mold constructed by the ruthless members of the Tower Society. His fate at the end of the novel recalls that of Mignon; although she can have no place in their world while she is alive, they seize upon the opportunity to turn her corpse into a grotesquely lifelike mummy. "Mignon's funeral is unspeakable kitsch," writes the Italian critic Giuliano Baioni. "[She] is artificially laid out and embalmed in a classical sarcophagus in the middle of the so-called 'Hall of the Past' in Natalia's villa, this true mausoleum of the future eclecticism of the nineteenth century."[42] Even the maxims that out of context testify to Goethe's wisdom serve to browbeat the beleaguered protagonist of his novel. " 'Understanding extends, but also immobilizes,' " intones Jarno, " 'action mobilizes, but also restricts.' 'Do desist from giving me any more of these wondrous observations,' Wilhelm interjected. 'Such verbiage has confused me quite enough' " {337} (7:550). " 'Heavens! No more maxims, please! I feel they are inadequate balm for a wounded heart' " {339} (7:553).[43]

Shortly before the conclusion of the novel, Wilhelm Meister suffers from depression that drives him to wander through the house while everyone else sleeps. "He could neither accept nor reject what surrounded

---

41. Hass comes closest to analyzing the *Lehrjahre* from this perspective. He claims that error is an essential component of Wilhelm's development, whose adventures are portrayed with a pervasive sense of irony; however, providential nature ensures a positive outcome for the hero ("Wilhelm Meisters Lehrjahre"). In addition to the objections raised later in this chapter concerning the questionable ethics of the *Turmgesellschaft* members, one might also question why the same nature fails to come to the aid of Mignon or the *Harfner*.

42. Baioni, "Märchen," 115.

43. "Das sententiöse Gehaben entspringt der an sich schon etwas komischen Pedanterie des Turms, der an sich schon grotesk anmutenden Überzeugung, daß man sich gewissermaßen mit einer aufrecht gehaltenen Stange durch das Gestrüpp der Welt schlagen könne—der Überzeugung, daß es zuletzt überall auf Begriffe, Grundsätze und Regeln ankomme..." (Schlechta, *Goethes Wilhelm Meister*, 168).

him, everything reminded him of something else, he could see the whole chain of his life, but at the moment it lay in pieces which would not join together again" {349-50} (7:570). Much to his astonishment, the Tower Society hammers the ring together by arranging for his marriage to Natalie. The sense of closure he had sought through his love for Mariane has finally been granted him by a third party. Wilhelm Meister's aesthetic education is complete.[44] He has not only learned the folly of identifying with fictional characters; he has also given up any attempt to take an active role in becoming the author of his own existence. In the place of the sensual and fertile Mariane he receives the ethereal, sterile Natalie in a marriage that, as far as we can tell, is never consummated. The ring is hammered shut, the novel reaches its conclusion, and a shell-shocked but obedient Wilhelm Meister is sent off toward Italy to begin a prolonged period of wandering and celibacy.

---

44. But not in the positive sense argued by Albert Berger (*Ästhetik und Bildungsroman*). He claims that as the theater disappears in the course of the novel, Meister learns to view the world itself aesthetically. Like the other critics mentioned above, Berger can only make this assertion by ignoring the sense of personal despair that characterizes Wilhelm's mood in the final pages of the novel. Rather than demonstrating the triumphant realization of the aesthetic condition in the person of Wilhelm Meister (Berger, 143), Goethe explores the negative aspects of the same aesthetics, as Meister finds it impossible to reconcile his perception of a purposeful order in his *Lehrjahre* with his ongoing problems in reality.

Professional Romanticism: Ludwig Tieck's *Franz Sternbalds Wanderungen* (1798)

5

Ludwig Tieck has been viewed with more suspicion, even outright hostility, than perhaps any other writer associated with the Romantic movement in Germany. Rudolf Haym set the tone for a century of Tieck scholarship with the following biographical sketch: a psychologically unstable child born into an unhealthy environment is corrupted at an early age by excessive and indiscriminate reading. Then two early mentors—Rambach and Nicolai—abuse the young man's glib facility with words by employing him in the production of pulp fiction. Far from resisting this literary "seduction," Tieck displays a remarkable virtuosity, but a disturbing lack of moral fiber, by producing whatever is demanded of him.[1] Thus he begins his career as a prolific but superficial hack, equally capable of producing elegantly didactic stories for Nicolai, in the tradition of the Enlightenment, and a sensational, hair-raising conclusion to Rambach's Gothic novel *Die eiserne Maske* (The Iron Mask). To be sure, the slightly older Tieck is grudgingly credited as the first to assemble what would become the familiar topoi of Romantic prose: "the

---

1. "In wahrhaft frevelhafter Weise wurde der achtzehnjährige Primaner um seine litterarische Unschuld gebracht, wurde er um das Gefühl der Würde des schriftstellerischen Berufes und der Heiligkeit der ersten Regungen des poetischen Genius betrogen" (Haym, *Die romantische Schule*, 29). Influential sketches of Tieck's career by both Gundolf ("Ludwig Tieck") and Staiger ("Ludwig Tieck") reproduce the essential elements of Haym's analysis. See Lillyman's opening chapter for a detailed look at this persistent trend in Tieck reception (*Reality's Dark Dream*).

'magical moonlit night' [*mondbeglänzte Zaubernacht*] of the Middle Ages, ... the German 'forest-loneliness' [*Waldeinsamkeit*], and ... romantic irony."² In later years, however, Tieck returned to his role as a popular writer with a series of now-forgotten novellas that catered to the taste of emerging *Biedermeier* society. Gundolf summarized this often-repeated assessment of Tieck's literary career with particular nastiness: "He began as a low-class popular writer.... he ended as an old man of literature [*Literaturgreis*] and high-class popular writer."³

Ironically enough, these critics take offense at those tendencies in Tieck's professional career that seem to contradict the notion of the artist he himself helped propagate in his most influential work, *Franz Sternbalds Wanderungen* (Franz Sternbald's Wanderings). Here we are told repeatedly that the artist is a rare and superior breed of humanity, whose autonomous works of art glorify God and the universe. Philistines, in contrast, concern themselves only with earning money and gaining social prestige. Trapped in a hostile world, it is not surprising that the young artist should suffer, as Dürer explains to his pupil Franz Sternbald: "There is something wonderful about the fact that we painters never really fit in with other people, that our activity and industry has absolutely no effect on the events of world trade, as is after all the case with other artisans."⁴ Thus Sternbald's sense of alienation from society becomes a virtue: the state demands uniformity among its members, but the artist celebrates his or her own uniqueness.

Viewed from this perspective, the young Tieck was guilty of two cardinal sins against his own philosophy: he not only agreed to betray his personal integrity by subordinating his opinions to the demands of his literary mentors, but worse, he did it for money. Even critics sympathetic to Tieck usually sidestep the problem by forgiving Tieck for his literary apprenticeship and basing his reputation on a handful of canonical works.⁵ Only Heinz Hillmann offers an interpretation that argues for the continuity of Tieck's literary development from producer and

---

2. Gundolf, "Ludwig Tieck," 139.
3. Gundolf, "Ludwig Tieck," 7.
4. *Franz Sternbalds Wanderungen: Studienausgabe*, 59. All subsequent references to this edition are included in the text.
5. Thalmann (*Weltmann*, 23), Ribbat (*Ludwig Tieck*, 19), Paulin (*Ludwig Tieck*, 18), and Lillyman (*Reality's Dark Dream*, 1-5) all defend Tieck against the charge of superficiality while regarding his earlier work as part of a useful apprenticeship for a professional author. Serious critical attention is reserved for Tieck's most familiar works. Thus Lillyman prefaces his study of Tieck by pointing out that he "is not concerned with all of Tieck's vast output of novels, fairy-tales and novellas, but only with his major achievements as a writer of narrative fiction" (vii). Ribbat also stresses the selective nature of his Tieck study ("Vorwort").

parodist of popular fiction to influential Romantic artist. In his insightful comments on Tieck's early novel *Peter Lebrecht* (1795/96) Hillmann shows how this comic novel parodies the popular fiction Tieck himself was quite capable of writing. In so doing, he points out, Tieck addresses the problematic status of literature that had become a substitute for and escape from the retrograde political situation in his contemporary Germany. Rather than representing an absolute break with this earlier work, Hillmann claims, *Franz Sternbalds Wanderungen* presents a subtler reworking of the same basic technique: "Thus the transformation of reality into the novelistic [*ins Romaneske*] by means of traditional schemata of the novel at the end of the eighteenth century corresponds, with slight variations, to the process of romanticizing. The high literature of Romanticism, at least that of Tieck, appears therefore as a more tasteful, refined, sublimated version of earlier popular literature."[6]

It is important that we do not mistake Hillmann's identification of the popular roots of Tieck's Romanticism for a disparaging interpretation that only gives "some modern sociological garb" to "the old fallacious and misinformed biographical approach."[7] Biographical criticism deserves to be rejected if it only serves to slander character, or if it reduces the literary work to a roman à clef. Nevertheless, literature *is* written by particular individuals in particular institutional contexts, and efforts to take this fact into account in the interpretation of a given text need not be dismissed out of hand in the misguided interest of shielding

---

6. Hillmann, "Ludwig Tieck," 116. Long before Hillmann, Robert Minder had pointed out that the multitude of literary forms in Tieck's work does not come from a richness of human experience, but rather from reading: "Sans jamais plagier au sens réel du mot, Tieck a toujours eu besoin, pour écrire lui-même, de stimulants livresques, de modèles littéraires" (*Un Poète Romantique Allemand*, 28). However, he bases his interpretation of Tieck's work on a psychological model that is unconcerned with the problems of literary sociology addressed by Hillmann.

7. Lillyman, *Reality's Dark Dream*, 19. It is true, however, that Hillmann's interpretation of *Sternbald* proves disappointingly dismissive, as he regards it primarily as the expression of Tieck's longing to escape from an unbearable reality (125-26). While his willingness to view Tieck's literary production in its institutional context marks a welcome new development in Tieck scholarship, his thumbnail sketch of the social function of literature in the 1790s remains simplistic and overly negative. "Entpolitisierung, Privatisierung und Ästhetisierung" (112) were only the negative consequences of a literary movement that also played a positive role in the transformation of popular consciousness. Ribbat offers a more balanced assessment of the transformation of the public sphere that affected the young Tieck: "In einem allmählichen, kaum je dramatischen Prozeß hatte sich hier das Bürgertum eine Plattform relativer Selbstbestimmung geschaffen und hielt mit ihr emanzipatorische Möglichkeiten für solche Jugendliche bereit, für die sich die altständischen Bindungen gelockert hatten—was, wie angedeutet, vor allem in Berlin aktuell wurde" (*Ludwig Tieck*, 13).

literature from the contamination of its historical setting. Tieck in particular lends himself to an attempt to understand literature in its institutional context for two reasons: First, he was not alone in his struggles to make ends meet as a professional writer. His career has a representative status that extends beyond the merely personal. Second, and more important, Tieck reflects on the problems that attended the emergence of the professional author in his literary works themselves. Rather than representing a clean break with Tieck's earlier career, *Franz Sternbalds Wanderungen* offers a subtle analysis of the economic pressures that continued to affect Romantic artists like himself, who insisted on the absolute distinction between their art and financial concerns.[8] Moreover, Franz Sternbald's journey toward the discovery of his identity follows the already familiar pattern of countless literary characters who preceded him on this path. As a result, the novel most responsible for the dissemination of the Romantic understanding of the artist contains a critical subtext that exposes the contradictions of its own position.

We first meet Franz Sternbald as he embarks on a European journey that he expects will last several years. During this time he plans to complete the apprenticeship as an artist that he began several years earlier with Albrecht Dürer. Of particular importance is his desire to view the works of the Italian masters at first hand before returning to Nuremberg. Yet he soon faces temptation from those who would prevent him from completing his mission. The businessman Zeuner, who had dabbled in the arts himself as a younger man, urges Sternbald to abandon his art for the wealth and social prestige available in the business world. Then his mother encourages him to give up his foolish plan to travel to Italy and instead to become a respectable farmer. Sternbald rejects both offers out of hand. He insists that being an artist is not like having the sort of profession where one considers the potential profit of one's activity. " 'I never think of my earnings when I think of art; indeed, I can hate myself when I sometimes fall into such thoughts' "

---

8. Even after his earliest years Tieck had to struggle to earn his living as a writer to a greater degree than his contemporaries like Goethe, Schiller, Novalis, and the Schlegels: "We must concede that Tieck's position was difficult, if not anomalous, from the very start. The Schlegels were fully engaged in high-class journalism and managing to fend for themselves, especially the provident August Wilhelm; Schelling and Novalis were salaried officials; Tieck alone, perhaps lacking Friedrich Schlegel's sheer energy or August Wilhelm's tidy organization, was plagued by the problem of where the next work was to be published and how much the publisher was likely to advance" (Paulin, *Ludwig Tieck*, 102-3).

(54). Significantly enough, however, what begins as an unqualified assertion trails off into guilty self-accusation. Apparently it is not so easy to suppress all thoughts of money even when trying to concentrate exclusively on art.

The topic emerges already in the midst of his sentimental departure from his best friend, Sebastian, who insists that he would not sell Franz's sculpture " 'even if someone were to offer me a lot of money for it' " (12). United in their love for art and respect for Dürer, Sebastian and Franz are not about to allow financial concerns to encroach upon their special relationship. At the same time, however, Sebastian reveals that the art produced in the sanctified atmosphere of Dürer's workshop *is* usually for sale. In fact, Sternbald admits to his mother that he is financing his journey with money earned as Dürer's apprentice: " 'I have scrupulously saved all of the money I could get for this purpose; what would Dürer say if I were to give up everything now?' " (53). The journey is an investment of the profits of his apprenticeship; to give up now would be to incur substantial penalties for early withdrawal.

In rejecting the offers of his mother and Zeuner, Franz avoids a life without art altogether. At the opposite end of the spectrum lies his encounter with a simple peasant family for whom art, life, and religion are still one. Sternbald delights in "the happiness of quiet domesticity, a modest calm" (29) that he finds in the circle of the old farmer's extended family, in a way that recalls Werther's praise of patriarchal times. After dinner the children gather around the old man and request stories of the old martyrs, "nothing new, but what he had told them many times before. The more they heard it, the more they liked it" (30). Tieck thus invokes a nostalgic image of a family that still practices the old "intensive" reading, or in this case, storytelling. The stories function as both entertainment and religious instruction; the audience is the family, not the public; payment is obviously not expected, and neither is novelty. Later that evening Sternbald writes to tell Sebastian that the legendary Golden Age is to be found in such scenes as he has just experienced, not in some distant realm. However, Sternbald remains an observer of a scene that charms him with a noble simplicity he cannot share, and his letter ends on a note of confusion and lament: " 'I no longer know what I am; my mind is completely confused' " (35).

This incident is only one of several in which Franz encounters images of simple wholeness that contrast with his own dissatisfaction. His trip to the retreat of an old hermit seems like an entry "into primeval times" (251); an evening meal with a simple family of colliers fills him with "the calm, pious feelings that had delighted him so often" (346-47); he hears of the mythical Arion's power (436-37) and dreams of a utopian world where all could be artists (76-77). However, these images serve to define rather than to solve Sternbald's problems. He is a professional artist, not a mythical singer from the past, nor a patriarchal storyteller in the present, nor an inhabitant of a future utopia where artists would have the enthusiastic support of an understanding community.[9] Any real solution to the inherent contradiction between his disdain for economic concerns and his need to make a living from his art will have to take the form of a compromise.

Midway through the novel the businessman and art collector Vansen presents Sternbald with the opportunity for just such a compromise. While Franz has rejected both Herr Zeuner's and his mother's suggestions that he abandon his art altogether, Vansen's offer proves more difficult to refuse. If Sternbald agrees to marry his daughter Sara, then Vansen will not only see to it that Franz can pursue his art without having to worry about money, but he will also finance Sternbald's trip to Italy. "'Then you can devote all your energies to your art, as you have always desired. You will become well known, even famous, my daughter will be happy with you, and all of my wishes will be fulfilled,'" summarizes Vansen (182). As it turns out, Sara is already in love with the young blacksmith Messys, whom Franz had met soon after leaving Nuremberg. Rather than accepting the offer himself, Franz convinces Vansen to sanction an engagement between Messys and Sara, on the condition that Messys recover from his illness and become the artist he now longs to be.

By rejecting Vansen's offer, Sternbald tries to avoid an unholy alliance between his art and capital gains of the business world. Although Vansen seems to respect the artist much more than the Philistines of the world, the narrator points out that his patronage of the arts is motivated by "vanity and a mania for collecting and accumulating" (172), rather than any deep understanding of art, "for Vansen's love of painting was nothing more than a blind impulse that happened to have thrown itself into art" (172). Although Sternbald chooses a life of adventure over marriage to Vansen's daughter, he *is* willing to accept "a handsome present" (189) from his would-be patron upon leaving Antwerp. Seen idealistically, Vansen gives Franz the money simply because he loves him like a son. Viewed from a more critical perspective, the gift is a reward for services rendered: while Sternbald refuses to prostitute him-

---

9. Hibberd examines Tieck's indebtedness to the eighteenth-century idyll, while noting correctly that the novel itself is more problematic than the idyllic tradition it occasionally cites: "His novel breaks way from the idyllic tradition and shows its limitations, but at the same time reveals the vigour of its spell" ("The Idylls in Tieck's *Sternbald,*" 249).

self and his art to the vanity of a second- or third-rate businessman (171-72), he is nonetheless willing to set up his young friend in the same position and take his share of the profits.

Thus while Sternbald loudly proclaims the utter incompatibility between the worlds of art and business, his actions indicate that the two realms stand in an uneasy relation of mutual dependence. A closer examination of his two role models reveals that they have attained artistic greatness only by sacrificing many pleasures of life. While Lukas presents himself as a happy-go-lucky sort of fellow, his life history reveals a man driven since childhood by his artistic impulses to the point that it seems he has no time for any pleasure beyond his work: " 'I've been like this since childhood. I have never enjoyed games, stories, or other pastimes' " (96). Both he and Dürer lead very "bourgeois" lives; they work at their art like a job and praise the middle-class values of diligence and thrift. Moreover, both artists are married to women presented as negative stereotypes of boorish housewives. " 'But my dears, stop your endless learned discussions. We women don't understand a word' " exclaims Lukas's wife as she turns to discuss Nuremberg fashion with Frau Dürer (116), who for her part is busy sending her husband to an early grave with her constant nagging about household finances.

By indicating the problematic conditions behind the artistic productivity of Sternbald's two mentors, Tieck transforms what seems like a wistful look back at the bygone days of Dürer's Germany into an investigation of the economic position of the artist within his own society, as noble benefactors are replaced by members of the business community, who obscure the contractual agreement between artist and patron beneath the rhetoric of their commonly shared humanity.[10] Tieck further explores the issues raised by Sternbald's encounter with Vansen in an anecdote told by an older art collector at Vansen's house.[11] In the story a rich patron of the arts becomes annoyed when an elderly painter refuses to sell him a commissioned work at the agreed price. The artist has grown so fond of what he correctly senses is his last major work that he is loath to part with it. The angry collector returns home and, on the way, buys an elaborately carved walking stick for a ridiculously

---

10. This process reveals another aspect of the "Strukturwandel des Mäzenats" that Christa Bürger analyzes in terms of Schiller's relation to the liberal noble Augustenburg (*Der Ursprung der bürgerlichen Institution Kunst*, 39-50). In *Sternbald* the patronage stems from the bourgeoisie, but is concealed under the same idealistic rhetoric.

11. The story had first appeared in Tieck's *Phantasieen* (1799) under the title "Eine Erzählung, aus einem italienischen Buch übersetzt." Tieck added it to the revised version of the novel published in 1843 (*Studienausgabe*, 431 n. 6).

low sum from another old artist, who also displays regret at parting from his creation.

Upon returning to the city, the rich man is about to mutilate the artist's carving by breaking it off from the staff that supports it, since he is embarrassed to be seen with such an ostentatious walking stick. Suddenly he realizes what the carving meant to the old man—and what the painting meant to the artist—and exclaims: "How lonely is the artist... whom we treat only like a valuable machine that produces artworks we love, while we neglect the creator himself: it is a base, damnable selfishness" (439). The collector realizes that what he had viewed as a simple exchange of money for a handmade object is to the artist a heartrending loss of his creation. Overcome with remorse, he rushes back to the home of the painter, begs his forgiveness, buys the painting at a much higher price than had been demanded or was expected, and allows the old artist to come visit his home whenever he wants. There they sit hand in hand in front of the work, sharing their pleasure until the old man dies six months later. But what has really changed? The bottom line remains the same: the rich collector buys the last completed work of an old painter and takes it home. The only difference is that he does so with a guilty conscience, which he seeks to appease with a combination of philanthropy and sentimentality.

Sternbald's rejection of Vansen's offer sets the stage for the second, prototypically "romantic" part of the novel, as Franz sets off toward Italy, encountering love and adventure along the way. Although he never explicitly criticizes Dürer or Lukas, his actions suggest that he is unwilling to make the sort of compromises they have made for the sake of their art. Rather than entering into the type of marriage he has observed in the two older artists, he sets off in the hope of finding his beloved Marie. Her attractiveness, however, is due at least in part to her probable unattainability. In a word, he rejects the predictable stability of marriage for a life dedicated to sensual pleasure, travel, and the indefinitely prolonged quest for his beloved: "But again he was afraid to determine the course of his life and to set limits on himself; yearning beckoned him into the distance again, strange sounds enticed him and promised golden happiness waiting for him far away" (182-83). The quest for the mysterious lover becomes a way of justifying the journey for its own sake. Life in the service *of* art is rejected in favor of a life *as* art.[12]

12. Anger summarizes the difference between the two halves of the novel in these same terms: "dort das Leben als opferbereiter Dienst an der Kunst—hier die Kunst zu leben, das Leben selbst als romantische Kunstwerk" ("Nachwort," 570). He does not, however, concentrate on how this new way of life compromises the integrity of Sternbald's art.

In the process, the concept of aesthetic autonomy is transferred from art to life. We recall that in the first half of the novel Sternbald had vigorously defended the autonomy of art against an old man's charge that art is something society could just as well do without. " 'I'll say it again,' " exclaims Sternbald in reply, " 'what is truly sublime cannot and must not be useful; this utility is completely foreign to its divine nature and to demand it is to denigrate the sublime and to degrade it to the vulgar needs of humanity' " (177). The same language is echoed in a different context in the second half of the novel when, surrounded by his good friends Roderigo, Rudolf, and Ludoviko, Sternbald laments the fact that he must continue on his journey: " 'I don't know myself how it happens that I have almost completely forgotten my objective.' 'One cannot forget one's objective,' interrupted Ludoviko, 'since the rational individual arranges matters so as to have no objective' " (322).

While Sternbald moves in hardworking bourgeois circles in the first half of the novel, he now moves in a world where characters have no pressing financial concerns: "Instead of having made his choice and having paid dearly and harshly for his devotion to the ideal, Sternbald gives the impression of moving through an almost fairy-tale landscape, where social and material contingencies no longer play any role."[13] The Duchess Adelheid, Roderigo's temporarily abandoned fiancée, has inherited wealth that enables her to turn her life into "a pleasant game" (467). "She was not willing to make do with the usual consolation of music, of diversions; she wanted to elevate her life itself into a poem" (479), complains the young Arnold to Franz in the revised edition of the novel, in which Tieck turns Adelheid into an irresponsible seductress. Florestan, Roderigo, and Ludoviko all have the time and money to devote their lives to carefree adventure. Even the hermit-artist whom Sternbald visits shows no concern for his finances. When Sternbald pays him for the picture of Marie, he simply pockets the money without even looking to see how much he has earned.

Although Sternbald had resisted the temptation to become integrated into bourgeois society in part one, in part two he refuses to abandon himself completely to the opposite extreme of the carefree way of life exemplified by these characters. His hope for a reunion with Marie restrains him from unbridled sensualism. His affair with Emma comes on the heels of Adelheid's false report that her sister is dead, and represents more of a desperate reaction to this disheartening news than

---

13. Fink, "L'Ambiguïte du message romantique," 64. See also Hillmann: "Geld haben diese wandernden Gesellen alle, meist weiß man nicht woher: genau das zeigt den unrealistischen Entwurf dieser Gestalten" ("Ludwig Tieck," 126).

an embrace of a live-for-the-day mentality or deep affection for Emma. He deserts the weeping Emma immediately after seducing her (279) and avoids the temptation of the beautiful and flirtatious Adelheid. Even in Florence, Sternbald remains distant from his bohemian friends. He alone finds Laura's "exceedingly merry stories" about her neighbors offensive (382), and in Rome he rejects his second mistress Lenore. "Franz found the frivolity of his way of life up to now insipid and dissatisfying; he regretted certain hours and resolved to devote himself more fervently to art" (397).

As this last passage indicates, Sternbald combines partial resistance to the loose morality of his companions with concern for the detrimental effect of this life-style on his artistic production. The artists in Florence encourage Sternbald to join their revels while neglecting his art. " 'Love is half of painting' " (375), Rustici assures him, and Andrea del Sarto seconds the notion: " 'Forget your paintings and be completely happy with us' " (377). Although the suggestion entices him momentarily, Sternbald is neither willing nor able to renounce his artistic calling completely. Lacking the money of the landed gentry, Sternbald is forced to accept work as a painter on projects that do not particularly interest him. In Antwerp he had painted Sara's portrait at his host Vansen's request (172); later Adelheid rewards him generously for his portrait of her and her absent lover Roderigo (271). He interrupts his journey to Italy again, on the advice of Bolz, who has secured him a job restoring a painting in a cloister for an abbess with little understanding of art. This commission occasions a crisis of conscience for Franz. "He felt that he had been hired as a mere artisan to make something for which his love for art, even his talent, was completely superfluous. 'What have I accomplished up till now?' he said to himself. 'In Antwerp I made a few portraits without particular interest; later I painted the Duchess and Roderigo because she was in love with him; and now I am here to touch up maxims, poorly drawn drapery, stags, and wolves' " (355).

Thus Franz's decision to reject Vansen's offer of a comfortable but dull life in the service of art for a life of romantic adventure results not in the solution of his original dilemma but in its inversion. Instead of leading an impoverished life for the sake of enriching his art, now Sternbald lives a richer life financed by an art that has degenerated into a mere job that pays for his adventures. At no time in the novel does he succeed in maintaining the clear distinction between the artist and the rest of society that is presented as inevitable by his mentor Dürer. Instead, the two worlds are necessarily connected in a uncomfortable alliance. The great artists celebrated in the first half of the novel produce their work at a price: they live like common laborers and receive their money from collectors like Vansen, who buy what they cannot comprehend. The noble adventurers of the second half of the novel can afford to hire the bourgeois artist, who can emulate their way of living at the risk of debasing his art to a mere job. His precarious position as a professional artist has been exposed, but not resolved.

Like the other romantic novels we will consider, *Franz Sternbalds Wanderungen* remains a fragment, despite Tieck's best intentions to conclude the work. Successive critics have attributed this defect to the incompatibility of the second half of the novel with the first, claiming that an explanation for this incompatibility can be found in the corrupting influence of Goethe and Heinse on a project conceived in the spirit of Wackenroder, in Tieck's own "loss of thematic control," or, more positively, in the emergence for the first time of what would become a familiar romantic way of life that could no longer be reconciled with the pious diligence represented by Dürer and his world.[14] By concentrating on the irreconcilability of the two halves of the novel as a source of its inconclusiveness, however, critics downplay the fact that the novel ends on a triumphant note that all but does away with any need for a continuation. Sternbald suddenly finds himself reunited with Marie shortly after the narrator asserts that he has also attained the personal maturity so obviously lacking throughout most of the novel: "Franz was now in the prime of his life. He was alert, his eyes sparkled, his cheeks were red, his gait noble, almost proud" (376). To be sure, the novel breaks off before the secret of his identity is revealed, but he has already encountered his (still unrecognized) brother Ludoviko, and we can easily anticipate the happy reunion of the family in Nuremberg at the conclusion of the novel, which Tieck described in 1843: "Everyone is happy: the story was to have ended in Nuremberg, in the cemetery where Dürer is buried, in the company of Sebastian."[15] All indications in the fragmentary novel point toward the successful outcome of Sternbald's triple

---

14. Haym formulated the first influential interpretation (*Die romantische Schule*, 130-40), while Sammons claims that the problem lies in Tieck's having lost sight of the original *Gehalt* of his work, namely Sternbald's struggle to turn artistic sensibility into artistic productivity ("Tieck's Franz Sternbald: The Loss of Thematic Control"). Anger represents the third point of view ("Nachwort").

15. Tieck, in *Dichter über ihre Dichtungen*, ed. Schweikert, 176. Anger lists a long series of questions that remain unanswered in the fragmentary novel ("Nachwort," 575-77), and yet, given the rapidity with which knots are tied already in the final pages of the second book, it seems clear that Tieck points toward a conclusion in which the divergent threads of the narrative are neatly knotted together: "die Vereinigung der Liebenden, das Wiederfinden der Verwandten, die Entwirrung aller Verwicklungen und die Lösung aller Rätsel" (Alewyn, "Ein Fragment der Fortsetzung," 68).

quest: to become a mature artist, to find his beloved, and to discover his true identity.

Not surprisingly, critics have complained that Tieck's attempts to tie up the various strands of his plot are "more than breathtaking," straining the credulity of the most generous reader.[16] Rather than pondering the potential conclusion of Tieck's novel, we are more apt to notice the forced nature of the solutions already present. Although the narrator suddenly asserts that Sternbald has reached the high point of his development, nothing in the text preceding this assertion indicates substantial maturation on his part.[17] Nor are we sufficiently prepared to accept his reunion with Marie as anything but a convenient way to end the second book of the novel on a positive note. In fact, a series of wildly improbable coincidences propel the plot of the entire novel. Sternbald's Europe seems to be populated by about a dozen mysteriously interrelated individuals who bump into one another in the most unlikely places and at the most unlikely times. No sooner does Sternbald lose his way in the forest than he is taken in by a zither-playing hermit or a blissful peasant family. Ludoviko jumps out of the bushes just after Roderigo has completed the tale of his long-lost friend, the hermit who shelters the pilgrim discovers that he had once lost his bride to that same pilgrim, and Vansen's daughter loves none other than the same blacksmith who happened to encounter Franz outside of Nuremberg. Franz's stepfather manages to live long enough to tell Sternbald that he is not his real father, but conveniently dies before he can complete the story, thus setting the creaky machinery of the plot into motion. In the wake of these coincidences the reader is hardly surprised when the allegedly dead Marie shows up alive, unmarried, and longing for Sternbald — although she has seen him only twice before in her entire life — just in time for a happy ending.

In response to complaints about the implausibility of the final pages of the novel, it should be pointed out that the rest of the novel is no less implausible. Nor should we place too much stress on Tieck's alleged inability to complete the work: its ending is already a foregone conclusion. Tieck left his novel a fragment *not* because he was incapable of providing it with a conclusion, but because it would have been too easy. To

---

16. Sammons, "Loss of Thematic Control," 42. Anger also points out that the sudden reunion with Marie is "kaum überzeugend" ("Nachwort," 583).

17. Sammons questions the plausibility of Sternbald's new personal maturity as it relates to his alleged growth as an artist: "But the development is not made clear. If this is so, how did it come about and what does it have to do with his ability to function as an artist? ... On what terms this new re-awakening takes place we do not know" ("Loss of Thematic Control," 41).

ridicule Tieck for his inability to produce a more realistic work of fiction misses the point. Surely the man who could reproduce literary clichés at will for his early mentors was well aware of the contrived nature of the plot in *Franz Sternbalds Wanderungen*. Reduced to its bare outlines, the plot of this prototypical romantic *Bildungsroman* looks suspiciously similar to that of Tieck's ironically subtitled *Peter Lebrecht: A Story without Adventures*. After mocking the sort of novelist who entices the reader with such standard elements of Gothic fiction as midnight storms around gloomy castles populated by ghostly figures, Tieck nevertheless sends his hero through a series of adventures taken directly from the sort of popular fiction he parodies.[18] He even includes the familiar motif of the mysterious family identity, which recurs in *Sternbald,* as Lebrecht discovers that his bride, who is abducted before they can consummate their marriage, is actually his twin sister, conceived by his otherwise celibate parents while on leave from their respective cloisters.

Although Tieck makes use of similar elements in the plot of *Franz Sternbalds Wanderungen,* he clearly intends that Sternbald's quest to discover his true identity be taken seriously as an important part of his personal and artistic maturation. The work emerged out of Tieck's collaboration with Wackenroder on the *Herzensergießungen eines kunstliebenden Klosterbruders* (Effusions of an Art-Loving Monk) (1797), and many of the passages on the quasi-religious role of art and the artist in *Sternbald* read like an extended version of the ideas set forth in the earlier work. Yet some readers might well have found it difficult to maintain their interest in four hundred pages of effusions on art, unrelieved by plot; by sowing the seeds of mystery in the opening book of his novel, Tieck helps solve the practical problem of holding the reader's attention through his considerably longer work of fiction. Thus *Franz Sternbalds Wanderungen* can be seen as a hybrid development out of the earlier *Herzensergießungen* and *Peter Lebrecht,* as Tieck uses the familiar plot of the latter to package the romantic ideology of the former. In the process, however, Sternbald's search for his identity drifts into uneasy proximity to the hackneyed plots parodied in the earlier novel. How can we tell the difference between the development of Sternbald's innermost self and Lebrecht's mass-produced identity?

Tieck signals his awareness of just this ambivalence by inserting an anecdote into the novel that mirrors the structure of the larger narrative. In the second book of the first part of the novel, Rudolf Florestan tells

---

18. "Peter macht also in diesem Roman alle Schicksale aller Helden der Bücher des 18. Jahrhunderts durch.... er kennt auch die literarischen Muster, nach denen sich sein Leben bewegt" (Hillmann, "Ludwig Tieck," 115).

Sternbald the story of a knight named Ferdinand, who finds a picture of a woman with whom he falls in love. To the dismay of his friend Leopold, he decides to devote his life to the search for this woman. Just as he is about to give up his fixation on the image of the woman as folly, Ferdinand rescues a beautiful maiden from the amorous advances of another man. He is delighted to discover that she is none other than the woman he has sought. They find refuge with a nearby hermit, who turns out to be her father, and the would-be seducer discovers that he is the long-lost son of the hermit, and thus the woman's brother! All turns out for the best—the family is reunited, incest has been avoided, and the lovers live happily ever after.

Given the obvious parallels between Florestan's story and Sternbald's own, it is not surprising that it affects him deeply. "He related almost everything he heard and saw to himself, and so he found his personal history in this story too" (161). The successful resolution of Ferdinand's search for his absent lover promises a happy conclusion to Sternbald's own search for Marie. Florestan's anecdote, however, is interrupted just as it reaches its climax. The hermit has just recognized his daughter, and explains to her that he had given her away to peasants when he was driven from his home by a conquering army. Suddenly Vansen wants to know *which* war Florestan means. Rudolf impatiently declares that it really doesn't matter, but eventually chooses the War of the Hussites to satisfy the curiosity of both Vansen and Sternbald. What is significant here is not so much which war is chosen—it is clear that the choice is arbitrary—but rather the way in which the brief discussion deflates any sense of suspense surrounding the conclusion of Florestan's story, which is summed up almost as an afterthought: "By the way, the ending of the story takes care of itself" (160).

While Sternbald identifies with the content of the story, the manner of its narration suggests distance is advised on the part of the reader. The conclusion that seems to have such deep significance for Franz repeats the familiar patterns of the fairy tale. As if to underscore the formulaic nature of this plot, Tieck embedded yet another story within Florestan's story, in the 1843 edition of the novel, which turns out to be a tragic variant of the same tale. In order to justify his own love for an unknown woman, Ferdinand tells Leopold the story of a medieval knight named Gottfried Rudell, who becomes so obsessed with the image of a woman he knows only by hearsay that he sets off on a crusade to the Holy Land to find her. Although the knight falls ill and meets her only on his deathbed, her beauty is such that he does not regret his journey. The woman, for her part, is so impressed with his fidelity that she becomes a nun. As in the first story, this second insert sets off a lively debate among the listeners concerning its plausibility. But even before the story is told, Vansen finds it annoying that the original narrative should be interrupted. After Florestan protests that Ferdinand really did tell this story to his friend Leopold at this point, Vansen grudgingly permits Florestan to continue, provided that he does not add still more stories to the story within the story, "because otherwise it could be continued forever" (425).

Thus the tales are viewed with different and conflicting claims as to their truth value. What to Sternbald seems a promising allegory of his own future is presented by Florestan as a unique historical occurrence. At the same time, threefold repetition of the same basic plot undermines attempts to fix the story's significance at either a specific time or for a particular individual, by highlighting instead the iterability of the conventional plot shared by narrative and frame alike. Seen from this perspective, what distinguishes the main plot of *Franz Sternbalds Wanderungen* from these inserted stories is the fact that they are brought to predictable conclusions, while the novel itself remains fragmentary.

Instead of a conclusion, we are given a discussion *about* conclusions toward the beginning of the second half of the novel. Florestan and Sternbald have just met with Adelheid and her hunting party. Challenged by the local poet laureate, Florestan climbs onto the table and sings a song in praise of wine, having already drunk a fair amount himself. After a few opening verses, Florestan suddenly interrupts himself, declares that he is no longer in the mood for poetry, and climbs back down off the table. When Sternbald urges him to complete the poem, Florestan responds with what seems to be a defense of the fragment, an affirmation of the open-ended, progressive, romantic work of art: " 'And why does everything have to have a conclusion?' "[19] Yet as soon as a few people begin to agree with him, he abruptly reverses his opinion: " 'Without a conclusion, without an ending, there can be no pleasure, no enjoyment at all.... In art, after all, the conclusion is nothing more than a completion of the beginning' " (230).

While such abrupt mood swings typify Florestan's volatile nature, the

---

19. Anger cites just this passage to argue that a conclusion to the novel would violate its own logic: "Müssen, ja können *Franz Sternbalds Wanderungen* überhaupt ein Ende haben?, so wollen auch wir fragen. Würde ein offener Schluß der inneren Tendenz des Romans und dem Charakter seines Helden nicht weit eher entsprechen?" ("Nachwort," 582). However, by citing the passage out of context he obscures the fact that Florestan takes back his original assertion. Ribbat also points out that Tieck repeatedly planned to conclude his novel, and that his indications of Sternbald's continued character development work against "das Prinzip der ständigen Wiederkehr 'romantischer' Momente" (*Ludwig Tieck*, 100).

content of his poem suggests that this play with its ending has deeper significance. Until the interruption, Florestan sings of the loss of the Golden Age, and of the scornful retreat of the gods. In the continuation, Bacchus takes mercy on the mortals and grants them the gift of wine as consolation. The humans rediscover a new sort of Golden Age in the inebriation of the wine; drunken, they compel Venus to come down to earth. Eventually all the gods return and request that thrones be built for them on earth—but to the astonishment and consternation of all present, Florestan ends his poem by having the humans reject the gods: " 'We can dispense with you without sorrow, / As long as we have wine and love' " (" 'Wir können Euch ohne Gram entbehren, / Wenn Wein und Liebe bei uns gewähren' ") (232). Thus Florestan's poem invokes the quintessential Romantic plot about the loss of paradise and the hope for its return only to reject the very gods who obey the humans' summons. Yearning for divine presence yields to a defiant assertion of human self-reliance. The particular conclusion Florestan gives his poem simultaneously subverts the desire for the ultimate conclusion, namely the transcendence of temporality in the return to the Golden Age.

Tieck nevertheless invokes just this dream of the end of time in the fragmentary continuation of *Franz Sternbalds Wanderungen*. United at last, Franz and Marie celebrate the successful conclusion of their personal journeys, as an Edenic experience of "presence" that transforms protracted longing into timeless fulfillment: " 'O happy present!' cried Marie, 'now past and future have disappeared, eternity has entered into time' " (496).[20] Yet just as Sternbald had left Marie in Rome almost immediately after he had found her, he now leaves her for the second time to wander off into the landscape again. Thus we cannot really speak of a true parousia, for we have not one but two such moments that

20. Thus Geulen asserts that the novel is meant to reveal "das Eindringen der Ewigkeit in die Zeit, das Ineins von Vergangenheit und Zukunft" ("Allegorie im Erzählvorgang," 290). Kern also sees in the work a secularized version of a redemption myth: "Sein [Tiecks] Thema ist der Verlust des Paradieses und die Erwartung des Erlösers" (41). "Tieck will das Abendland auf sein Wesentliches zurückführen, wenn er Historisches anbietet. Er will keinesfalls die Zeit zurückschrauben" (*Ludwig Tieck*, 21). Ribbat stresses the cultural function of this religious paradigm in Tieck's novel: "Vielmehr liegt dem Romankonzept ... das Wunschbild einer immanenten Eschatologie zugrunde, deren Organon die Kulturbewegung von Nation zu Nation ist, wobei der Patriotismus des 18. Jahrhunderts darauf insistierte, daß die nächste Stufe der Manifestation von Humanität in Deutschland Ereignis werde" (*Ludwig Tieck*, 104). While Tieck may well long for the return of the Golden Age, or at least hope for progress toward greater humanity in Germany, the novel itself stops short of exemplifying the timeless world it invokes. Like the idyllic interludes inserted into the novel, this projected conclusion reads like a self-conscious citation of a familiar romantic idea that does not resolve tension in the body of the text itself.

are both interrupted by the resumption of desire. The ending that seems to be conclusive turns out to be only provisional, which is to say that it is no ending at all. In the place of a true sublation of time we have repeated narrative gestures toward closure that are immediately broken open again. As in the case of Florestan's poem, the finality of the ending is undermined by its self-conscious presentation as an iterable narrative.

To sum up: in *Franz Sternbalds Wanderungen* Tieck presents us with the first of several *Bildungsromane* that problematize the very understanding of the artist they propagate, by reflecting on the tension between Romantic ideology and the demands of artistic professionalism. While Tieck repeatedly emphasizes the special status of the artist and the incompatibility of genius and economic concerns, his text reveals that the artist is in fact bound to the rest of society in an uneasy alliance obscured by idealistic rhetoric. Like Wilhelm Meister before him, Sternbald struggles to reconcile his artistic desires with financial need. The solutions are formulated in terms of a compromise between bourgeois capital and a noble, hence "artistic," way of life. Wilhelm Meister's family wealth finances his dalliance with the bohemian theater troupe; his inheritance later enables him to exercise the social graces learned on stage among the nobles of the Tower Society.[21] Sternbald confronts the dilemma of having either to sacrifice his life to produce great art or to debase his art to live like a noble. Tieck further complicates the distinction between the artist and the rest of society through his self-conscious use of literary conventions. Although he traces the progress of his hero toward the discovery of his true identity, he displays an awareness that this quest follows the well-worn paths of the popular fiction Tieck and others wrote primarily for profit. By exploring the inherent contradictions between his aesthetic ideals and pressures of the literary market on the artist in both the form and content of *Franz Sternbalds Wanderungen,* Tieck produced the prototypical *Bildungsroman* of a generation of professional Romantics.

---

21. Janz has pointed out the irony behind Wilhelm Meister's apparent rejection of his middle-class roots: "Das Vermögen, das Wilhelm erlaubt, ohne materielle Not der Kunst sich zu widmen, ist entstanden gerade aus dem Verkauf der Kunstsammlung. So ermöglicht die Freiheit, die sich der Bourgeois nimmt, die Kunst zu verbannen, indem er sie kapitalisiert, die Freiheit Wilhelms, für die Kunst zu optieren. Der Künstler, der sich in selbstgewählter Distanz zum bürgerlichen Leben wähnt, übersieht, daß es die verachtete Ökonomie ist, die ihm diese Distanzierung allerest ermöglicht" ("Zum sozialen Gehalt der 'Lehrjahre,'" 329-30).

Nostalgic and Progressive Utopias in Novalis's *Heinrich von Ofterdingen* (1800)

6

In recent years our understanding of Novalis has undergone considerable revision. Two studies in particular have significantly altered the persistent willingness to view him as the prophet of a new Golden Age, Germany's most influential spokesman for a secularized, poeticized version of Christian salvation history.[1] For Alice Kuzniar, Novalis, like Hölderlin, is a protodeconstructionist, a prophet of *différance* rather than parousia. "Derrida, along with Hölderlin and Novalis, focuses upon this production of intervals and interims, not upon what is absent or remains hidden. None of the three articulates a negative theology or a belief in pure absence."[2] Géza von Molnár agrees that Novalis lends himself to this sort of deconstructive analysis: "Such [Derridean] readings of Novalis are undoubtedly justified since his concept of *Poesie* and his practice of it are not based on the premise that our thoughts and their expressions refer to an extraconscious reality. This type of a metaphysics of presence is as foreign to him as it would be for Derrida and, one should add, for Fichte as well."[3] As his inclusion of Fichte in the above

---

1. Influential books by Mähl (*Die Idee des goldenen Zeitalters*) and Hiebel (*Novalis: Deutscher Dichter, europäischer Denker, christlicher Seher*) typify earlier studies of Novalis. While Hiebel stresses Novalis's role as a modern-day Christian visionary, Mähl views his work in the context of the classical topos of the Golden Age.
2. Kuzniar, *Delayed Endings*, 6. She provides a lucid introduction to major trends in traditional Novalis scholarship (72-80).
3. Molnár, *Romantic Vision*, 157.

passage indicates, however, Molnár argues that Derrida is not as radical as he seems, in that his concept of *différance* remains within the grasp of the metaphysics it seeks to deconstruct. He concedes the possibility of a Derridean analysis of Novalis, that is, only to the extent that it coincides with the traditional view of him as a mystic who takes the *via negativa* to express the ineffable: "In other words, the divine as perfection, as absolute unity and comprehension, is only negatively present, present only through its absence; however, negative presence is presence, nonetheless."[4]

At this point the critics reach an impasse that has less to do with Novalis's works than the presuppositions they bring to the act of interpretation. The very nature of the argument makes it unlikely that either side will convince the other; when debating whether negative presence is really presence or just absence we enter a realm where faith has to take over for logic. However, Molnár also introduces a more pragmatic aspect to his argument. While conceding language's inability to speak directly of the ineffable, he emphasizes its ethical quality in its function as that which binds together the "unlimited community of communicants."[5] As the title of his monograph indicates, he is less concerned with mystical theology than ethics; while taking the negative presence of God as a given, he concentrates primarily on the way in which the novel encourages the establishment of a productive dialogue among members of a universal linguistic community.

In basing his study on the recent work of Jürgen Habermas and Karl-Otto Apel, however, Molnár uproots Novalis from his historical setting to incorporate him in the "community of communicants" whose "membership is limitless and includes all of humanity," representing "the state of perfect mutual understanding or the completion of the dialogue that functions as the normative horizon within which all communication takes place."[6] While Molnár's decision to stress Novalis's place within a community marks a welcome shift away from the irresolvable debate concerning the presence or absence of God, it remains on an extremely abstract, theoretical plane. Even the most cursory glance at the "community of communicants" in which Novalis

---

4. Molnár, *Romantic Vision*, 165. "Even Derrida, despite his expressed denial that his philosophy is 'negative theology,' circumscribes nothing else but the dynamics of the *via negativa* with his key concept of '*différance*'" (*Romantic Vision*, 223). See Molnár's conclusion, "Novalis in Contemporary Context" (193-202), for an explicit discussion of the theoretical issues at stake.

5. Molnár, *Romantic Vision*, 201.

6. Molnár, *Romantic Vision*, 200.

actually lived reveals that it was neither limitless nor characterized by "perfect mutual understanding." We can begin to bring the discussion of Novalis into historical focus by viewing his work in the context of the situation he shared with other writers discussed in this book.[7]

In contrast to the struggle faced by bourgeois writers like Schiller, Tieck, and Jean Paul in their attempt to survive as professional authors, Novalis had the luxury of modest but adequate family wealth that was sufficient to cover his needs. "I have caused him considerable expenditures," writes Novalis of his father to Julius Wilhelm von Oppel in June 1799, "I have been out of the house for more than eight years now and have unfortunately used far more than my share during these first years.... I am now over twenty-seven years old and still a burden to my father."[8] This confession occurs in the context of Novalis's delight at having been appointed to a position in the local mines, a position that promised him

7. Most of the more recent Novalis scholarship has moved away from the theological/ eschatological focus of earlier criticism to place his work in its historical context. A number of critics have viewed Novalis's poetic work as an indirect commentary on his contemporary economic theory. As Beck points out, *Ökonomie* in the eighteenth century was a broad term that encompassed the relation between means and ends, parts and the whole in both aesthetics and what we would call "economy" (Beck, *"Friedrich von Hardenberg 'Oeconomie des Styls,' "* 85). Thus Stadler reads the Arion myth as an allegorical confrontation between two socioeconomic models: "Eine auf Dankbarkeit, Freundschaft und Liebe basierende Gesellschaft wird mit einer anderen, historisch späteren Gesellschaftsformation konfrontiert, welche auf dem Warentausch und einer Art Gesellschaftsvertrag beruht" (*Die theuren Dinge,* 141). While these studies reflect the influence of the Frankfurt School, the work of Lacan and Foucault informs Kittler's innovative studies of *Heinrich von Ofterdingen.* In "Die Irrwege des Eros" he continues the application of poststructuralist psychology to the history of the family begun in his study of *Wilhelm Meisters Lehrjahre:* "Das ist weder eine zeitlose Notwendigkeit noch ein unableitbarer Wunsch zu sprechen, sondern der diskursanalytisch bestimmbare Effekt einer Recodierung der bürgerlichen Familie" (459). His more recent study, " 'Heinrich von Ofterdingen als Nachrichtenfluss,' " interprets the novel as "Information über die Informationsnetze von 1800" (483); "Hardenbergs Roman—klarer wäre es kaum zu sagen—spielt nicht im Mittelalter seines Stoffs, sondern in der Gegenwart seines Diskurses" (499). However, Kittler understands the "presence of Novalis's discourse" primarily in terms of the psychological model he develops at length in the first half of his *Aufschreibesysteme;* in contrast, I situate Novalis's novel in the context of his comments on the German literary institution developed most explicitly in his first "Dialog." In a work influenced by Kittler, Schreiber offers an interesting account of Novalis's understanding of the absolute book in the context of the transformation of the German literary market (*Symptom des Schreibens*). However, he is primarily concerned with psychological aspects of *Heinrich von Ofterdingen* in his highly speculative analysis of the novel.

8. Novalis (Friedrich von Hardenberg). *Schriften* 4:286. Further references to Novalis's works are cited from this edition in the text.

financial independence; it is most significant that Novalis does not consider his activity as a writer to be a potential source of income. Quite the contrary: when his friend Just encourages him to be more considerate of the public in his enigmatic fragments, Novalis responds that they are merely "texts for the amusement of friends" (4:266), "texts to ponder" (4:270). "Writing is a matter of minor importance—You should judge me according to the main thing, namely practical life" (2:266). The publication of Novalis's poetic works, both during his life and posthumously, was due in large measure to the efforts of his friends, rather than any attempt on his part to supplement his income through writing. For example, when Friedrich Schlegel writes to inform Novalis that his collection of fragments entitled "Glauben und Liebe" (Faith and Love) is already in the midst of being published, it becomes clear that Novalis has never brought up the question of payment: "The publisher asked about terms. I told him that you hadn't brought up the issue; should you be interested at all, he should give you the usual amount." With a trace of exasperation, Friedrich goes on to urge his friend to accept the money: "I really don't see why you would want to give it to him for free" (4:493).

Thus Novalis's activity as a writer seems to fit into a pattern more common during the first half of the eighteenth century than the second, as he considers his works private productions for himself and friends, written in his spare time and only incidentally for publication and profit. Friedrich von Hardenberg's choice of an old medieval family name as his public pseudonym seems to emphasize his identification with an earlier generation of writers. Nevertheless, it would be inaccurate to view Novalis's activity as a writer as a mere anachronism. However unconcerned he may seem about receiving remuneration for his publications, Novalis was hardly unaware of the contemporary literary scene. Through both his personal contacts and his voracious reading, Novalis stood at the center of the literary and philosophical developments of the 1790s. If he chose not to enter into the acrimonious public debates of the sort that characterized relations between enlightened Berlin, classical Weimar, and romantic Jena and Dresden, it was not from ignorance, but rather due to personal choice.[9] While there is no record that Novalis ever intended to support himself exclusively as a professional writer, it becomes clear in his final years that what he had termed a sideline (*Nebensache*) in 1798 was rapidly becoming his primary concern

9. Thus Novalis was able to maintain cordial relations with Schiller even at the height of hostilities between Schiller and the other early Romantics: "Das Verhältnis Hardenbergs zu Schiller war und blieb ein anderes als das Friedrich Schlegels und seines Kreises" (Kluckhohn, "Friedrich von Hardenbergs Entwicklung," 1:6).

(*Hauptsache*). "I now think of nothing but novels and comedies. I will take up the Apprentice at Saïs as soon as I finish the above-mentioned novel.... I will be collecting material for an intellectual journal until Michaelmas."[10] Even a few days before his death his brother Karl reports that Novalis continued to speak of future plans: " 'As soon as I recover you'll see what poetry is; I have wonderful poems and songs in my mind' " (4:535).

The increased scope of Novalis's literary endeavors in his final years is matched by a greater awareness of the practicalities of publication and the place of his own work in current literary developments. *Heinrich von Ofterdingen* was originally to have appeared from the same publisher and in the same format as *Wilhelm Meisters Lehrjahre,* clearly with the intention of emphasizing both Novalis's indebtedness to and his implicit repudiation of Goethe's work.[11] Novalis's encyclopedia project also reveals a willingness to engage issues in the contemporary literary scene. Precisely what Novalis's encyclopedia would have looked like is impossible to determine, as we have only his extensive collection of fragments toward such a work in *Das Allgemeine Brouillon.*[12] However, his correspondence with Friedrich Schlegel in the fall of 1798 gives some indication of what Novalis had in mind. Schlegel had written that "the goal of my literary projects [is] to write a new Bible, to follow in the footsteps of Mohammed and Luther" (4:501). Novalis responds with delighted surprise that he too was engaged in a similar project. "A developed theory of the Bible would result in a theory of writing or word-sculpting [*Wortbildnerey*] in general—at the same time, it would yield the symbolic, indirect construction-principles of the creative spirit [*Constructionslehre des schaffenden Geistes*]" (4:263). Novalis conceives the project as a sort of metabook, "as a critique of the Bible project—an experiment of a universal method of Biblicizing [*Universalmethode des Biblisierens*]—the introduction to a genuine encyclopedism" (4:263). Instead of writing another collection of fragments, Novalis attempted to construct a text that would bring together various fields of discourse into a productive dialogue with one another.[13]

---

10. 4:318. Several weeks later Novalis writes: "Ich bin würcklich sehr fleißig.... der Kopf wimmelt mir von Ideen zu Romanen und Lustspielen" (4:322).

11. "Als Gegenstück zu Goethes Roman sollte der 'Ofterdingen' ganz in der Gestalt des 'Wilhelm Meister' mit gleichen Lettern und gleichem Format beim gleichen Verleger (Unger) erscheinen" (Kluckhohn and Samuel, "Einleitung," 1:186).

12. See Mähl's introduction to this work for a reconstruction of Novalis's intentions for his unfinished project ("Einleitung," 3:237-41).

13. "Ihm ging es um eine Grundlegung aller Wissenschaften, um eine Wissenschaftslehre

It has been maintained that this new Bible or encyclopedia was meant "as a preventative measure against the industrial degradation of the book to a wholesale product. Its esoteria was directed against easy consumption. The universal and absolute claim in this plan was supposed to counter the disappearance of religion in society; in the case of Novalis this poetic plan was even to be developed into a utopia."[14] On the other hand, however utopian Novalis's ambitions may be, he does *not* advocate retreat into the private sanctity of a new religion. Rather, his plans are formulated in terms of transforming the existing literary institution. Thus he links his encyclopedia project with specific plans for a new literary journal: "I intend to engender truths and ideas in large format—genial thoughts—to produce a living, scholarly organon— and to pave the way to genuine practice—to the true reunion process— through this syn-critical politics of intelligence [diese synkritische Politik der Intelligenz]" (4:263). The journal, in turn, is conceived in combination with the establishment of a writers' union. "My new plan is very extensive," he writes to Friedrich Schlegel in his next letter. "It concerns the establishment of a literary, republican order—which is thoroughly mercantile-political—a true Cosmopolitan [Masonic] Lodge. A printing press—a book trade must be the first thread of the web. Jena—Hamburg, or Switzerland, if peace comes—must become the central office" (4:268-69). This community of writers would be able to escape the tyranny of the current literary market: "You should no longer be literarily and politically dependent on booksellers, so to speak" (4:269).

These fragments contain the seeds of a discussion of the contemporary institution of literature that Novalis developed at some length in the first of six unpublished *Dialogen*.[15] The dialogue is constructed as an exchange between speakers A and B that focuses on the significance of the expanded book market in Germany in the second half of the eighteenth century. When A voices the typical complaint that the new annual catalogue (*Meßkatalog*) provides further evidence of the book plague

---

als 'System des wissenschaftlichen Geistes' (Nr. 56), die das Verbindende zwischen den verschiedenen Zweigen und Sachgebieten der Wissenschaften aufsucht und diese auf ihre tiefere Einheit zurückführt" (Mähl, "Einleitung," 3:238). See also Kesting ("Aspekte des absoluten Buches"), Heftrich (*Vom Logos der Poesie*, 26-53), Blumenberg (*Die Lesbarkeit der Welt*, 233-66), and Schreiber (*Das Symptom des Schreibens*, 118-81) for general introductions to Novalis's encyclopedia project.

14. Kesting, "Aspekte des absoluten Buches," 429.

15. The dialogues were written in 1798. Their careful preparation indicates that Novalis valued them highly, although they were not published during his lifetime (Samuel, "Einleitung," 2:655).

(*Bücherseuche*) that infects Germany, B comes to the defense of the same phenomenon with metaphors drawn from economic theory. Books are Germany's most valuable commodity, he claims; their exportation brings the country international respect, while importation of foreign books only further profits the Germans. Against A's objection that such luxury articles represent a needless expense, B responds that money is meant to be kept in circulation: "'My friend—isn't money there to stimulate—?'" (2:662). B thus defends the publishing industry in terms that recall Novalis's own plans for a new literary journal and writers' guild, which would be bound together by the "genuine mercantile spirit" Novalis praises in *Das Allgemeine Brouillon:* "The historical spirit of commerce—which acts slavishly in accordance with given needs—with the circumstances of the time and place—is only a bastard of the genuine, creative spirit of commerce" (3:464).[16]

A admits that his objections sound like those of the Philistines; he too sees the value of the new literature, but he would like to regulate the trade. "'Yes, but what if it were a *methodical progress?* if every book filled in a gap somewhere—and if in this way every book fair were at the same time a systematic link in the chain of *Bildung?*'" (2:661). In the long run, he goes on to argue, wouldn't it be better to concentrate on one good book than to skim through a hundred? Not at all, responds B; every single book in the new catalogue is valuable, even if it pleases only the author and a few friends. In fact, there should be even more books: "'For me, bookmaking is not nearly carried on to the proper extent.... *Wilhelm Meister's Apprenticeship* is all we have now—we should possess as many Apprenticeships as possible, written in the same spirit—all the Apprenticeships of all the people who have ever lived—" (2:664).

Thus this debate further develops issues concerning the contemporary expansion of the book market raised in Novalis's encyclopedia project. A is an intensive reader who seeks to police literary production and reading habits by imposing restrictions on the quantity of new material in the hope of increasing its quality. He argues for the construc-

---

16. "Der 'ächte' Handelsgeist erscheint hier als Inbegriff des Tätigen Lebens. Er wird gelobt, weil er alles in Bewegung setzt und alles in Verbindung bringt. Indem er dies tut, transzendiert er sich selber und wird produktiv: Werkzeug ist er, und zugleich wundertätig. In seiner historischen Ausformung hingegen bleibt er bloß mechanisch" (Stadler, *Die theuren Dinge,* 149). He interprets Heinrich's lute and sword as allegories of this "genuine mercantile spirit" and its "bastard" counterpart (220). Stadler develops this interpretation in the context of what he identifies as Novalis's primary achievement, namely the construction of an aesthetic model in which the alienation between subject and object in the modern world is overcome (9). In contrast to this general philosophical model, I stress the relation between this concept and Novalis's reflections on the place of literature in the public sphere.

tion of a new, secular literary canon, both in his conception of a select number of texts filling out the gaps in a master plan of general *Bildung*, and in his willingness to apply intensive patterns of reading to these works. As such A's position recalls Goethe and Schiller's attempt to impose enlightenment on a recalcitrant public from above. In contrast, B speaks for Novalis's "universal method of Biblicizing" (4:263), which eschews any limitations on literary quantity and quality in envisioning a society freed of financial and political restraints, where texts could circulate unrestricted in the true spirit of commercial exchange.

B's position does not go unchallenged, however. At one point in the dialogue A raises an objection that checks B's exuberant affirmation of the recent proliferation of literature: " 'Haven't you often spoken of the unfortunate addiction to printed nature?' " (2:662). B responds with a series of apologies that culminate in a plea that A not blame signs for the weakness of the humans that create them: " 'This [world of ciphers] is not to blame for the fact that we eventually only see books but no things, and that our 5 physical senses are all but useless' " (2:663). B has maneuvered himself into an untenable position, as he wants to absolve the human-created world of signs of the human weakness to perceive these signs rather than reality. B's uncharacteristic lament at the end of this exchange reveals his awareness of this contradiction: " 'Why do we cling so exclusively, like miserable moss, to the printing block?' " (2:663). Thus what seems to be an unqualified affirmation of current literary production in its entirety is in fact tinged with the awareness that the new encyclopedia comprises a totality that differs from the way Jung-Stilling viewed the Bible in that it remains infinitely perspectival, cut off from the direct apprehension of reality: "We see nature, as perhaps the spiritual world, *en perspective*" (3:450). Novalis's Bible project, in other words, has passed through the Copernican revolution of Kantian philosophy, to emerge at a position hovering between an unqualified affirmation of all the new literature and a nostalgic yearning for a distant realm of former plenitude.

The same fluctuation marks his extensive comments on the nature of language. Novalis frequently espouses the familiar theory of historical and linguistic decline. In the beginning, writes Novalis in the "Hymns to the Night," "rivers, trees, flowers, and animals had human sense" (1:141). In *Die Lehrlinge zu Saïs* he asserts that the original words were adequate expressions for the things they represented (1:82-83). Since then, however, we have gradually lost the connection: "Our language—was much more musical in the beginning and has only gradually become so prosaic—so *toneless* [*enttönt*]" (3:283-84). "We have lost the meaning of the world. We have stopped at the letter" (2:594).[17] While Novalis identifies one of the basic ideas of *Kabbalistik* as the "sympathy of the sign with what it signifies" (3:266), he also points out that "words are a deceptive medium of prethinking [*trügliches Medium des Vordenckens*] —unreliable vehicles of a certain, specific stimulus" (2:522). At other times, however, Novalis reverses this lament into an affirmation of the noncoincidence of the sign with what it signifies. This opinion is expressed most forcefully at the beginning of his "Monolog": "proper conversation is a mere word-game. We can only marvel at the ridiculous mistake of people who think they are speaking for the sake of things" (2:672). Thus Novalis can assert in the *Lehrlinge zu Saïs* that "genuine Sanskrit would speak for the sake of speaking, because speaking would be its delight and its essence" (1:79).

Novalis grants neither of these contradictory positions the last word. No matter how abstract language may be in principle, in practice it functions on the basis of a communal consensus. "All language is a postulate. It is of positive, free origin. You have to agree to think certain things with certain signs, to create something particular intentionally within yourself" (2:558). Rather than being viewed as an inadequate medium for the expression of preexisting ideas, language derives its power from its ability to *create* reality among its community of users.[18] "Four letters designate God [*Gott*] to me; a few lines a million things. How easy the manipulation of the universe becomes, how visible the concentricity of the spiritual world! Language theory is the dynamic force of the spiritual realm. An order moves armies; the word freedom moves nations" (2:413).[19] Even the concept of a purely nonreferential language can only be expressed by means of a paradox, for one must rely on language to refer to itself in the process of communicating this

---

17. "Ehemals war alles Geistererscheinung. Jezt sehn wir nichts, als todte Wiederholung, die wir nicht verstehn. Die Bedeutung der Hieroglyfe fehlt. Wir leben noch von der Frucht besserer Zeiten" (2:545).

18. "In other words, the decisive criterion for knowledge is not that it refers to autonomous objects, nor that it must refer its objects to the transcendental apperception of self-consciousness, but rather that it may occur only within the context of its potential as shared communication. Once language is no longer regarded in the traditional sense as a vehicle subordinate to a fully independent reality ... the relationship can now be considered to have been reversed and it may be argued that reality depends on language" (Molnár, *Romantic Vision,* 134). While Molnár's comments accurately reflect *this aspect* of Novalis's comments on language, there are numerous other passages of the sort quoted above that reveal a more traditional understanding of language as a poor medium for representing a preexisting reality.

19. "[Jedes Wort ist ein Wort der Beschwörung. Welcher Geist ruft—ein solcher erscheint]" (2:523). "Denken ist Sprechen. Sprechen und thun oder machen sind Eine nur modificirte Operation. Gott sprach es werde Licht und es ward" (3:297).

idea.[20] We are left in the world of fallen language after all, where we can long for an Adamic past and speculate about free-floating, purely abstract signs, but where we remain within a communally created/community-creating linguistic world. Taken as a whole, then, Novalis's comments on language reproduce the dilemma traced in his reflections on his contemporary literary scene, combining wistful longing for an unattainable past with a utopian affirmation of an equally unattainable world of unrestricted literary and linguistic circulation. There is either too much literature or not nearly enough, either language that swerves away from direct expression or language that falls short of the desire for unrestricted abstraction.

Given Novalis's lack of experience in the practical matters of organizing such a community of writers and the failure of similarly ambitious projects, like Schiller's *Die Horen,* it is most probable that nothing would have come of these plans had Novalis lived longer.[21] His encyclopedia project also remained incomplete. However, there is some indication that his fragmentary novel, *Heinrich von Ofterdingen,* was to take the place of the new Bible he was unable to finish. In *Das Allgemeine Brouillon* Novalis had written, "Every person's story should be a Bible—will be a Bible.... A Bible is the highest task of writing" (3:321). In late February of 1799 we find a reference to Novalis's plan to turn his own life into such a Bible in a letter to Caroline Schlegel: "... for I want to devote my entire life to One novel—which by itself is meant to comprise an entire library—perhaps to contain the *Lehrjahre* of a nation" (4:281). One month later Friedrich Schlegel reports to Friedrich Schleiermacher the latest news from Novalis with the following terse comment: "We miss Hardenberg badly, but I hope that you or I will arouse his jealousy, so that he writes a Bible or a novel" (4:625).

20. See Strohschneider-Kohrs's brilliant analysis of Novalis's "Monolog," where she demonstrates that the meaning of the work arises negatively, in the tension established by the meaningful assertion that language cannot convey meaning. The very self-cancelling nature of the statement paradoxically enables Novalis to express the alleged truth about language by demonstrating the impossibility of making such a statement directly. The original meaning is both cancelled and preserved, i.e., preserved by the very act of its self-cancellation (Strohschneider-Kohrs, *Die romantische Ironie,* 250-73; also Link, *Abstraktion und Poesie,* 87-91).

21. Heftrich suggests that the project was so ambitious that its almost inevitable incompletion provided a convenient way of avoiding hard questions of practicality: "Oft aber, und gerade bei den höchsten, ausgreifendsten und auch ausschweifendsten Plänen, wirkt die Hoffnung auf die Gruppe wie eine Flucht vor der Alternative, das Projekt verwirklichen oder sein Scheitern eingestehen zu müssen.... Flüchtet nicht auch Novalis in ähnlicher Weise vor den Schwierigkeiten ihrer Methode, nur in das neue Projekt des literarischen Ordens?" (*Vom Logos der Poesie,* 47).

Novalis maintained that his *Heinrich von Ofterdingen* was to counter the increasingly prosaic *Wilhelm Meisters Lehrjahre,* and the contrast between the two works is indeed striking. Goethe sets his novel in contemporary Germany; his protagonist is an avid reader and theatergoer who serves as a vehicle for Goethe's examination of the changing function of his contemporary institution of literature. Novalis goes beyond the Renaissance world evoked in Tieck's *Sternbald* to place his protagonist into an idealized version of the Middle Ages. Although Heinrich knows how to read, he has seen only a few books (1:203), and knows nothing of either poetry or poets. By setting his work in the hazy past, and by deliberately emphasizing his protagonist's ignorance of his own contemporary writers, Novalis seems to create a deliberately anachronistic image of the "good old days," when poets were born, not made, and when the written word was painstakingly and lovingly inscribed in illuminated manuscripts.

Given Novalis's awareness of developments in the book market and his (admittedly nebulous) plans for a new journal and an organization of professional writers, it seems unlikely that he should restrict himself to a mere sentimental longing for an idyllic past in his major literary work, and this is indeed not the case. However, to an even greater extent than was the case with *Franz Sternbalds Wanderungen,* this engagement with contemporary issues takes place beneath the surface of an idealized past. Like *Wilhelm Meisters Lehrjahre, Heinrich von Ofterdingen* is as much about itself as it is about the content of its narration, and it is through analysis of the self-reflexive moments in the text that we can best understand its significance for Novalis's own times. We begin therefore with a look at the most striking point of comparison between the two texts, namely the fact that both protagonists read another version of their own novel within the novels themselves.

Toward the end of *Wilhelm Meisters Lehrjahre* Meister tries to write his autobiography when proposing to Theresa. As we have seen, he is unable to complete the project until he has read the *Lehrjahre* composed for him by the Tower Society. This self-reflexive moment in the text illustrates the mixture of success and failure that characterizes his development: While the biography helps him to perceive order in his past life, it does not enable him to act more decisively in the present. In direct contrast, Heinrich von Ofterdingen's encounter with a written version of his own life takes place in a realm where the normal progression of time has been suspended.

In the fifth chapter Heinrich meets an old miner who leads an expedition to the caves in the nearby hills. The journey takes on the significance of an archetypal descent to the underworld that recalls passages in Homer's *Odyssey,* Virgil's *Aeneid,* and Dante's *Inferno,* while anticipating Faust's journey to *die Mütter* in the second half of Goethe's drama. In each of these descents the hero encounters a world at once far removed from normal reality and yet central to that reality as the source of its transient appearances. A series of reversals of the normal order of things signals the special status of this experience for Heinrich. The landscape is a "dreamworld brooding within itself," in which the moon hangs suspended like the dream of the sun. This inversion of night and day, waking and dreaming, opens up the present to the past, guiding us "back to that mythical primeval age" {77} (1:252).[22] Finally, the dissolution of the ordinary time in the dreamworld results in the breakdown of the distinction between subject and object, the observer and the observed. Already in the opening chapter Heinrich has defended the importance of dreaming as "a remarkable phenomenon, which apart from any notion of its being sent from God is a significant rent in the mysterious curtain that hangs a thousandfold about our inner life" {19} (1:198-99). Now the journey through the magically transformed landscape becomes inverted into a journey into the world contained within him: "The fairy night mirrored itself in [Heinrich's] soul. He felt as though the world lay unlocked within him and was revealing to him as to an intimate friend all its treasures and hidden charms" {77} (1:252).[23]

Having entered this dreamworld, Heinrich begins to discover the interconnectedness of the events of his own life and history in general. In a remarkable image, Heinrich's new perception of time is likened to his having opened the door of his little room to reveal an allegorical cathedral of time next door: "He saw his own little room hard by a lofty cathedral from whose stone floor the solemn past arose while from the dome the bright and cheerful future soared singing in golden cherubs toward the past" {77} (1:252). All creatures enter the music-filled structure, and their original language is once again immediately comprehensible. Heinrich is flooded by memories of the merchants' tales, "and a thousand other recollections of his life strung themselves on a magic thread" {78} (1:252). This personal epiphany prepares the reader for the discussion of history that follows, in which the role of the historian is defined as the ability to discover the hidden links between different events:

22. References to *Heinrich von Ofterdingen* are listed in the text with the page number of the English translation in brackets followed by the volume and page number of the German edition in parentheses.
23. Mähl selects this passage as a good example of what "Novalis (verstand) unter der 'Romantisierung' der Welt im Medium der Sprache.... immer ist das Äußere nur Hinweis und Zeichen für Inneres, Geistiges, Unsichtbares" (*Die Idee des goldenen Zeitalters,* 422).

"Only when one is able to survey a long series of events... does one notice the hidden interlinking of the past and the future, and learn how to piece history together out of hope and memories" {83} (1:257-58). If Heinrich is not yet capable of actually composing a historical narrative and discovering "the simple rule of history" {83} (1:258), then the flash of insight precipitated by his entry into the caves has at least given him an intuitive grasp of the mystical unity of past, present, and future.

The chapter culminates in the description of Heinrich's encounter with an illuminated manuscript in the library of the old hermit. While the hermit and the old miner go off to explore more caves, Heinrich remains behind with the books. "At length he came across a volume written in a foreign language.... It had no title, but as he looked through it, he found several pictures. They seemed wonderfully familiar to him, and as he looked more sharply, he discovered a rather clear picture of himself among the figures" {90} (1:264). The contrast between this scene in *Heinrich von Ofterdingen* and the similar passage in Goethe's novel is already striking. While Meister requests the Tower Society's manuscript after having failed in the attempt to write his own autobiography, Heinrich von Ofterdingen remains passive, encountering the manuscript only by chance. Moreover, the work, termed only "a book" or "a novel," seems to have nothing to do with him: it records the life of a poet at a different time, in a distant setting, and in a foreign language. Yet Heinrich soon begins to recognize himself in the manuscript's illuminations. First he sees an image of the present: "He hardly trusted his senses when soon after he discovered in another picture the cave, the hermit, and the miner at his side." Next he recognizes familiar characters from his past: "Zulima, his parents, the landgrave and the landgravine of Thuringia, his friend the court chaplain, and several other acquaintances of his; yet their clothes were altered and appeared to be those of another age" {91} (1:264-65). Finally he sees a series of figures who are unfamiliar to him, but who turn out to be images of individuals he will encounter in the future, including Klingsohr, Mathilde, and himself as a poet.

The inclusion of Heinrich's future in the hermit's manuscript constitutes the most significant difference between his experience and Wilhelm Meister's encounter with the Tower Society's biography. Time remains linear in Goethe's novel; Wilhelm Meister twice perceives organization of his past life, only to blunder further in the present. Heinrich von Ofterdingen does not have to face the problem of reconciling retrospection with activity, for the manuscript reveals that each new event has already happened. Throughout the novel, in fact, his new experiences trigger a feeling of déjà vu: when the merchants tell him about poets and poetry for the first time, Heinrich feels "as though I had heard about them at some time in my earliest youth" {32} (1:210). When the miner finishes his song it again seems to him "that he had heard the song somewhere before" {75} (1:250). When he meets Mathilde later on, she too feels that it is as if she had already known him "time out of mind" {116} (1:287). The presence of the prophetic manuscript within the novel becomes a way of representing the mystical dissolution of time into "an eternal now," where the journey out leads one back home.[24]

However, the very concept of mystical unity suggested by this passage is simultaneously undermined by its means of representation. For the figure in the manuscript is also *not* identical with Heinrich von Ofterdingen in a number of significant ways. Heinrich cannot understand the language of the text, the figure wears strange clothing, and most important, he has already experienced the events that constitute Heinrich's future. In other words, Heinrich sees not his own life but a previous version of a life he will repeat. The "eternal now" can only be represented in terms of eternal repetition. Thus Heinrich and Mathilde can also claim that their love is something new: " 'Henry, never can two people have loved each other so.' 'I cannot believe it either, because there has never been a Mathilda before.' 'And no Henry.' 'Ah, swear to me again that you will be mine forever; love is an endless repetition' " {119} (1:289-90). Heinrich's own life will repeat the life re-presented in the prophetic manuscript, and could in turn become the model for future poets—after all, both the manuscript and the novel itself lack conclusions.[25]

So which interpretation of the passage is correct? Does Novalis create an image of mystical union or demystified *différance* by introducing the prophetic manuscript into his text? The answer is both: as we have seen, he demystifies the mystical moment in the process of representing its simultaneity as a succession of iterable narratives. At the same time, as Molnár and others have argued, it is impossible to speak of difference, "whether it be spelled this way or any other," without having an implicit

---

24. Molnár, *Romantic Vision*, 143. Molnár's assertion that the "sequential order" of events has been transformed into "simultaneity" (144) in this scene echoes many critics who have insisted on the identity of the manuscript with the novel and the figure in the illuminations with Heinrich. See for example Hiebel (*Deutscher Dichter*, 322), Mahr (*Übergang zum Endlichen*, 148), Frühwald ("Nachwort," 243), and Link: "Die Poesie realisiert durch ihre formale Struktur, was sie inhaltlich immer nur andeuten konnte: die Aufhebung der Zeit" (*Abstraktion und Poesie*, 166).

25. Unlike most critics who assume the identity of the two texts, Kuzniar points out that the manuscript's "relationship to the narration is sketchy, suggestive, and not fully explicit. It also thematizes this hermeneutic incompleteness by lacking both an ending *and* a beginning: the Provençal book has no title" (*Delayed Endings*, 106).

concept of unity.[26] In a logic that will be familiar to readers of poststructuralist thinking, the critical subtext needs the primary text it undermines, just as the parasite needs the host it destroys.[27] Whether or not the end result is an example of a "negative theology" depends on the convictions of the reader and leads us away from what is in the text to speculate on what may or may not lie beyond. What we can determine, however, is the relation of this passage to Novalis's reflections on language and the literary market discussed above.

From this perspective the book within the book generates two diametrically opposed models in response to the current state of affairs. Instead of imposing an aesthetic order on past events, Heinrich von Ofterdingen discovers that his entire life is already contained within a preexisting order. The manuscript takes on a significance analogous to that of the Bible in a religious autobiography, or of Shakespeare's "folios of Fate" for Wilhelm Meister: Unlike the sort of extensive reading that draws the individual out into a series of rapidly changing new perceptions of reality, this text reveals to Heinrich the central unified core of his identity. The intimate bond that Heinrich discovers between his own life and that of the figure represented in the text suggests that he has entered that realm of "presence" evoked in the image of the cathedral of time: His life and its representation, the sign and what it signifies, coincide. Thus the book within the book looks both backwards and forwards. As a handwritten manuscript it recalls a nostalgic image of better days, before literature was debased to "paper money" (2:462) in the modern world. At the same time it already fulfills for Heinrich the potential function of the finite canon of literary texts for society in general conceived by speaker A in the dialogue discussed earlier. While A dreams of a literary market in which each new season would function as "a systematic link in the chain of *Bildung*" (2:661), Heinrich discovers in the manuscript "the hidden interlinking of the past and the future" {83} (1:257) in the events of his own life.

However, this reading of the scene remains incomplete unless we account for the split that emerges between the reader and the text in the process of depicting the mystical moment. This fragmentation of the self into a series of infinitely iterable texts qualifies the combination of

---

26. Molnár, *Romantic Vision*, 198.
27. Culler provides a lucid account of the "logic of the supplement" in his explication of Derrida's reading of Saussure: "But the operation of deconstruction or the self-deconstruction of logocentric theories does not lead to a new theory that sets everything straight. Even theories like Saussure's ... do not escape the logocentric premises they undermine; and there is no reason to believe that a theoretical enterprise could ever free itself from those premises" (*On Deconstruction*, 109).

nostalgic longing and utopian hope that the scene offers upon first reading. Instead of the fusion of the observer with the representation, we are reminded that the concept of unfallen language is projected onto the past by modern, "sentimental" individuals. The handwritten, illuminated manuscript is only present in the text in the form of a typeset description. Even as it anticipates a regulated book market where each new text would contribute toward the systematic construction of a finite canon, the book within the book creates a model where each new text generates further texts in an uncontrollable flurry of literary production. At this point we have come full circle to the other pole of Novalis's reflections on language and literature. What speaker B sometimes laments as a loss of "presence" can also be affirmed as an anticipation of Novalis's alternative utopia, where language would be divorced from its referent to speak for its own sake in the free play of pure sign, where literary production could be liberated from the constraints of the current market to circulate uninhibitedly in the genuine spirit of commercial exchange.

The encounter with the illuminated manuscript stands at the center of *Heinrich von Ofterdingen,* as it formulates an experience of mystical unity in a way that simultaneously reveals that experience to be centered on an empty focal point surrounded by anticipations and repetitions that recede into infinity. Thus it is logical to begin a reading of Novalis's novel in the middle, since each new beginning already repeats a previous beginning that anticipates future repetitions.[28] This pattern is nowhere more evident than in the opening chapter. The linear unfolding of time suggested by the ticking clock in the first sentence of the novel is systematically undermined as this chapter progresses. Heinrich's dream anticipates the events of the novel to come, much as the manuscript will indicate his future experiences. At the same time, Heinrich's dream already repeats his father's dream. Both dreams, in turn, are set off by stories of former times told by mysterious strangers. The confusion of the normal temporal sequence is further complicated by the order in which the events are presented, as the narration of Heinrich's dream precedes the narration of his father's dream that it repeats.

This narrative technique undermines the frequently repeated contention in Novalis scholarship that the dreamworld grants Heinrich access

---

28. For this reason too I have opted to concentrate on the completed first part of *Heinrich von Ofterdingen,* rather than engage in speculation about the possible direction the continuation would have taken. As Link has argued, the self-reflexive structure of the text ultimately renders such speculation irrelevant, as any given moment looks simultaneously back to the past and ahead to the future (*Abstraktion und Poesie,* 166-67).

to a more profoundly accurate understanding of reality than he can achieve in his waking hours.[29] Like his father, Heinrich has heard " 'of the days of old, how animals and trees and cliffs talked with people then' " {15} (1:195), and it seems as if the dream is about to reintroduce this era. Yet Heinrich remains on the brink of revelation: " 'I feel just as though they might start any moment now and I could tell by their looks what they wanted to say to me' " {15} (1:195). Even if nature did begin to speak, Heinrich would not be able to comprehend or to articulate the experience: " 'And to think I can't even talk about my singular condition!' " {15} (1:195). Thus the erasure of origins in the opening chapter corresponds to the novel's lack of narrative closure; in the place of the confident depiction of the three-phase, Christian theory of history, Novalis leaves us instead suspended in an infinitely regressing series of reflections.[30]

Is there then no distinction between the dreamworld and waking reality? Here we must turn to the conversation between Heinrich and his father, situated between the narration of the two dreams in the opening chapter. Although Heinrich awakens profoundly moved by his final dream, his parents chide him for sleeping too long and deride the notion that dreams could still be divine messages. " 'The nature of dreams as well as of the world of men must have been different in those days,' " asserts Heinrich's father. " 'In the age we live in there is no longer any direct intercourse with heaven' " {18} (1:198). Quite significantly, Heinrich does not contest his father's claim directly, but rather substitutes psychology for religion in his defense of dreams: " 'Is not every dream, even the most confused one, a remarkable phenomenon, which apart from any notion of its being sent from God is a significant rent in the mysterious curtain that hangs a thousandfold about our inner life?' "

---

29. Most critics have viewed the events of the novel as an objectification of Heinrich's inner development: "Alle äußere Aktion dient nur als Sinnbild für innere Geschehnisse" (Hiebel, *Deutscher Dichter*, 315; also Mahr, *Übergang zum Endlichen*, 24; Molnár, *Romantic Vision*, 121). Thus the dreams and the fairy tales in the novel are understood to be revelations of the higher truth that lies beneath the surface of normal waking reality: "The freer the imagination is in forming its images, the more clearly do they display their function of serving to reveal the self's true nature. Objects may assume such symbolic transparency in dreams, when the self lies suspended in sleep and for this very reason achieves a keener state of awareness than the distortions of waking reality would permit; actually, the dreaming self is awake and the waking self asleep to the truth of its reality" (Molnár, *Romantic Vision*, 104).

30. Kuzniar is the one critic who doubts the revelatory status of Heinrich's dream. As she points out, Heinrich's dream may be understood in psychological terms as a mere repetition of his father's dream, or it may be simply "opaque and uninterpretable" (*Delayed Endings*, 105).

{19} (1:198-99). After appealing to the evidence of written records and personal experience, Heinrich goes on to define the therapeutic benefits of dreaming: " 'Dreams seem to me to be a defense against the regularity and routine of life, a playground where the hobbled imagination is freed and revived and where it jumbles together all the pictures of life and interrupts the constant soberness of grown-ups by means of a merry child's play' " {19} (1:199).

Two aspects of this statement deserve notice. First, Heinrich defends dreams not because of their oracular nature, but rather because they provide an escape from the dull routine of daily life. The result is a striking parallel to the defense of the theater by both Anton Reiser and Wilhelm Meister. The dream is conceived as an aesthetic, not a religious experience. Second, Heinrich does not claim that the images of the dream world are essentially different in kind from those of waking reality. Dreams merely jumble up already present images, thus transforming the deadly seriousness of the adult world into the joyous play of childhood. These statements about the nature of dreams indirectly characterize the text in which the dreams are narrated. To express the point negatively, the dreams bear out the father's assertion that direct access to the divine is no longer possible, or, more radically, that the Golden Age itself was never more than a concept used to gesture toward an inarticulable realm that can only be defined negatively. From a positive perspective, however, the complex interweaving of anticipation and repetition in both the content of the dreams and the order of their narration transforms the text itself into a dreamlike structure, "where it jumbles together all the pictures of life." While the text refuses to articulate the ineffable, it does disrupt the *Selbstverständlichkeit* of conventional reality. Once again we recognize the two aesthetic models produced by Heinrich's encounter with the illuminated manuscript, where the promise of direct access to the one master text generates instead an infinitely receding structure that inspires a combination of lament over lost unity with affirmation of potentially unrestricted verbal and textual plurality.

Heinrich's interpretation of dreams as aesthetic experiences, at the end of chapter one, leads into the merchants' comments on the nature of poetry, at the beginning of chapter two. They formulate these comments by contrasting poetry with music and painting. The latter two types of art are mimetic; just as we enjoy the sights and sounds of nature, we also enjoy the representation of these sensual stimuli in art. However, music and painting are more than inferior substitutes for the real thing; nature is said to enjoy its own reflection in art as much as the human beings: " 'Nature herself also wants to derive a pleasure from her great artfulness and hence transformed herself into human beings; thereby she takes delight in her own glory' " {31} (1:209). The Platonic notion of art as a copy of nature, which is itself merely a copy of the eternal forms, becomes instead a reciprocal relation between art and nature, based on mutual reflection for mutual pleasure. As a result, music and painting are no longer distinct from and subordinate to nature; rather, they are the crowning achievement *of* nature, nature come to self-consciousness through the creations of *its* supreme creation, human beings.

The merchants go on to explain that poetry, unlike painting and music, is not a mimetic art. Its building blocks are words rather than sounds or images, and thus arbitrary rather than natural signs. This does not mean that poetry is inferior to the visual arts, however. Precisely because it does not merely reflect reality, it is able to conjure up nonexistent worlds in the mind of the listener: " 'Within us as out of deep caverns there rise ancient and future times, countless people, *marvelous* regions, and the strangest occurrences, snatching us away from the familiar present' " {31-32} (1:210). If the language of poetry were utterly foreign to us, however, we would never be able to follow its imaginative flights. At this point we reenter our discussion of Novalis's views on language. We saw how Novalis situates normal language between an Adamic past and the total abstraction of a "genuine Sanskrit" that would exist for its own sake. Neither option is open to us, however. While language is arbitrary enough to prevent us from equating its signs with what they signify, it nevertheless always exists in a communal context that assures its (inevitably imprecise) referentiality. Thus the poet can introduce us to unfamiliar foreign words, which nevertheless seem comprehensible to us, which is to say that we are able to embed them in a meaningful context. " 'One hears alien words and yet knows what they are intended to mean' " {32} (1:210). Poetry delights its audience not only because it enables the assimilation of the radically new, but also because, like a dream, it recontextualizes and revitalizes what is already present: " 'The sayings of poets exert a magical power; they make even common words take on enticing sounds and intoxicate the spellbound listener' " {32} (1:210).

The merchants follow this theoretical discussion of poetry with the story of Arion and the dolphins. This combination of discussion and storytelling typifies Heinrich's development in the ensuing chapters. While his experience consists outwardly of a journey to visit his mother's family in Augsburg, the trip is really more of a pretext for allowing Heinrich to encounter new individuals and hear their stories, which gradually reveal to him further aspects of his own latent character.

Three times in the course of the first book these encounters take the form of his listening to inserted fairy tales. The merchants follow the story of Arion with a tale of forbidden love in Atlantis. Then the first part of the novel concludes with Klingsohr's fairy tale. Each of these stories centers on the theme of the redemption of society through poetry: Arion suffers injustice at the hands of the greedy sailors, but saves himself through the power of his song. The young man's poetry overcomes the hostility of the king and enables his marriage to the princess, bringing joy to Atlantis. Finally, Klingsohr's fairy tale tells of the rebirth of poetry through love in a mythical kingdom.

As there is often little or no commentary in the text regarding the relation between these fairy tales and the primary narrative, we are forced to determine their significance ourselves. The discontinuity between the various elements of the text had already troubled Friedrich Schlegel, who complained that parts of the novel were to him "completely incomprehensible, and since everything is interconnected, actually everything [is incomprehensible]" (4:655). One month later Novalis conceded that his primary difficulty lay in making the transition from one section of the novel to the next.[31] One might well argue that these tales are meant as a form of instruction for Heinrich, or perhaps more accurately as a form of revelation of his destiny as a poet. Like the dreams of the opening chapter and the hermit's illuminated manuscript, these tales can be viewed as anticipations of Heinrich's future, in that they reveal what has always been present. As in the case of the dreams and the manuscript, however, the analogy stops short of identity. These stories are set in a mythical realm as far removed from Heinrich's world as his world is distant from that of Novalis. While the novel itself remains incomplete, each of the narrative inserts comes to a resoundingly happy conclusion. Thus it is equally possible to stress the discontinuity between these tales and the fragmentary narrative, viewing them as "inverted projections of present deficiency,"[32] rather than as prefigurations of future plenitude.

This stress on the tension between comic resolution in the subplots and persistent fragmentation in the main plot can be extended to characterize the function of poetry within the fairy tales themselves. The merchants begin the story of Arion by recalling a distant, happier past: " 'In days of old, all nature must have been more alive and meaningful

---

31. Although Schlegel's comments have not been preserved, Novalis reformulates his critique in a letter dated 18 June 1800: "Deinen Tadel fühl' ich völlig—diese Ungeschicklichkeit in Übergängen, diese Schwerfälligkeit in der Behandlung des wandelnden und bewegten Lebens ist meine Hauptschwierigkeit" (4:333).

32. Kuzniar, *Delayed Endings*, 110.

than today'" {32} (1:210). However, Arion's own world is no earthly paradise; greed and violence already exist, as the sailors plan to murder Arion for his treasure. Nor are we led to believe that the evil has resulted from a previous fall from grace. Here as elsewhere in *Heinrich von Ofterdingen,* the earliest times are described as being more barbarous than blissful. When Heinrich's trip to the caves in chapter five is likened to a journey back into "that mythical primeval age," this original era is characterized by lack rather than fullness: It was a time "when every bud and germ still slept by itself, lonely and untouched, yearning *in vain* to unfold the obscure wealth of its own immeasurable existence" {76} (1:252; emphasis added). Heinrich's own "reflective and romantic period" represents a positive development away from "the rough and crude times of barbarism" {25} (1:204). Nor is Arion's ancient world a "healthy world" (*heile Welt*) of the sort sketched by Schiller in his description of "naive" peoples, but rather a "*healed* world," (*eine ge-heilte Welt*) where harmony is created, not given. Arion's song redeems a world characterized by adjectives like "desert," "waste," "dead," "ferocious," and "wild" {33} (1:211). But the redemptive power of Arion's song is limited. Not only are the majority of the pirates allowed to murder each other in the fight to possess Arion's treasure; worse, some of these evil men escape, and there is no indication that they have been cured of their asocial tendencies. Thus the harmony created by Arion's song stands in deliberate *opposition* to the primal discord of the world; it presents us with an "inverted projection" of a *past* deficiency that continues to exist in the present of the narrative frame.[33]

The second tale told by the merchants confirms the suspicion that the harmony established by Arion was both incomplete and transitory. Arion's world has become a distant memory to the king of Atlantis. To be sure, his court has become something of a national center for the performing arts, but the king's devotion to the arts is compulsive, causing him to neglect "the most important affairs, indeed even the necessities of life" {36} (1:214). In this artificial paradise conflict is preserved in "only the ancient legends of poets" {37} (1:214), whereas in Arion's day poetry created images of harmony in a discordant world. The king's daughter epitomizes the spirit of the land: "Grown up amid singing," she herself has become "an exquisite song" (1:214). Like the

---

33. While Kuzniar differs from most critics in her stress on the discontinuity between the inserted narratives and the frame, she remains traditional to the extent that she views these tales as evocations of "happy bygone days" (*Delayed Endings,* 110), whose "closed, self-contained, timeless structure[s]" (108) contrast with the fragmentary novel in which they are embedded. My point here is that the same antagonistic relation between harmonious poetic constructs and discordant society exists *within the fairy tales themselves.*

society her father has created, however, she too is threatened with sterility. Certain that he and his wife are of stock superior to the rest of his subjects, the king finds no suitor fit to marry his daughter and thus to perpetuate his noble lineage.

If we take this situation at face value, then we can see in the king's plight a parable of historical decline. The time of heroes and demigods has passed; he alone remains as the last link to a bygone era. However, there is enough of an ironic undertone to the narration to suggest that the king may well be enamored of a fiction produced by the incessant singing of his sycophantic court poets. "His bards had constantly celebrated his kinship to former semidivine rulers of the world, and in the magic mirror of their art the superiority of his lineage over the origin of other men and the glory of his dynasty appeared to him to shine even more, so that he thought himself related to the rest of mankind only through the nobler class of poets" (38) (1:215). Just as the Golden Age of the previous myth was a momentary creation of Arion's song rather than a spontaneous overflow of harmonious nature, the king's conviction that he is the last descendent of this Golden Age can also be understood as a self-serving fiction rather than as impartial history.

The limitations of her father's world become apparent to the princess only after she encounters the man and his son who live in deliberate isolation from the court. In keeping with her own characterization as "an exquisite song" their courtship takes the form of mutual instruction in poetry: while she teaches him songs of the court, he sings to her of the secrets of nature and primeval history. Their clandestine affair is consummated in what at first glance seems a refreshing outburst of young passion in a protective cave during a thunderstorm. Yet this encounter contains an unmistakable allusion to the fourth book of Virgil's *Aeneid*, when Aeneas and Dido also find shelter and love in a cave during a thunderstorm. Moreover, like Gottfried's Tristan and Isolde before them, who sing of Aeneas and Dido while in *their* secluded cave, the young man and the princess entertain each other with the lute he has happened to bring along. At this point the opposition between the artificiality of the court and the unstudied natural world represented by the young man and his father begins to break down. The love nurtured by shared poetry culminates in an embrace staged as a quotation of a medieval quotation of classical literature.

One year later the young man effects a reconciliation between the king and his daughter with a plea for mercy and a song that sketches a myth of universal history from "the primeval golden age and its sovereigns—love and poetry; with the emergence of hate and barbarism and their battles with those benevolent goddesses; and finally with the coming triumph of those divinities, the end of calamities, the rejuvenation of nature, and the return of an everlasting golden age" {48} (1:225). Universal rejoicing breaks out among the people, and life in Atlantis is transformed into perpetual celebration. It seems, in other words, as if the song about the regaining of the Golden Age has actually created that paradise in Atlantis. The life-denying exclusivity of the king's private pleasure dome has been opened up and regenerated through the theme of love and forgiveness in the young man's song.[34]

Unfortunately, however, this harmonious moment is short-lived: Atlantis and its inhabitants are swallowed up by destructive floods, and their memory is preserved only in legends. This tragic conclusion to a fairy tale of poetic redemption gives us pause. Clearly the Golden Age that seems to be embodied at the end of the story is no less transient than that moment of harmony inspired by Arion's song. The fragility of the restored health of Atlantis, in turn, raises questions about the status of the young man's verses. As with the court poets, his own myth is not without personal motivation. The Golden Age he evokes in his song is also a self-serving fiction, created in the interest of receiving royal sanction for his secret marriage and his illegitimate child. The impending total destruction of Atlantis and its inhabitants indicates that the true Golden Age had in fact not returned. This is neither to suggest that the general celebration at the end of the young man's song is not genuine, nor to downplay the significance of the change of heart that overcomes the selfish king at the end of the fairy tale. What should be clear, however, is that we cannot simply read this fairy tale through the lens of the familiar tripartite pattern of history invoked in the young man's song. Both here and at the beginning of the tale, this theory of history is clearly identified as a poetic fiction created by human beings for personal motivations, rather than as an unqualified account of the way things really are. Hence I have stressed the moment of self-conscious artifice even in the spontaneous mutual seduction of the two lovers, who to the reader at least merely reenact a literary topos. If from the perspective of the frame the myth of Atlantis provides a nostalgic image of a happier world, from the perspective of this world itself we see that even the myth of Atlantis is a product of human imagination conceived in self-interest and impotent against the forces of a hostile nature.

Klingsohr's fairy tale is the third and longest narrative insert in

34. Thus Molnár reads this story as a tale of the king's redemptive deliverance from the " 'prison house of language' " (*Romantic Vision,* 134): "The youth's inspired composition revolves around the central theme that love of poetry remains mere self-indulgence in aesthetic delight, unless it also is love of the fellow human being in whose name the poet speaks and whom he addresses in each member of his audience" (136).

Heinrich von Ofterdingen. Drawing on the vocabularies of Greek, Germanic, and Arabic mythology, as well as elements of his autobiography, Novalis creates his own version of the familiar Romantic paradigm of secularized salvation history that had already appeared in more traditional form in the first two fairy tales. As in the myths of Arion and Atlantis, Klingsohr speaks of the establishment of the Golden Age through the triumph of love and poetry over the forces of evil. Once again, it is possible to see his tale as an anticipation of Heinrich's future, as a transformation of the private dream-vision of the opening chapter into the universal language of myth.[35] As in the previous tales, however, the image of attained harmony at the end of Klingsohr's fairy tale contrasts markedly with the open-ended, fragmentary frame of the novel itself. Moreover, this harmony does not represent the spontaneous expression of a world without strife. Instead, the idyll is again achieved through the active assertion of the will over the forces of evil that remain present, but spellbound, on the magic chessboard.

The salvation narrative is further undermined by its iterability. Just as Heinrich encounters another version of the novel in the hermit's cave, Eros and Ginnistan are treated to a magical performance at the castle of the moon that prefigures the resolution of the fairy tale itself. By promising to repeat the performance for the entertainment of the court at the end of the tale, the moon further undermines the uniqueness of the event. The metanarrative of the Bible that contains within it all personal histories has been transformed into a fiction that can be reproduced at will.[36] The self-reflexive structure of the fairy tale extends further to reflect the novel within which it is narrated. The plot of Klingsohr's fairy tale corresponds quite closely to the plot summary of the song that the young man sings to the king at the end of the Atlantis myth, which in turn anticipates the probable course of the novel's continuation.[37] Moreover, the story of Eros bathing at the court of the

---

35. "Dreams are, however, a purely subjective, or internal, experience that must be communicable if it is to have validity. Poetic statements are such dreams shared in common and fairy tales, as least referential to a pragmatic context, come closest to being objective, or external, counterparts to dreams. Consequently, part I of *Heinrich von Ofterdingen* begins with a dream and ends with a fairy tale, which completes the complementary arch of mutual validation that extends from internal to external vision" (Molnár, *Romantic Vision*, 104).

36. Once again, my reading of this fairy tale is indebted to Kuzniar's excellent interpretation (*Delayed Endings*, esp. 114-15). We differ primarily in terms of the conclusions drawn from the analysis: while she works to subvert the persistent tendency among critics to impose a Christian model of salvation history onto Novalis's work, I attempt to view the text in the context of Novalis's comments on language and literature in his contemporary society.

37. "In dieser Inhaltsangabe ist Novalis' ganze Geschichtsschau zusammengefaßt; sie

moon repeats events of Heinrich's dream, themselves a repetition of his father's dream.

Taken as a whole, the three narrative inserts stand in an analogous relation to the frame, as do the illuminated manuscript in the fifth chapter and the dreams of the first chapter. From one perspective, they anticipate Heinrich's future role as a poet who will create order in his own life and harmony in society by recalling stories of poets who succeeded at this task in the past. As in the case of the manuscript, this poetic order stands in a positive relation to the seeming chaos of present events. In terms of the novel itself, this chaos refers to the disorienting experiences that confront Heinrich during his first trip away from home. Viewed in the broader cultural context in which the novel was written, *Heinrich von Ofterdingen* addresses both the growing sense of "transcendental homelessness" common to the early Romantics, and the disorienting effect of the explosive growth in literary production in the public sphere. The novel formulates a utopian model of restored harmony based on a nostalgic image of an idealized past designed to guide German society back to its metaphysical home with a literature that has taken on the role of a secular scripture.

While this interpretation of the novel recalls speaker A's desire to create a limited German canon that is to cure cultural chaos, the text also encourages an alternative reading that reminds us of speaker B's call for even more literary production. The infinite iterability of the redemptive narrative accelerates the current disorder into the swirling confusion of images in a dream, "where it jumbles together all the pictures of life." To the extent that this process identifies the Golden Age as an unattainable fiction, the result is to be regretted; but as the narrative equivalent of that dreamlike liberation from the stultifying order of everyday reality, the process may be affirmed. The perpetually deferred harmony of the Golden Age gives birth to "the chaos of completed creation" (3:281) in the text. Granted, Novalis's combination of nostalgic longing for mystical presence with a utopian desire for absolute difference does not represent a very practical response to the transformation of the public sphere, but is a response nevertheless. Whether conceived as a limited canon of texts promising total coherence, or as an alternative model of infinite textual circulation, Novalis's literary utopias define contemporary deficiencies in the institution of literature while suggesting possibilities for its productive transformation.

---

wird in Klingsohrs Märchen symbolisch dargestellt und sollte in der Fortsetzung als Romanhandlung durchgeführt werden" (Samuel, "Novalis: Heinrich von Ofterdingen," 273).

Self-Engendering Fictions
in Jean Paul's *Flegeljahre* (1804-5)

7

In Jean Paul's *Flegeljahre* (adolescent years) we encounter the motif of the book within the book for the third time. Unlike Wilhelm Meister and Heinrich von Ofterdingen, who read biographies composed by someone else, the twin brothers Walt and Vult decide to write their own novel. The project gradually gathers steam until the fourth and final part of the *Flegeljahre,* when the brothers move in together and devote all their energies to writing their book and getting it published. They first send the unfinished manuscript to the publisher Dyck in Leipzig, specifying not only their price (which they set at four times what Milton received for *Paradise Lost*), but also "paper, print, format and size of the edition—the master was permitted to print 3,000 copies."[1] To their surprise, Dyck returns the manuscript with an insulting letter, claiming that he would be happy to publish "pleasantries" by the popular authors Rabener or Wezel, "but never ones like *this*" (2:1009). After the bookseller Paßvogel refuses to look at their manuscript the brothers send it off to Berlin, bastion of the Enlightenment, where they hope the critic Garlieb Merkel will pass it on to Friedrich Nicolai. This time the response is openly hostile. Merkel returns their book "with real contempt," finding "Walt's contributions still bearable, but Vult's not only tasteless... but even imitating the cuckoo Jean Paul, who already sounds boring enough

---

1. Jean Paul, *Werke,* 2:988. Unless otherwise noted, all subsequent references to Jean Paul's works are taken from this edition and included in the text.

himself without the cuckoo clock of imitation" (2:1031-32).[2] Not to be deterred, the brothers try a notorious publisher of pirated editions in Vienna, who sends their work on to another disreputable publisher in Cologne, with the explanation that he rarely prints anything that hasn't been published already. Unfortunately, the Cologne address turns out to be inaccurate, and the novel is once again returned to its authors.

Unlike Goethe, who has his protagonist read the biography kept in the archives of a secret society, or Novalis, whose hero leafs through an illuminated manuscript in a hermit's cave, Jean Paul brings Walt and Vult into direct contact with authors, publishers, and reviewers living in contemporary Germany. He writes openly about the problems of finding a sympathetic publisher, receiving sufficient payment for the manuscript, and dealing with hostile reviewers and pirated editions. Jean Paul shared these concerns with the hundreds of writers like himself, who struggled to establish themselves as professional authors. In characteristic fashion, however, Jean Paul addressed these common problems in terms of his personal experiences. A decade older than Novalis, Tieck, and the Schlegels, Jean Paul had gone through an unusual and particularly difficult development as a writer. He began his career as a satirist in the Enlightenment tradition of Swift and Voltaire. However, his *Grönländische Prozesse* (1783) met with little response, and his next work, the *Teufelspapiere*, proved even less of a popular and critical success when it finally appeared in 1789.[3] In contrast to his failure as a satirist, Jean Paul's turn to fiction in the 1790s brought him personal fame and popular success. In an unfortunate paradox, however, the popularity of works like *Die unsichtbare Loge* (1793), *Hesperus* (1795), and *Siebenkäs* (1796-97) created expectations among the readers that led to the widespread rejection of his most ambitious novel, *Titan* (1800-1803). His short-lived commercial success had only prepared the way for renewed difficulties with the public. Although he remained famous throughout his life, he never regained the celebrity status that reached its zenith in the 1790s, nor did his late fiction sell at the rate of his earlier work.[4]

2. See Theiss for information about Merkel's generally unsympathetic response to Jean Paul's work ("Garlieb Merkel als Rezensent Jean Pauls").
3. Harich, *Jean Paul*, 118, 126, 140, 170. See also Berend, "Jean Paul—der meistgelesene Schriftsteller seiner Zeit?" Köpke provides the best introduction to the young Jean Paul in his aptly titled study *Erfolglosigkeit*.
4. "Dabei scheint die Arbeit der letzten Jahre ergebnislos. Für die Leserwelt ist er immer noch der Verfasser des 'Hesperus.' Selbst der unendlich reifere und größere 'Siebenkäs' hat sich neben dem den Instinkten der Zeit entgegenkommenden 'Hesperus' nicht durchsetzen können" (Harich, *Jean Paul*, 528-29). The reception of *Titan* was further hindered by the fact that the novel was published only gradually in yearly installments (Harich, *Jean Paul*, 602-3). Berend supports this general sketch of the rise

On the most direct level, then, the twin protagonists of the *Flegeljahre* reflect Jean Paul's concern with the lack of public response to varying aspects of his literary production. Both Walt and Vult are artists who prove singularly inept at establishing effective communication with their audience. Vult has already published a collection of satirical sketches which is identified as none other than Jean Paul's own first work, *Die Grönländischen Prozesse*. And yet, as he tells Walt, he would be lying if he claimed that " 'the publication of these volumes . . . had made either me or the material itself known in the slightest' " (2:654). With the exception of a few negative reviews, he continues, " 'unfortunately not a soul knew or criticized my writing' " (2:654). Vult has since responded to the public's rejection of his work by treating them with contempt. This disdain for the public manifests itself most clearly in his role as musician. " 'Like cattle, the masses only hear the present, not both polar-times [*Polar-Zeiten*], only musical syllables, no syntax' " (2:756). The common lot is only satisfied when the music suddenly swells from pianissimo to fortissimo, or when the lead violinist plunges from a sustained high note to the lowest, or when both happen at the same time: " 'In such moments the burgher loses control of himself and sweats with praise' " (2:757). As a result, Vult delights in the cynical manipulation of this undeserving public by feigning blindness to heighten the effect—and increase the profit—of his flute performance: " 'People deserve to be deceived' " (2:671).

Walt is a sensitive, introspective individual who uses literature to retreat from a hostile environment. As a child he liked nothing better than curling up with an exciting book: "The more grimly cold I found everything in the geography books or the wilder in the historical ones, the more comfortable and cosier I felt" (2:1001). Walt's own literary productions seek to compensate for the sacrifices of adulthood by recapturing the security of his youthful reading experiences. We are first introduced to Walt as the author of a dreamy idyll, "Das Glück eines schwedischen Pfarrers" (The Happiness of a Swedish Pastor), in which he imagines the delights of a profession that has been denied him. Although he is deeply moved by his own "polymeters" (*Polymeter*) or "extended verses" (*Streckverse*), his works do not inspire similar feelings among his fellow citizens. The court treasurer Knoll finds them "a real waste of time," an unseemly activity for a young professional: " 'Capitalists or lords of the manor, who have nothing to do and a sufficient livelihood, can indeed write and read as many poems as they want, but not a

---

and fall of Jean Paul's popularity with statistics on the number of copies and editions of his various texts ("Der meistgelesene Schriftsteller?"). See Wiethölter for further works on the subsequent history of Jean Paul's reception ("Jean Paul: Flegeljahre," 189 n. 8).

mature person in a good, respectable field who wants to appear as a rational lawyer'" (2:626). To Vult's delight, Walt emphatically defends his right to continue writing these prose poems for his own pleasure and for his immediate circle of family and friends, but they remain primarily a private, compensatory activity. If Vult's satires fail to find the audience they address, then Walt's polymeters become "endangered idylls," poetic interludes that tend toward narcissistic escapism.[5]

Perhaps, however, the brothers' joint project of writing a novel entitled *Hoppelpoppel oder das Herz* (Hoppelpoppel or the Heart) suggests a way of transcending their respective problems. In his sensitive analysis of the *Flegeljahre,* Herman Meyer argues that we should understand the novel's structure in terms of Friedrich Schlegel's early romantic theory. Citing the 116th *Athenäum* fragment, he maintains that the novel is "definitely romantic poetry. And in the structure of the *Flegeljahre,* Walt and Vult's double novel is just the sort of reflecting mirror that Schlegel has in mind."[6] Although significant differences obtain between

---

5. I allude of course to the title of Wuthenow's essay. Although he concentrates on the endangered idyll of "Schulmeisterlein Wutz," the phrase accurately captures the sense of Walt's precarious isolation. Gansberg argues that Walt and Vult together represent two equally ineffective protesting stances against the German political situation in the wake of the French Revolution. Walt's dream of a better world remains divorced from reality, while Vult's clear-sighted critique of social conditions becomes "barocke[r] Lebensnihilismus" in the face of his inability to effect change ("Welt-Verlachung," 390-91). The "truth" of the novel, in her view, lies not in its implied vision of future harmony, but rather in Jean Paul's unwillingness to obscure a historical dilemma with the false harmony of an artificial happy ending (395). Sprengel comes to similar conclusions: "Hier konnte es nur Pseudo-Synthesen wie Raphaelas verlogene Sentimentalität oder Walts unsinnige Bürgschaft geben.... Der Autor Jean Paul war zu ehrlich, solche Notlösung als Lösung anzubieten" (*Innerlichkeit,* 293).

6. Meyer, "Jean Paul: Flegeljahre," 233. Wuthenow echoes Mayer on this point: "Hier erscheint das Buch im Buch als die Möglichkeit einer unendlichen, sich wiederholenden Spiegelung" (*Im Buch die Bücher,* 102). In an article roughly contemporary to that of Meyer, Gerhart Mayer approaches the novel with stylistic categories taken from Jean Paul's own aesthetics; he maintains that the seemingly irreconcilable positions of the two brothers are sublated into the higher wisdom of the narrator, who speaks from the perspective of Jean Paul's concept of humor: "Er ist sich einerseits durchaus des antinomischen Gegensatzes von Ideal und Wirklichkeit bewußt, zum andern aber glaubt er an dessen Überwindung und Versöhnung in einer fernen, metaphysischen Zukunft" ("Die humorgeprägte Struktur," 424-25). Neumann's meticulously detailed analysis of the novel remains firmly within the tradition of these formalist critics (*Jean Pauls 'Flegeljahre';* see in particular his introduction and 56-57). Similarly, Tönz views the "Wirtshaus 'Zum Wirtshaus'" as a reflection of Jean Paul's "deepest desire": "ins Unendliche zu gelangen" (122). Although more psychologically oriented, Maurer's study of the dialectical link between the characters' disappointing reality and their desire to escape that reality through projection of the self into poetic masks does not go beyond an intrinsic analysis of the work. For Furst, romantic irony in the *Flegeljahre* has the primary effect of rendering

Schlegel's understanding of irony and Jean Paul's conception of humor,[7] both are united in their opposition to satire. As a classical rhetorical strategy — *dissimulatio* — irony involves saying one thing while meaning another in order to develop an implicit critique of a particular aspect of reality.[8] The romantic ironist, in contrast, seeks the self-cancellation of any fixed point of view in the desire to articulate the ineffable. As Schlegel writes in his *Philosophische Lehrjahre*, "Everything that does not annihilate itself is not free and [therefore] worthless."[9] Satirists are serious, writes Jean Paul in his *Vorschule der Ästhetik* (Preschool of Aesthetics) (1803-4); "even the accidental contrasts of their paintings cut short laughter with bitterness, whereas the comic plays its poetic game with the triviality of nonsense [*mit dem Kleinen des Unverstandes*] and makes [one] happy and free" (5:115). The "world humor" (*Welt-Humor*) of Gozzi, Sterne, Voltaire, or Rabelais arises "not *by means of,* but rather *despite* its allusions to current events" (5:126). Satire drags the work of art into direct, contaminating contact with the world it seeks to transcend. Thus humor liberates, while satire enthralls: "There one finds oneself chained by custom, here poetically liberated.... It is an accident when something lashes out satirically in a genuinely comic work; indeed, it disrupts the mood" (5:116).

Despite these comments in the *Vorschule,* Jean Paul never eliminated

---

our perception of reality ambiguous: "Truth, identity, reality, and narration too dissolve in an indeterminacy that admits alternatives without reconciling them. So nothing is definite, everything possible" (*Fictions of Romantic Irony,* 156).

7. Whereas Berend had underscored the proximity of Jean Paul's humor to Schlegel's irony in his study of the *Vorschule* (*Jean Pauls Ästhetik,* 228-42; esp. 240), Strohschneider-Kohrs carefully distinguishes between the two concepts in her monograph. For Schlegel, romantic irony *is* the activity, tension, relation in the work that points toward the infinite through negation of the finite; Jean Paul's humor involves the negation of the finite from the fixed position of the infinite. Infinite approximation is replaced by "einen einmaligen Aufschwung zu einer weltverlachenden Ansicht" (*Die romantische Ironie,* 150). Thus Jean Paul's humor substitutes a reconciliatory perspective on life's vicissitudes for an aesthetic theory of incessant progression through annihilation. Nevertheless, Jean Paul conceded his increased indebtedness to Schlegel in a letter of 1803: "Mein poetisches System hat sich weit von meinem alten und von der Bewunderung für Leute wie Wieland, Haller, Ramler, Gesner etc. verloren; und ist sehr Schlegelisch geworden" (*Sämtliche Werke: Historisch-Kritische Ausgabe,* Section 3, 4:217). Strohschneider-Kohrs provides an excellent discussion of the various concepts of irony and humor among the early Romantics as they developed out of Fichtean philosophy. Behler places the romantic ironists in the broader context of their relation to both classical rhetoric and world literature (*Klassische Ironie, romantische Ironie, tragische Ironie*). Both Mellor (*English Romantic Irony*) and Furst (*Fictions of Romantic Irony*) provide more recent summaries of Schlegel's theory in English.

8. Behler, *Klassische Ironie, romantische Ironie, tragische Ironie,* 15-16.

9. *Kritische Ausgabe,* 18:II, 628.

satire from his novels.[10] Here, as in his other works, he reserves particular venom for his critique of the nobility. At the same time, Jean Paul clearly alludes to contemporary romantic theory by introducing *Hoppelpoppel oder das Herz* into his novel; the brothers agree to collaborate on the project at the "Inn of the Inn" (*Wirtshaus zum Wirtshaus*), and Vult originally suggests that they entitle their work *Flegeljahre*. However, the repeated rejection of the novel within the novel inverts the effect of the romantic irony it creates. When the motif is first introduced it emphasizes the autonomy of the work of art: rather than reflecting external reality, the *Flegeljahre* turns its attention inward, to reflect upon itself. But *Hoppelpoppel oder das Herz* returns quite literally in the final section of the *Flegeljahre*, as the rejected manuscript keeps arriving on the authors' doorstep. The result is neither the dialectical progression toward the infinite through the negation of the finite (Schlegel's irony), nor the negation of the finite from a fixed perspective of the infinite (Jean Paul's humor), but rather the grounding of the text in its social context. The *Flegeljahre* remains trapped within itself, not in self-sufficient plenitude, but rather in its isolation from the public it seeks.

Vult's image of the transparent glass that distorts communication between Walt and himself expands into a metaphor for the gap between writer and public around the turn of the nineteenth century: "We both were completely open to one another, and inclined to one another anyway; as transparent to one another as a glass door. But, brother, I write my character with legible characters onto the outside of the glass

---

10. As Lindner has pointed out, Jean Paul's literary practice reveals contradictions that he tries to obscure in his literary theory: "Die 'Ideologie' Jean Pauls ... hat sowohl die Funktion, die eigenen subversiven Tendenzen metaphysisch zu harmonisieren, wie sie zugleich die Möglichkeit schafft, diesen Tendenzen auch nachgeben zu können. Jean Paul interpretiert die eigenen ästhetischen Erfahrungen der Innerlichkeit, der Sentimentalität, der Satire und des Witzes im Diesseits-Jenseits-Schema einer zu seiner Zeit eher anachronistischen Glaubensmetaphysik, die ihn vor den Widersprüchen der historischen Realität schützen soll" (Lindner, *Scheiternde Aufklärung,* 104). Lindner contends that Jean Paul's embrace of autonomy aesthetics was a defensive strategy meant to compensate for the loss of the enlightening function of literature demonstrated by the public failure of his early satires (151). Caught "zwischen dem literarischen Marktgesetzt" and "dem ideelen Anspruch des Genies," the separation of intellect and economy was proclaimed as compensation for the failure of the Enlightenment (52). The concept of genius became a method of immunizing Jean Paul from literary criticism while raising "zugleich Universalitätsanspruch der Dichter, Menschheit schlechthin zu repräsentieren" (137). Sprengel concludes his discussion of Jean Paul's engagement with the literary marketplace by asserting that he was painfully aware of the contradiction between his ideals as a writer and the pressures of publication, without ever coming to a satisfactory solution to the dilemma (*Innerlichkeit,* 146).

in vain, for you can read nothing and see nothing but the reverse on the inside. And so the entire world almost always gets to read very legible, but reversed writing" (2:1058). *Hoppelpoppel oder das Herz* reflects both the brothers' alienation from one another and their mutual isolation from their potential audience. Its rejection anticipates the conclusion of the fragmentary novel within which it is inscribed; like the *Flegeljahre*, the novel conceived within the novel is never brought to term.[11]

Although the twins' collaboration on *Hoppelpoppel oder das Herz* constitutes an important part of the *Flegeljahre*, large portions of the novel focus exclusively on Walt. An earlier generation of critics hailed the introspective Walt as the incarnation of "German humanity" (*des deutschen Menschentums*) in a work said to represent "a transcendent high point of German poetic writing [*Dichtertum*] altogether."[12] More recent work by Peter Sprengel has helped to historicize these earlier appeals to German essence, as he views the bourgeois retreat to "inwardness" as a lamentable response to the retrograde political situation in late eighteenth-century Germany.[13] From another perspective, however, the same character often cited as a typical representative of German *Innerlichkeit* has thoughts and desires so thoroughly mediated by other works of literature that his seemingly private self becomes merely the point of intersection for a variety of literary quotations. Even though Walt fails to reach the public with his writing, the public has already come to him through his reading.

His trip through the northern Bavarian countryside in volume three of the novel provides the best example of this tendency: "He traveled

---

11. The fate of *Hoppelpoppel oder das Herz* was to prove prophetic for that of the *Flegeljahre*. Although Jean Paul *was* able to publish the novel, it was not an immediate commercial success: "Der von dem Dichter selber lange vorher als sein Hauptwerk angekündigte *Titan* (1800-1803) war buchhändlerisch ein ausgesprochener Mißerfolg, noch mehr die folgenden *Flegeljahre* (1804-5), die großenteils aus diesem Grunde unvollendet geblieben sind" (Berend, "Jean Paul—der meistgelesene Schriftsteller?" 182). The evidence presented in Freye's valuable collection of earlier drafts of the *Flegeljahre* suggests that Jean Paul's work is a fragment of a different sort than *Heinrich von Ofterdingen*. Novalis died before he could complete his planned multivolume novel, whereas Jean Paul seems to have reached a dead end in the process of composing the work, as successive versions further developed an increasingly irresolvable opposition between the two brothers (*Jean Pauls Flegeljahre: Materialien und Untersuchungen*).

12. Borcherdt, *Der Roman der Goethezeit*, 454. Similar comments on Walt's representatively "German" inwardness in Berend, "Einleitung," *Sämtliche Werke: Historisch-Kritische Ausgabe* 10:v-vi, and Harich, *Jean Paul*, 648-49.

13. Thus Sprengel concludes that Jean Paul's response to the French Revolution ended in a "Kult der Innerlichkeit" which "erwies sich als geschichtsfremde, als schlechte Negation" (*Innerlichkeit*, 85).

with unspeakable pleasure, particularly into unknown regions, because he believed it was possible while he was under way that one of the most romantic, delightful adventures he had read about would flutter his way" (2:827). He literally reads and writes his way through the landscape, stopping to decipher every engraved stone bench and then pausing to record his adventures in his diary (2:842). Like Don Quixote, who moves through a landscape where it "seems as if from behind every roadside bush and every wooded hill another author is waiting to spring out, clutching a sheaf of verses,"[14] Walt travels through a Bavaria populated with readers, like the "high school student sitting on a border marker with a borrowed novel before his eyes to create a poetic picture of the world and youth" (2:859). Not surprisingly, Walt is more than ready to believe that a man he encounters is none other than "the unforgettable poetic Man of Tockenburg" (2:861).[15] Evening brings on a change from "epic" to "romantic" feelings (2:860), while the next morning Walt sets off from the "land of prose" (*Prosa-Land*) of the inn in search of the "land of poets" (*Dichter-Land*) inhabited by the theater troupe (2:877). His decision to pursue Jakobine is partially motivated by the fact that he has received "oracular" hints from his brother, since he has learned the importance of paying attention to divine signs by reading Homer and Herodotus (2:876).

Walt's love for Wina provides another example of a desire that is both nourished and displaced by writing. We have encountered this theme already in *Wilhelm Meisters Lehrjahre,* where Wilhelm's love for the theater mediates his desire for Mariane. In the *Flegeljahre* the mediating role of literature becomes greater even as the degree of sexual intimacy declines. Shortly after the infatuated Walt has admired Wina in her blue dress at his brother's concert, her father, General Zablocki, hires him to copy his *mémoires érotiques.* Walt's job as Zablocki's "erotic secretary" (2:882) provides him access to the home of his beloved Wina. What follows might be termed love by metonymy, as Walt gradually approaches Wina through his role as first copyist and then poet. After his first meeting with Zablocki, Walt tries to leave the room, but mistakenly opens the door to the closet where Wina's blue dress hangs. The close proximity of this fetishistic object preoccupies him during his first day on the job: "He seriously considered whether he ought to break into the wardrobe and lightly touch the sky-blue dress as the blue ether of his distant senses, with his hand or mouth" (2:813). On the fourth day he

---

14. Alter, *Partial Magic,* 5.
15. Jean Paul refers to Ulrich Bräker's *Lebensgeschichte und natürliche Abenteuer des Armen Mannes im Tockenburg* (1789), the unusual autobiography of a poor Swiss man.

hears the maid singing in the background, which reminds him of Wina, and a few days later while Wina herself sings, "he [makes] a fair copy [*ins reine schrieb*] of an extremely brash letter of a certain Libette with unspeakable pleasure" (2:817).

However obvious this sort of sexual sublimation may seem to the reader, Walt remains blind to his own desire. " 'How do you like wild Libette?' " asks Zablocki. " 'Like the current song, so true, so intimate, and so deeply felt,' responded Gottwalt. —'I think so too,' said Zablocki with an ironic facial expression that Walt took for listening-transfiguration [*Hör-Verklärung*]" (2:819). To Walt's astonishment some days later, Vult determines that Walt is in love on the basis of his contributions to their novel. Although Walt is secretly pleased to discover that his brother has correctly guessed his feelings, he finds it difficult to speak of them directly: "... he kept more to the general and his *mémoires érotiques,* in order to cover his own" (2:825).

Later Walt moves closer to declaring his love for Wina. They share a tender, but silent moment by a waterfall toward the end of the journey described in volume three, after which Walt rereads his contributions to *Hoppelpoppel oder das Herz* in a new light. For the first time he grasps the extent to which his love had inspired his writing, and he begins to produce imaginary descriptions of Wina's feelings that same evening, followed by a series of poems to her. "Then he held the papers full of Eden in the tallow candle and burnt everything, because, he said, he did not see with what right he should reveal so much of her to her or to others without her knowledge" (2:920). Thus Walt destroys the very writing that is meant to bring the lovers closer together; like Wilhelm Meister's monologue in the presence of the sleeping Mariane, Walt's imaginary narrative is produced and consumed in narcissistic isolation.

This practice of deflecting desire into writing reaches a climax toward the end of the novel. For the last time Walt sits in Zablocki's room to finish copying the memoirs. Just as he writes about the feelings he would have if Wina were to enter the room—she does enter. They actually converse, but the conversation consists of a series of misunderstandings. She asks him if he has visited the baths in Leipzig. Falsely assuming that she refers to disreputable student baths, he avoids a direct answer, whereupon "Wina [misunderstands] his misunderstanding" (2:1016). The General brings in a portrait in which Wina has sat as a model for her mother, and Walt is embarrassed by the thought that Wina is holding her own child. Further confusion is added when Walt mistakenly interprets Wina's comment about the fact that his brother has moved in with him as a disparaging remark about the poor quality of the tea served in his bourgeois surroundings (2:1019). Finally, Wina reads Walt one of his own sentimental *Streckverse* printed in the local newspaper, under the mistaken assumption that it was written by his brother. When he shyly confesses the truth, both are deeply moved, but they are brought no closer together: "Hidden from one another behind the happily streaming tears, they were like two notes that quiver invisibly to a single pleasant sound; they were two inclined mayflowers, more moved in unison by an unfamiliar spring breeze than brought closer together" (2:1020).

Thus it is only fitting that Wina should finally confess her love (in Polish!) to a person she assumes is Walt in disguise, but who in fact is Vult dressed up in Walt's costume. While it is possible that Walt and Wina might have been united if the work had been completed, the novel as we have it leaves their love unfulfilled. Instead we are left with the double movement traced here. On one level, Wina gradually moves closer to Walt. What begins with the suggestion of her presence with a dress or her distant voice culminates in the scene in which she reads Walt his own sentimental love poetry. However, increased proximity never leads to physical intimacy, and even at the height of their emotions they remain alienated from each other. The writing that promises to unite the lovers becomes a wall that prevents their actual contact.[16] Indeed, the content of the writing itself is gradually emasculated, *ins reine geschrieben* (literally, "written into purity"), as Walt moves from the salacious contributions of Libette to the *mémoires érotiques* to his own slightly saccharine *Polymeter*.

Walt comes closest to realizing his love for Wina when he hears his own prose poem from her lips. Desire is realized only to the extent that it becomes literature. In an analogous way, Walt undertakes his literarily inspired journey in the hope that he will experience an adventure during his journey "that someone else could dig up with roots and blossoms and transplant into a novel" (2:861). In fact, ever since he agreed to contribute to *Hoppelpoppel oder das Herz* he has begun to view experiences as " 'nothing but freight and trade fair goods for the novel' " (2:722). Life is subordinated to literature to the extent that it merely provides source material for his narrative: "No adventure, even the worst, is ever so blissful to experience as to narrate" (2:918). Taking charge of his actions for Walt means selecting the proper quotation from his collection of reading experiences. For example, he decides to follow the attractive Jakobine into a store, because he knows that markets are like coaches for

16. Günter de Bruyn argues that Jean Paul also sublimated his sexual desires into writing throughout his prolonged bachelorhood: "Er erträgt die Sexualnot, weil deren Umformung seine Dichterstärke ausmacht. Was er wie kein anderer beschreiben kann, ist nicht die Liebe, sondern der Traum von ihr.... Er zieht die Entladung durch Schreiben der durch Erleben vor" (*Das Leben des Jean Paul Friedrich Richter,* 188).

the novelist, namely places where a number of disparate people can be brought together plausibly; "so he treated himself as his auto-novelist [*sein Selbst-Romanschreiber*] ... in order to establish some sort of a link between himself and the blue-eyed one" (2:864). Indeed, one of Walt's primary activities in the novel is writing on projects like his *Streckverse,* the idyll about the Swedish pastor, his diary, the novel, and Zablocki's memoirs; he also works as a proofreader of Paßvogel's manuscript.

A life described in the text becomes a life *as* text; thus Walt's "biographer" comments that his love for Wina "is strange and cannot possibly last without the biggest storms that rage in volumes from one book fair to the next" (2:912-13). Walt is delighted with the prospect of becoming a coauthor of *Hoppelpoppel oder das Herz,* since he equates publication with birth. "Nothing moves a person more—particularly the well-read person—than the first thought of his publication. Old deep desires of the heart grew up suddenly in Walt and were in full blossom.... he saw himself enriched and famous and on the poetic birthing-chair for weeks" (2:655). For Vult's part, writing a diary becomes an act of self-creation: "Out of what else should God's own image consist, than that one—to the extent that one can—is one's own little *aseitas* (to be your own cause), and—since there are enough *worlds* already—creates and enjoys *oneself* every day, like a priest at Mass the Host-God?" (2:978).

Here Jean Paul picks up the theme we encountered already in *Anton Reiser* and *Wilhelm Meisters Lehrjahre,* as both protagonists struggle to shape their lives into a coherent narrative. But there is a crucial difference in the *Flegeljahre:* while Wilhelm Meister and Anton Reiser try to give form to their own lives, Walt's life is already a copy of someone else's. The novel begins with the reading of a certain van der Kabel's will, the richest man in the city of Haßlau. He has unexpectedly chosen Walt as his heir, provided that Walt fulfill a series of unusual requirements spelled out in the will, that amount to having him repeat episodes in van der Kabel's life. However, becoming van der Kabel's heir merely substitutes a superior model for the novels he read as a child: "Walt's life-novel would have quickly shrunk together into a university-novel that he played out in the armchair at home by reading novels ... if it had not been for the van der Kabel will; but this uplifted the notary with his story" (2:649). Authorship becomes merely the act of writing down the events that were inspired by reading in the first place. Thus Vult writes in his diary that Walt would be a suitable subject for a literary work, since his life is already a text that merely needs to be copied: "It is only imperative that I, as the describer of his life, skillfully unwind him like a Herculean scroll and then copy" (2:978).

Vult deserts his brother before he has the opportunity to perform this task. Instead, the writing of Walt's biography is left to none other than Jean Paul Friedrich Richter. He has been chosen by the executors of van der Kabel's will in accordance with the stipulation that a biographer should be hired to record Walt's life. With the introduction of this biographer into the novel Jean Paul further complicates the relation between himself and the text. As noted above, Walt and Vult have close ties to Jean Paul the idyll-writer and Jean Paul the satirist respectively.[17] Now we are invited to consider the relations between these characters, the historical Jean Paul, and the biographer Jean Paul. To make matters still more complicated, van der Kabel's original name was Friedrich Richter, and the will stipulates that Walt must change *his* name to Friedrich Richter after he fulfills its other requirements!

We have clearly come a long way from Jung's decision to portray himself as Stilling in his autobiography, as Jean Paul is in some sense author, biographer, benefactor, heir, and satirical brother in this novel. Within the text itself, however, Jean Paul maintains careful distinctions between the various self-portraits. The biographer Jean Paul presents himself as being identical with the author Jean Paul, dating his correspondence in the historical present and situating himself in contemporary Germany. At the same time, he goes out of his way to distance himself from the other characters in the text. While Walt travels through the landscape of Jean Paul's own childhood, including the village Joditz, the biographer Jean Paul is quick to add a disclaimer in a footnote to his own narrative: "To be sure, there is a second Joditz in the same region — the childhood village of the present writer—, but it is not in Haßlau, but rather in the *Vogtland,* where the notary certainly did not go" (2:879). He claims that his biography of Walt will be acceptable to the highest government officials, "since I *might* be related to the late van der Kabel, alias Richter" (2:584; emphasis added).

Rather than presenting himself as an inspired romantic artist, the biographer admits that he is one of 55,000 contemporary authors who could have written Walt's life history (2:583). Kuhnold, one of the executors of the will, chides him for acting as a mere editor who composes his narrative by simply cutting and pasting together the

---

17. The biographer comments on the tendency of authors to portray themselves in their works: "'Mich dünkt, ich und sämtliche poetische Weberschaft haben oft genug bewiesen, wie gern und reich wir jedem Charakter—und wär' er ein Satan oder Gott—von unserem leihen und zustecken'" (2:975). See also the following comment in Jean Paul's *Vita-Buch:* "Erzähle, wie du dich in den Flegeljahren als V. u. W. darstellen wolltest" (quoted from Berend's introduction to the *Flegeljahre, Sämtliche Werke: Historisch-Kritische Ausgabe,* 10:vi, n. 2).

available documents: "'I do not believe that van der Kabel's heirs will accept the mere filing of prepared documents, as is the case with Vult's diary, for a sufficient fulfillment of the biographical conditions under which you were willed the natural history collection'" (2:980). The objection seems warranted, for the biographer constructs his narrative out of source material that he presents as having an existence independent of his text. For example, he claims to adapt the story of Walt's youth from a previously published account by the innkeeper and Schomaker (2:596). Other inserts include Walt's "The Happiness of a Swedish Pastor," excerpts from the brothers' diaries and novels, Walt's *Streckverse,* and Jean Paul's correspondence with the city councillors of Haßlau. At one point Jean Paul breaks off a passage by Vult destined for *Hoppelpoppel oder das Herz,* "since the 'Hoppelpoppel' belongs in his own book and not in this one" (2:747). As he explains to the councillors, in a letter from Koburg dated 23 October 1803, he would have written a very different sort of novel if he had had the chance: "O critics! Critics, if it were my story, how I would invent it and twist it and confuse it and crimp it for you!... but it is a wretched state of affairs and a still indeterminable misfortune for all belles lettres that it is true" (2:913).

Why doesn't Jean Paul either write a first-person confession in the tradition of Augustine and the Pietists of the eighteenth century, or a novel without any obtrusive elements of his own autobiography? And having introduced himself in various guises in the novel, why does he coyly deny any autobiographical significance to clearly autobiographical details? The technique goes beyond any attempt to gain distance from the past by assuming just one pseudonym, as could be argued in the case of Moritz's *Anton Reiser,* since Jean Paul has scattered fragments of his autobiography into a multitude of characters throughout the text. Moreover, Jean Paul extends his portrayal of Walt as a character whose identity consists in the reception and reproduction of literary texts to include himself. In doing so he complicates the rather traditional description of genius that he develops in the *Vorschule der Ästhetik:* "In the genius *all* strengths blossom simultaneously" (5:56). The genius combines *Besonnenheit* (levelheadedness) (5:56) with instinct, consciousness with passion. Moreover, the genius is unique: "... indeed, already as a child the genius must have taken in the new world with different feelings than the others and have spun the web of future blossoms differently, since without the earlier dissimilarity no mature one would be conceivable" (5:64). However, as Jean Paul reminds us in the preface to the first edition of the *Vorschule,* the proliferation of writing in modern times has made it difficult to distinguish between one's own thoughts and what one has read. Although he claims that his treatise presents original material, he immediately qualifies his assertion: "... to the extent to which a person, in this age of printed paper, where the desk is so close to the bookshelf, can speak of a thought as one's own" (5:25).

Jean Paul's disclaimer about the originality of his literary theory characterizes the notion of authorship that informs the *Flegeljahre*. To become a writer is to reproduce and reassemble the fictions that have helped shape the self, not to speak in a language that is exclusively one's own. In Mikhail Bakhtin's terminology, the novelist acts as a ventriloquist, speaking through an assemblage of quotations: the "author does not speak in a given language (from which he distances himself to a greater or lesser degree), but he speaks, as it were, *through* language, a language that has somehow more or less materialized, become objectivized, that he merely ventriloquates."[18] From this perspective the graffiti that Walt discovers on the wall of an inn takes on particular significance. It reads: "J.P.F.R Wonsidel: Martii anno 1793" (2:886). Jean Paul was born in Wonsidel, but 1793 marks the publication date of his first novel, *Die Unsichtbare Loge*. What Jean Paul records, in other words, is not the date of his real birth, but rather, the date of his birth as novelist. We recall that both Walt and Vult speak of writing and publication as a form of self-engendering or birth. In his private correspondence Jean Paul also used the metaphor to express his pride over his new baby girl: "I would like to have my beautiful, calm, vigorous, but not passionate Emma-Idoine properly printed, so that the world could only see her."[19] Elsewhere in his correspondence Jean Paul regularly identifies himself with his literary works. "*I* am being read the most now in Germany," reports an excited Jean Paul after his first meeting with Herder in Weimar, "the entire court right up to the Duke is reading *me.*"[20] However, Jean Paul's sudden fame as a novelist carries with it the same ambivalence that distinguishes the status of his characters. The novel establishes his public identity as an author, but at the same time it effaces his private life outside of writing. He exists publicly, that is, to the extent that he transforms his autobiography into fiction.

---

18. Bakhtin, "Discourse in the Novel," 299. Bakhtin mentions Jean Paul frequently in this essay and in his later essay on the *Bildungsroman* as a comic novelist in the tradition of Rabelais, Sterne, Dickens, and others, without, however, going into a close reading of any given text.

19. Jean Paul to Thieriot, 18 June 1803, *Sämtliche Werke: Historisch-Kritische Ausgabe*, Section 3, 4:224. The girl's name was Emma; Idoine is a character from Jean Paul's novel *Titan*.

20. To Christian Otto, 12 January 1796, *Sämtliche Werke: Historisch-Kritische Ausgabe*, Part 3, 2:206.

This transformed perception of the writing self also changes our understanding of the novel's relation to reality. Initially the biographer's montage technique increases the sense that the story is true, in a way familiar to readers of Jean Paul's earlier novels. Thus he appears as the one-legged tutor and *Lebensbeschreiber* of Gustav in *Die unsichtbare Loge,* the biographer and cousin of the hero in *Hesperus,* and the *Geschichtschreiber* in *Siebenkäs.* Having created the impression that his text is woven together out of a variety of subtexts that come from outside the novel proper, however, Jean Paul then collapses the distinction he has so carefully established. For example, at the end of the twelfth section Vult sets off to meet his brother. " 'Now,' said Vult figuratively, as he went down the stairs toward his brother, with a pounding heart, 'a completely new chapter is beginning.' It is happening literally in any case," adds the narrator (2:642), whereupon the text breaks and we move to section thirteen. The activity recorded in the text parallels the activity of recording itself; the narrative is at once performative and constative, a biography and an event.

In an earlier example of the same tendency, Walt's biographer includes his letter to the city council in the novel. From his perspective, this letter is not part of the novel proper. Rather, it is the cover letter that Jean Paul includes along with the first chapter of the novel, which we have just read. The letter will also be included in the completed novel, and Jean Paul requests that it be copied for that purpose. But he introduces a new twist at the end of the chapter: "The copy of the same for the reader, promised in the letter to the executors, is probably no longer necessary, since he just read it" (2:586). Until now Jean Paul has maintained a seemingly clear distinction between the actual subject of his "biography" and the details of his "contract" with the city council. With the sudden reversal at the end of the letter, however, the distinction between frame and content disappears. The letter that seemed to be about the writing of the novel is now a part of the novel itself.

The technique recalls the sort of trick black-and-white drawing that produces two completely different pictures depending on whether we interpret the black as foreground or background. What from one perspective creates the illusion of pictorial depth can suddenly flatten out to remind us that we are still looking at a two-dimensional surface. In terms of the *Flegeljahre,* we fluctuate between the impression that the text represents an external world and the sense that reality and the text are one—or, as we suggested above, the fiction established about the writing of the biography of one individual becomes a displaced form of autobiography, in which the private self is revealed as a construct of public discourses. The personal narrative suddenly expands to become an encyclopedia, a new "book of nature": "The work—just to anticipate a little—is to include everything that one finds much too scattered in libraries; for it is to become a little supplementary volume to the book of nature and a preliminary report and the first folio to the Book of the Blessed [zum Buche der Seligen]" (2:584).

The motif of the book of nature recurs at several points in the course of the *Flegeljahre*. At one point Walt wanders through a park that has been quite literally transformed into a legible text by Raphaele. "The notary [Walt] read down the instructions for use bound to the world like those found on medicine bottles, which prescribed how one was to ingest beautiful nature, in which spoonfuls and hours. Walt liked the feeling-institute [*Gefühls-Anstalt*]; they were after all inaugural- or Easter-programs of spring-nature, consignment notes of the seasons, second, secretly printed title pages of the Nature-Picture-Bible [*Natur-Bilderbibel*]" (2:738). Later, when Walt wants to write about spring during the winter, he naturally makes a trip to the local library, where he reads "attentively in the works in order to imagine the spring-things that came up in them" (2:993-94). Walt's tendency to prefer books about nature to nature itself indicates his distance from the Greeks Jean Paul describes in the *Vorschule der Ästhetik*. Whereas their mythology transformed the world into "a deified nature" (*eine vergötterte Natur*) (5:74), both modern life and poetry are impoverished: "The Greek saw and experienced life for himself; he saw the wars, the countries, the seasons, and did not read them.... We moderns, in contrast, get our art of poetry from the bookstore" (5:74). The result is a transformation of the traditional trope of "reading the book of nature."[21] Instead of a natural world that reveals God's presence to those who know how to "read" its "text," Jean Paul's nature becomes an assemblage of various discourses that resist transcendence: "Earlier in ancient Rome, libraries were preserved in temples, but now temples in libraries (for our worship services are now generally held in books)" (5:177).[22]

These references to the book of nature recall Novalis's plans for an absolute book, a new Bible. His project took two forms: in *Das allgemeine Brouillon* he gathered "materials for an encyclopedia," a massive collec-

21. See Curtius on the European adoption of this classical topos ("The Book as Symbol," *European Literature and the Latin Middle Ages*, 302-47).
22. Ohly sums up the transformation this trope undergoes in the work of Jean Paul in terms of the human inability to perceive the divine: "Ist der Mensch nur eine und am Ende wohl nicht einmal bedeutende Letter unter vielen anderen des Buches der Natur, kann—da Buchstaben sich nicht selber lesen—dieses ihm nicht mehr von Gott zum Lesen aufgegeben und kann er darum auch nicht mehr der Empfänger dieser seiner Offenbarung sein" ("Das Buch der Natur bei Jean Paul," 177).

tion of cryptic fragments that attempted to establish connections between traditionally distinct disciplines. He then wrote *Heinrich von Ofterdingen* in a deceptively simple style where he created textual plurality primarily by disrupting the chronological order of narration. In contrast to Novalis, Jean Paul develops the productive chaos of association that characterizes *Das allgemeine Brouillon* in the novel itself. In the *Vorschule der Ästhetik* Jean Paul defines this ability to perceive likeness between two seemingly disparate things as wit (*Witz*). "'I am not without wit'" (2:655), declares Vult to Walt, and indeed his comments bristle with allusions to a remarkably wide range of subjects.[23] To take only one example: just before he suggests that he and Walt collaborate on a novel, Vult admits that he wrote the unsuccessful *Grönländische Prozesse*. He then launches into a tirade against reviewers in general. In the space of about one page he compares reviewers to painters, gods, and actors, while alluding to cookbooks, mathematics, ship navigation, classical mythology, and a treatise on how to pickle meat (2:654-55). In this context Herman Meyer examines the "diffusion-space of the chapter headings" (*Diffusionsraum der Überschriften*) in the *Flegeljahre* as another example of Jean Paul's delight in combining words to produce strange hybrids that stand in an often oblique relation to the text.[24] To these chapter headings we can add the footnotes as a further example of how Jean Paul expands the scope of his fictional biography into an encyclopedia. Here he alludes to church history (2:598), the history of civil law (2:617), onomastics (2:649), mathematics (2:654), art history (2:670), biology (2:679), Nordic mythology (2:693), numismatics (2:726), social history (2:752), military law (2:760), calligraphy (2:766), horticulture (2:786), Persian mythology (2:791), Greek philosophy (2:817), contemporary philosophy (2:871), his own novels (2:729), and his own aesthetics (2:906).

Jean Paul assembled the material for these far-flung allusions from his collection of excerpts drawn from his years of voracious reading.[25] At first glance these notes give the impression that Jean Paul was an immensely erudite novelist who presupposed similar knowledge on the

---

23. "Der Witz, wie ihn die 'Vorschule' definiert, entspringt einer geistigen Haltung, die derjenigen Vults frappierend ähnlich ist.... Indem Vults Witz alles mit allem verbindet ... hebt er mit spielerischem Ernst die konventionellen Denkschemata seiner spießbürgerlichen Umgebung auf" (Mayer, "Die humorgeprägte Struktur," 413).

24. Meyer, "Jean Paul: Flegeljahre," 242-50.

25. See Berend ("Jean Pauls Handschriftlicher Nachlaß") and Müller's "Nachwort" to the recent index of *Jean Pauls Exzerpte* for information on Jean Paul's reading habits. Further information in Rehm ("Jean Pauls vergnügtes Noten leben") and Soffke (*Jean Pauls Verhältnis zum Buch*).

part of his readers. However, the longer one looks at Jean Paul's footnotes, the more obvious it becomes that no one could possibly know all of the odd facts that he assembles. As Walter Rehm pointed out, the word *bekanntlich* (as is known) in a footnote generally signals one of these impossible bits of trivia.[26] Jean Paul's ability to write this sort of footnote stems from the way he took notes on his reading material. Rather than reproducing a quick summary of the major points of a given work, he would select the odd fact or two that struck his fancy. These excerpts would then be catalogued according to his own eccentric system, and combined to produce surprising analogies in his literary works. While it may seem that he simply parodies scholarly texts with these peculiar footnotes, he claims in the *Vorschule* that his witty allusions are part of a project to unify the earth and its inhabitants: "In the end, namely, the earth has to become *one* country, humanity *one* people, the times a part of eternity; the sea of art must connect the regions of the world; and so art can expect a certain erudition" (5:205).

While Jean Paul may seek to establish a new, universal human order, he goes about it by taking apart the old order of things and putting it back together in an extremely idiosyncratic way. "The prerequisite for the new construction of the links between things is the complete dismantling of conventional as well as scientific discourse with its limiting and exclusive rules."[27] Here we have a further inversion of the situation noted earlier: there the personal narrative turned out to be constructed of public discourses, whereas from this perspective these same discourses have been deconstructed and then reconstructed into a new sort of personal order. "Such a gifted spirit looks around brightly and boldly in his world in a most peculiar Oriental manner, creates the strangest connections, joins the incompatible in such a way that a secret ethical thread runs through, which leads the whole thing to a certain unity."[28]

Goethe's late assessment of Jean Paul's work as a whole serves as a fitting characterization of the paradoxical fusion of disparate elements in the *Flegeljahre*. Here Jean Paul reflects on the relation between audience and writer in Germany as the public sphere begins to split into mass-produced works of *Trivialliteratur* and largely inaccessible works of genius. Rather than producing a scholarly treatise on the internal contradictions of the Enlightenment, he embeds his analysis in the dualistic structure of the *Flegeljahre*. This dualism appears in three

26. Rehm, "Jean Pauls vergnügtes Noten leben," 70. He includes many examples.
27. Müller, *Jean Pauls Exzerpte,* 346.
28. Goethe, "Noten und Abhandlungen zu besserem Verständnis des West-Östlichen Divans," *Hamburger Ausgabe* 2:184.

different guises in the novel: First, the protagonist Walt exists both as an introspective romantic artist alienated from bourgeois society and as an individual whose perceptions and desires are determined by the fictions that circulate within that society. Second, the novel itself fluctuates between biography and montage, between description and performance. Third, the "biography" of the protagonist is both the personal confession of the author and an impersonal assemblage of quotations, both autobiography and encyclopedia. The primary reading of the novel depends on the notions that individuals are unique, that reality can be distinguished from fiction, and that romantic artists are essentially different from their contemporaries and therefore condemned to a difficult life. The secondary reading argues that these distinctions are illusory: seemingly private selves are constructed out of public discourses, fiction creates what is perceived as reality, and the existential crisis of the artist is merely the reenactment of a literary cliché.

This is not to say that the second aspect of the *Flegeljahre* effectively "annihilates" the first. In a logic that we have already encountered in our reading of *Heinrich von Ofterdingen,* the subversive countertext needs the romantic myth it undercuts; it cannot exist on its own. Thus, identifying the simultaneous presence of irreconcilable dualisms in the text should not lead us to the reductive conclusion that the novel is "about" linguistic and epistemological crisis. The implicit negative theology of a poststructuralist reading of the *Flegeljahre* would only invert the position of those formalist critics who interpret the text as evidence of Jean Paul's desire to transcend the physical world through humor. Instead, Jean Paul turns the metaphysical striving of romantic irony into critical commentary on the precarious situation of the professional German writer. Like Walt, Jean Paul is alienated both from the surrounding society that rejects his work and from himself, as he is the product of the fictions that circulate in the public sphere. It stands as a tribute to Jean Paul's integrity that he not only denies his novel the false harmony of an artificial happy ending, but that he also undercuts the self-congratulatory pathos of the romantic artist's lament over life in the land of the Philistines.

From Cultural Renaissance to Political Reaction: E.T.A. Hoffmann's *Kater Murr* (1819-21)

8

At the end of his largely futile search for the nineteenth-century German *Bildungsroman,* Jeffrey Sammons speculates that the genre's alleged absence may stem in part from the wider gap between popular literature and recognized masterworks in Germany than elsewhere in Europe. Whereas novels by Scott and Dickens enjoyed both immediate popular success and lasting critical acclaim, "those books [in Germany] that now have canonical standing were obscure and were read, if at all, only by a thinly populated intellectual elite."[1] Part of the problem lies in the fact that the German novels require a considerable investment of intellectual energy before they yield the rewards that the English texts grant more immediately. As Roy Pascal put it, "even for Germans, to read the great German novels is mostly a 'cultural task'—infinitely rewarding, I believe, but never likely to become a dangerous passion in the reader!"[2]

E.T.A. Hoffmann's *Lebens-Ansichten des Katers Murr* (*The Life and Opinions of Kater Murr*) seems calculated to refute these rather gloomy

---

1. Sammons, "Mystery of the Missing *Bildungsroman,*" 239.
2. Pascal, *The German Novel,* 303-4; cited by Sammons, 239. Pascal goes on at some length pointing out the "flaws" of the German novels, terming them "provincial," and "philistine," full of "heavy, hazy symbolism," and marked by "an extraordinary paucity of incident" (*The German Novel,* 302-4). Mahoney concludes his remarks on the *Bildungsroman* with similar observations: "Zur Aufgabe wurde die Romanlektüre, nicht unbedingt zum Vergnügen—was schließlich auch im Begriff 'Bildungsroman' impliziert wird" (*Der Roman der Goethezeit,* 54).

assessments of the teutonic ponderousness of the *Bildungsroman*. In the autobiography of his genial tomcat Hoffmann combines scathing social satire with a delightfully irreverent parody of the language and sentiments of the Enlightenment and Idealism, of Classicism and Romanticism, in short, of the entire cultural blossoming of late eighteenth- and early nineteenth-century Germany frequently dubbed "The Age of Goethe." Surprisingly enough, however, critics have been quite hostile to Kater Murr. Most readers maintain that the real hero of the novel is Johannes Kreisler, the suffering romantic artist whose biography has been inadvertently published in bits and pieces scattered throughout Murr's autobiography. Murr's narrative is said to inspire universal loathing among readers: "Murr appears unbearably self-satisfied.... His vanity knows no bounds, his self-righteousness is imperturbable, his hypocrisy disgraceful."[3] Murr's character flaws are indeed blatant, others have conceded, but he is, after all, just a cat, and thus hardly worth the sort of moral indignation his admittedly shameless egotism has inspired.[4] It is less Murr's person than the object of his parody that has offended some of his critics; his major crime is less ethical than cultural: "He [Hoffmann] undertakes nothing less than the methodical negation and destruction of the entire phenomenon of culture and society of the most splendid period of German intellectual history, the Age of Goethe."[5]

But can a skillful parodist actually "destroy" the cultural achievements of an entire epoch? Is it not more likely that Hoffmann merely records the unfortunate outcome of a process that had begun with such hope some thirty years earlier? The French Revolution encouraged the Germans to reflect on the political significance of the literary renais-

---

3. Singer, "Hoffman: Kater Murr," 302. Similar criticisms of the Philistine Murr versus the genuine artist Kreisler are repeated frequently in the pertinent secondary literature. For Herman Meyer, Murr anticipates the *Bildungsphilister* while Kreisler embodies "das wesentliche Menschentum" (*Zitat*, 115, 122). "Kreisler [ist] ein authentischer romantischer Künstler" (Feldges and Stadler, *Epoche—Werk—Wirkung*, 233). "Vor allem in den Gegensätzen authentisch—nicht authentisch, genuines Talent und angeeignete Fertigkeit, Kunstwerk oder Kunststück, wirkliche Kunst und Handwerk bestimmen solche Bezugspaare den ganzen Roman" (Hartmann, "Geschlossenheit der 'Kunst-Welt,'" 162). Brief comments by both Blackall (*The Novels of the German Romantics*, 236-37) and Safranski (*Hoffmann*, 260-61) question the persistent tendency to value Kreisler over Murr; my own work further develops this approach. Both Daemmrich ("Hoffmann: *Kater Murr*") and Feldges and Stadler (*Epoche—Werk—Wirkung*) survey earlier criticism of the novel and provide extensive bibliography.

4. "Aber so böse wie Herbert Singer vermögen wir trotzdem nicht auf ihn [Murr] zu sein," protests von Wiese; not Murr, but the Philistine he represents, deserves our scorn ("E.T.A. Hoffmanns Doppelroman," 257). Similar comments in Müller-Seidel, "Nachwort," 684; also Steinecke, "Nachwort," 498.

5. Singer, "Hoffmann: Kater Murr," 305.

sance that had been under way for a generation. With Schiller's *Aesthetic Education* and Goethe's *Wilhelm Meisters Lehrjahre* the Germans had been given theoretical and literary texts that seemed to indicate the possibility of achieving through cultural evolution what the French had sought through political revolution. Hoffmann, writing in the reactionary climate of post-Napoleonic Berlin, registers in *Kater Murr* the failure of the German cultural revolution to prepare the way for a truly democratic "aesthetic state." In the Kreisler episodes he portrays an anachronistic court that has become a caricature of the prerevolutionary governments it seeks to imitate. Murr's ill-fated association with the *Katzburschentum* directly recalls Hoffmann's own persecution by the Prussian authorities for his too liberal defense of the so-called "demagogues" (*Demagogen*), a broad term for those who resisted the state's authority.[6] In the place of Schiller's "aesthetic man" we have the jealous professor of aesthetics, Lothario, and the decadent aesthete, Baron von Wipp. The liberal association of writers that Novalis had once imagined has turned into the literary salon Murr visits, where ignorant aristocrats occasionally invite an artist into their midst to flatter themselves with the illusion that they are serious patrons of the arts. In short, Hoffmann's novel does not so much destroy the cultural blossoming of the previous two generations as it registers the failure of this literary renaissance to realize its political ambitions.

In the fall of 1814 E.T.A. Hoffmann moved back to Berlin to resume the career as lawyer and judge that had been interrupted by the Napoleonic takeover of East Prussia in 1806.[7] During this enforced leave of absence he had finally begun to earn his living as a multitalented professional artist, but the transition had not been easy. His disastrous debut as *Musikdirektor* in Bamberg forced him to earn his money there primarily by giving music lessons and publishing his own compositions. A second position with Joseph Seconda's opera company in Leipzig and Dresden ended abruptly in February 1814, when Hoffmann was fired for having cut short a poorly attended performance. Later that same

---

6. "'Demagogen'—das waren Burschenschaftler, Turner, Patrioten, Demokraten; alles zählte dazu, was sich in der einen oder anderen Weise unzufrieden zeigte mit den politisch-restaurativen Verhältnissen, wie sie der Wiener Kongreß, der Deutsche Bund und die Heilige Allianz hervorgebracht hatten" (Safranski, *Hoffman*, 456). See also Steinecke, "Nachwort," 498.

7. French troops entered Warsaw on 28 November 1806. Hoffmann lingered on in the city until June 1807, when he refused to swear an oath of allegiance to Napoleon and left Warsaw for Berlin (Safranski, *Hoffmann*, 174-79). In 1808 Hoffmann moved on to Bamberg.

year, however, there were signs that Hoffmann's artistic career was about to take off. Hoffmann anticipated his breakthrough as a composer would come with the upcoming performance of his opera *Undine,* now complete with a libretto by Friedrich de la Motte Fouqué. Meanwhile he discovered that he had already achieved literary fame with the recent publication of his *Fantasiestücke.* On the first night after his arrival in Berlin the man who had been reduced to publishing anti-Napoleonic caricatures after his break with Seconda found himself the guest of honor of a group that included Fouqué, Ludwig Tieck, and Adalbert Chamisso.[8]

Not surprisingly, Hoffmann reentered the legal profession with some reluctance: "Now I can no longer give up art, and if I did not have to take care of a dearly beloved wife and to provide her with comfortable circumstances after all she went through with me, then I would rather be a musical schoolteacher again than to let myself be spun around in the legal fulling-mill!"[9] This sort of passage encourages us to view Hoffmann as a suffering romantic artist forced to work at an unpleasant job by day in order to support his inspiration at night, an interpretation Hoffmann himself had encouraged years earlier in a letter to his friend Hippel: "On weekdays I am a lawyer and at most something of a musician, on Sundays I draw, and in the evenings I am a very witty author late into the night."[10] The same paradigm has also been applied to the interpretation of Hoffmann's literary works. As Hans Mayer put it in an influential essay, Hoffmann really only had one theme, "the relation between artistry and a society hostile to art."[11]

Hoffmann experienced the prejudice between these hostile camps from both directions. In Bamberg his abilities as composer and conductor had been doubted by those who knew he had recently worked for the Prussian courts; upon the resumption of his legal career in Berlin Hoffmann met with suspicion due to his growing fame as an artist. To the surprise of his colleagues and superiors, however, Hoffmann soon distinguished himself as an exceptionally capable judge, whose diligence was rewarded with regular raises and promotions: "There is probably no one who has more thoroughly refuted the prejudice that a genial writer is not fit for serious business, than he."[12] Hoffmann's

8. Safranski, *Hoffmann,* 353. Safranski also describes in detail the other events in Hoffmann's life mentioned here.
9. To Hippel, 12 March 1815, *Briefwechsel* 2:45.
10. To Hippel, 23 January 1796, *Briefwechsel* 1:78.
11. Mayer, "Die Wirklichkeit E.T.A. Hoffmanns," xxix.
12. Trützschler's annual report on Hoffmann's performance of 2 January 1820 (Schnapp, ed., *Hoffmann in Aufzeichnungen,* 520).

professional acumen at court carried over into the management of his literary career. Although he wrote a story like *Das Fräulein von Scuderi*, in which a Parisian goldsmith murders those who profane his artistry by buying his artworks, Hoffmann himself was more than willing to profit from his literary fame. "On the whole, my writing not only furnishes me with a cheering diversion, but also with a source of income, without which it would be impossible to subsist in overly expensive Berlin."[13] The same concerns are reflected in his work as a composer for the opera *Undine*, as Hoffmann points out that both he and Fouqué "find it necessary to consider the pecuniary profit of [their] intellectual endeavors."[14]

Unlike Kafka, who financed his largely unpublished writing by working at an insurance company, Hoffmann approached his literary career like a man who had to hold down two jobs in order to meet his considerable expenses. He lived well, drank heavily, and may well have had substantial gambling debts.[15] "He aptly termed his current life a double authorship [*ein doppeltes Autorleben*], in that he had to provide manuscript for the registry in his business capacity, and manuscript for the press as a poet."[16] If Hoffmann's double career caused him personal anguish, it was the self-doubt that attended his reluctance to commit himself fully to life as a professional artist, not the crisis of an artist in a hostile environment: "As a boy—as a youth I should have committed myself entirely to art, and never have thought of anything else. Of course, it was also due to an improper education."[17] Although *Undine* proved moderately successful, Hoffmann never really attained the fame he sought as a composer. Instead, somewhat to his own surprise, he became a remarkably popular writer.[18]

---

13. To Hippel, 27 January 1819, *Briefwechsel* 2:194. See also Trützschler's yearly report of 24 December 1815: "Ich glaube auch, daß ihm sein Dienstverhältniß im KriminalSenat zusagt. Aber die Ueberreste seiner kümmerlichen Ersparnisse ... sind ... rein aufgezehrt. Er muß daher die Stunden der Muße und der Nacht dazu verwenden, sich durch litterarische und musikalische Arbeiten die nöthigsten Subsistenz-Mittel zu verschaffen" (Schnapp, ed., *Hoffmann in Aufzeichnungen*, 319).
14. To Brühl, 9 August 1816, *Briefwechsel* 2:95.
15. Safranski, *Hoffmann*, 112-13.
16. Hitzig, "Aus Hoffmanns Leben und Nachlaß," cited from *Hoffmann in Aufzeichnungen*, ed. Schnapp, 598.
17. To Hippel, 12 March 1815, *Breifwechsel* 2:45. Safranski argues that this self-doubt followed Hoffmann throughout his life: "Wer doch noch neben der Kunst ein anderes Berufsgeschäft verrichtet, wie Hoffmann das die meiste Zeit seines Lebens tat, gibt der nicht allein schon dadurch zu erkennen, daß es ihm an wahrem 'Genie' fehlt?" (*Hoffmann*, 151).
18. Safranski has advanced the interesting hypothesis that it was precisely *because* Hoffmann had relatively few literary ambitions that he was able to achieve such easy success as a writer. "Mit derselben Bedenkenlosigkeit hat er übrigens auch seine großen

As was the case in Jean Paul's *Flegeljahre,* both protagonists of *Kater Murr* reflect certain aspects of their author's artistic career.[19] Kreisler's biography takes place in a tiny court and an isolated cloister in provincial Germany, reminiscent of Bamberg and its surroundings, while Murr lives in a large city that seems very much like the Berlin in which the novel was written.[20] Here again I do not mean to reduce the literary work to mere autobiography. Obviously we cannot identify the respected Berlin judge exclusively with either the manic provincial musician or with his creative pet. In both cases Hoffmann draws on his own experiences as an artist to address commercial and political problems he shared with his contemporaries. The above sketch of Hoffmann's various careers does indicate that we should hesitate to interpret his novel in terms of the familiar opposition between "the artist" and "society." Rather than assuming the superiority of Kreisler over Murr in the battle of artist versus Philistine, we begin by recalling that *both* are artists, and that both work in different institutional contexts. Only Murr writes his autobiography for the bourgeois public; Kreisler works for the nobility in the first half of the novel and composes his music for the church in the second.

Hoffmann's satirical portrait of Prince Irenäus's artificial court in Sieghartsweiler clearly recalls the situation he had encountered when he moved to Bamberg in 1808. Here the Duke Wilhelm of Bavaria maintained his court even though Napoleon had shifted the real government to Munich.[21] More than a decade later this hollow court had become a convenient metaphor for the general state of affairs in Europe, as a series of reactionary governments sought to turn back the clock to a prerevolutionary era.[22] Hoffmann alludes to this earlier period in his

---

Werke geschrieben. Für den *Kater Murr* oder die *Prinzessin Brambilla* hat er sich nicht mehr Zeit gelasssen als für irgendeines seiner hastigen Almanachprodukte. Wenn er besser getroffen hat, so lag das jedenfalls nicht daran, daß er sorgfältiger gezielt hätte" (*Hoffmann,* 407). While there is certainly some truth to this assessment of Hoffmann's attitude toward his literary productions in general, Safranski overstates the case with regard to *Kater Murr,* where Hoffmann did aim more carefully: "Was ich jezt bin und seyn kann wird *pro primo* der Kater... zeigen" (to Hitzig, 8 January 1821, *Briefwechsel* 2:288). In a letter to his publisher Dümmler later that year Hoffmann requested more money "für den Kater, an den ich ganz besonderen Fleiß wende" (2 September 1821, *Briefwechsel* 2:313).

19. Hoffmann signed his letters as both Kreisler and Murr. See for example his letter to Fouqué, 22 December 1814, *Briefwechsel* 2:33 ("Der Ihrigste Hoffmann auch Kreisler genannt") and to Johanna Eunike, 2 March 1820, *Briefwechsel* 2:240.

20. Feldges and Stadler summarize the apparent inconsistencies between the settings and characters in the two halves of the novel (*Epoche—Werk—Wirkung,* 224-27).

21. Safranski, *Hoffmann,* 216-17.

22. Steinecke, "Nachwort," 500.

fictive history of Sieghartsweiler. Under the elder Prince Irenäus the court had been legitimate, if insignificant. This prince had engaged Meister Abraham, an organ builder and dabbler in magic, to amuse the court with his tricks. After his father died the younger Irenäus tried to do without Abraham's services, but soon discovered that he fulfilled an important function in his ability to exorcise "a certain evil spirit which only too readily makes itself at home in little courts—namely, the hellish spirit of boredom."[23] As such he fulfills the role of the typical court artist of the eighteenth century, providing *divertissement* at a court that has ceased to occupy its members with useful activity. As Wolf Lepenies has argued in his *Melancholie und Gesellschaft* (Melancholy and Society), boredom at the French court signaled repressed dissatisfaction with the absolute power of the king: "The nobleman who betrays his boredom emphatically documents his impotence, whereas the king, for his part, senses in boredom the threat of rebellion."[24] In the same way, Abraham's tricks help "to kill time respectably" at this petty German court, "since there is nothing else to do."[25]

Kreisler's passionate devotion to his music for its own sake signals him as a member of a younger generation no longer willing to play the role expected of him by the increasingly ridiculous court. He first appears at Sieghartsweiler after having fled his position as court musician at the *Residenz*. There he had refused to compromise his artistic principles when ordered to defend Italian over German music. This particular incident triggers deep-seated dissatisfaction with his role as a bourgeois artist in the service of the nobility. He formulates his objections negatively in an ironic outburst to the *Rätin* Benzon: "'Let the worthy composer become a conductor or musical director, let the poet become a court writer, the painter a court portraitist, the sculptor a creator of court likenesses, and you will shortly have no more useless visionaries in the country, nothing but useful citizens of good education and gentle manners!'" {64} (357). The best way to produce a docile *Bürger* is to channel his artistic energies into the service of the nobility.

From Kreisler's perspective, however, the representational art demanded of him by the court involves a double betrayal: First, the artificial order of the court itself is not worth being glorified. As Meister Abraham puts it, Kreisler "'does not wish to recognize the eternity of the treaties which you [members of court society] have drawn up for the organiza-

---

23. Hoffmann, *Kater Murr,* 39; German 331. All further references to the novel are included in the text, with the English page number in brackets and the German page number in parentheses.
24. Lepenies, *Melancholie und Gesellschaft,* 56.
25. Lepenies, *Melancholie und Gesellschaft,* 56.

tion of life; yes, he [Kreisler] thinks that a gross delusion under which you labor prevents you from seeing reality'" {198} (499). Second, he feels that the utilitarian application of art debases its quasi-religious status: "'Let me forego the description of how, gradually, through the vacuous, childish playing with sacred art to which I was forced to lend a hand, through the idiocies of the soulless dabblers in art, through dilettantes without taste, through the whole crazy activity of a world peopled by puppets, I came to recognize the wretched uselessness of my existence'" {65} (357-58). This particular lament identifies Kreisler as a member of a new generation of romantic artists. He resists an anachronistic form of noble patronage with an appeal to the bourgeois concept of autonomous art that has taken over the role of religion in a secular age.

If subservience to the court represents the profanation of Kreisler's holy art, perhaps the cloister can provide him with a proper refuge, a setting in which his art will find integration into a more appreciative society. At first this seems to be the case. The monks respect and admire his work, and soon Kreisler finds himself calmer and more productive than he has been in years. It would seem that he has taken one step further back in time to preserve the sanctity of his bourgeois art by producing it within the protective confines of a medieval cloister. However, a number of factors prevent him from finding lasting satisfaction in the service of the church. When Chrysostomus encourages him to take vows as a monk, Kreisler responds with a sarcastic rejection of celibacy. In fact, his religious music has been inspired by his love for Julia, not love of God or the church. Moreover, the seemingly paradisal world of the monastery represents only an enclave of calm in a decadent society, rather than the Christian community of the Middle Ages idealized by Novalis. Thus Kreisler speaks of being "buried in this solitude" {215} (518), and Chrysostomus likens the cloister to "an asylum to which he [Kreisler] had fled" {235} (539). As it turns out, this seeming idyll was never safe for Kreisler. Cyprianus remains in close touch with the corrupt court of Sieghartsweiler, and his pious overtures to Kreisler are actually part of the sinister plots hatched by Irenäus, Hektor, and Benzon.[26]

Kreisler's fragmentary biography breaks off just as Abraham encourages him to flee the monastery. As a crowning insult to the indignities

26. "Die Musik wird—so wirkt es erst—als 'heilige' Kunst sakralisiert, das Kloster erscheint als idealer Fluchtpunkt. Allerdings wird die wahre Kunst damit von vornherein in die Isolation verwiesen, Schritt für Schritt dann auch das Problematische des Rückzugs aus der Welt aufgedeckt. Was nicht gelingt, nicht gelingen kann, ist die glückliche Einpassung von Existenz und Kunst ins 'wirkliche Leben'" (Hartmann, "Geschlossenheit der 'Kunst-Welt,'" 165; similar comments on 185).

Kreisler suffers in Sieghartsweiler, Irenäus and Benzon are about to marry off Julia to the retarded Ignatius.[27] Abraham does what he can to turn the command performance in celebration of this marriage into the fiasco described in the opening fragment of Kreisler's biography, but neither he nor Kreisler can effectively combat the decadent court. Kreisler remains isolated from Julia, while Abraham still suffers from the loss of his wife Chiara to the evil machinations of Irenäus and Benzon. As a result, their efforts to resist Irenäus have an air of hopelessness that recalls Vult's futile attacks on noble privilege in the *Flegeljahre*. One can only speculate about the intricate developments Hoffmann planned for the third volume of the novel, but it seems clear that Kreisler has already reached a dead end as an artist: having refused to profane his art in the service of a corrupt state, he has discovered that the monastery cannot provide him with a lasting haven for the production of his music. We leave him caught in the grasp of an utterly corrupt caricature of a court that nevertheless still has the power to crush those who get in its way.

In the end, the frequently praised artist Kreisler produces very little in the way of art. With the exception of his compositions at the cloister, he only sings a few songs with Julia, gives Hedwiga a music lesson, and strums his guitar by the lake before throwing it into the bushes. In contrast, the writer Murr, like Hoffmann, floods the market with his literary works. In addition to his autobiography Murr has also composed poetry, a tragedy (*Kawdallor, King of the Rats*), a novel (*Thought and Presentiment or Cat and Dog*), and "a political work entitled *Concerning Mousetraps and Their Influence on the Attitudes and Energy of Catdom*" {33} (324). While Kreisler resists the notion that his biography should be "dissected" in a "who's who" of contemporary musicians {83} (376), Murr eagerly records his glorious life for the benefit of other *Katerjünglinge* like himself {229} (532). Although Kreisler voices sublime sentiments about the value of music, Murr comes closer to exemplifying Hoffmann's actual artistic practice as a writer. While Kreisler can be viewed as Hoffmann's tragic self-portrait as a largely unsuccessful musician, Murr stands as a comic self-parody of his unexpected commercial success as an author.

However unproblematic Murr seems to himself, he fears that the public may not recognize his genius: "What can cause a genius greater pain than to see himself misunderstood—yes, mocked; what can embit-

---

27. While Ignaz is modeled on Duke Wilhelm's retarded son Pius (Safranski, *Hoffmann*, 218), Hoffmann uses this detail to stress the increasing decadence of the petty court. As Safranski and others have pointed out, Hoffmann's social criticism is not always particularly subtle.

ter a great spirit more than to meet obstacles where he expects every assistance! {72-73} (366). Murr's literary and philosophical masterworks may never see the light of day due to the prejudice of publishers against unconventional authors like himself: "... and, I repeat, had I Lichtenberg's humor and Hamann's depth, I would still get the manuscript returned.... O prejudice, outrageous prejudice, how you delude people, especially those called publishers!" {124} (420). It seems that his early novel was not published and his tragedy not performed {33} (324). Only the intervention of an anonymous friend enables the publication of his autobiography, a friend who convinces a skeptical E.T.A. Hoffmann to recommend the work to his reluctant publisher, Dümmler, in Berlin.

Kater Murr's talent has aroused suspicion and jealousy among humans from the beginning. When the professor of aesthetics, Lothario, first suggests to Abraham that his cat has been secretly composing poetry, Abraham angrily asserts that Murr should be chasing after mice, not knowledge {72} (365). Sarah Kofman speculates that Abraham's hostility is motivated by the threat that a writing animal poses to human pride in the powers of the intellect, although Abraham never explicitly expresses this fear.[28] What *is* clear is the professor's concern that the writing cat poses a financial threat to him as an author: "'Sooner or later he will appear as a writer and, being a novelty, find a publisher and readers and grab good honorariums away from us'" {128} (425). Following the same logic, Meister Abraham toys with the idea of profiting from his pet's unusual abilities: "Hm-m! I would imagine he could make me rich, richer than my Invisible Maiden did. I could put him in a cage; he would have to perform his tricks for people who would gladly pay a generous fee" {90} (384). While Murr finds the professor's suggestion flattering—"I already felt the little doctoral hat on my forehead and saw myself on the lecture stand!" {129} (425-26)—he understandably feels threatened by Abraham's plan: Murr the genius as a circus sideshow! Abraham's other idea is no more flattering, as he plans to turn Murr into his scribe, just as Murr's mother Mina had warned: "'As soon as your Meister Abraham finds out that you can write, he will make you his copyist, and what you now do for pleasure will be demanded of you as an obligation'" {42} (334).

Although presented comically, Murr's plight reflects difficulties facing the professional writer in general and Hoffmann in particular. When

---

28. "Schreiben heißt, sich eines menschlichen Privilegs bemächtigen, heißt, dem Narzißmus des Menschen einen bösen Schlag zu versetzen und ihn als Herrscher über die Welt zu entthronen" (Kofman, *Schreiben wie eine Katze,* 51).

Murr complains that publishers don't like cats, we are likely to smile at the allusion to the familiar romantic motif of the writer as social outcast. In fact, publishers liked Hoffmann very much, as his stories guaranteed a good profit. However, he drove a hard bargain: Hoffmann's correspondence consists largely of aggressive exchanges with publishers who solicit stories, receive promises and demands for advance payment, and then have to badger him to get the overdue final copy for their journals. Unwilling to turn down a good offer, Hoffmann would overcommit himself to the point where he would have to write furiously on several stories at once in the hopeless attempt to make up long-past deadlines.[29] Thus Hoffmann represents the most extreme example of a commercial artist yet encountered; he worked as a willing contributor to the growing "entertainment industry." Jean Paul and Tieck, the two writers most dependent on their professional success before Hoffmann, each went through a literary apprenticeship before turning to the works that made them famous. To be sure, neither artist made a complete break with his earlier years: Jean Paul's unprofitable satire lives on in the digressions of his fictional works, and Tieck's Romanticism of the late 1790s draws on the storehouse of popular literary motifs he had reproduced during the earlier part of the decade. There is relatively little development in Hoffmann's brief career as a writer in terms of his relation to the public. Even at the height of his literary fame, Hoffmann continued to churn out prose for popular publications. In the end, Murr manages to avoid becoming Abraham's secretary, but all too often financial concerns forced Hoffmann into literary production that resembled Mina's description of the "alienated labor" of a scribe.

Abraham's unfulfilled plan to parade Murr as a curiosity points to a different danger facing the bourgeois artist. While Kreisler struggles against the devious plots of the provincial nobility, Murr allows himself to be seduced by their decadent urban counterparts. Although he disapproves of Ponto's self-serving devotion to Baron Alzibiades von Wipp, Murr cannot resist the opportunity to capitalize on his literary fame at a gathering of aristocratic aesthetes. In visiting the canine literary salon, however, Murr realizes that he only serves as an amusing diversion that caters to the dogs' sense of self-importance: "It is a special case with artists such as poets and writers, whom the aristocrat occasionally invites into his circle in order to bestow a kind of patronage according to ancient custom" {325} (640). As has often been noted, Murr craves

---

29. Safranski suggests that the double novel itself can be understood as Hoffmann's ironic allusion to his tendency to work simultaneously on a series of different publications (*Hoffmann*, 392).

the recognition from these circles that Kreisler disdains;[30] Murr even becomes infatuated with a young greyhound "girl" who praises his works. Nevertheless, a cold shower brings him to his senses and he too realizes that he has no business among individuals "who, because of the meaninglessness of their being, had to limit themselves to the form and could offer me nothing more than the shell without the kernel" {330-31} (646).

While Murr's attendance at the literary salon reduces him to an entertaining curiosity, his brief association with the *Katzburschen-Gesellschaft* exposes him to open persecution. The initial target of Hoffmann's satire would seem to be the *Burschenschaft* movement itself, as Murr crawls out of bed with a terrible hangover after an evening of too much *Katzpunsch*. Meister Abraham scolds Murr for his dissolute behavior, but echoes Hoffmann's tolerant views when he claims that Murr will soon grow out of this passing adolescent phase. While Hoffmann disapproved of the excesses of the student radicals, he insisted that the state could only legitimately punish crimes, not opinions. These liberal ideas were enough to cast suspicion on his role as state judge; worse, he continued his critique of the government in his literary works. In *Kater Murr* Lothario condemns Murr in tones that anticipate the blind zeal of Knarrpanti in the slightly later "Meister Floh" (Master Flea), a literary satire that involved Hoffmann in a dangerous legal battle that remained unresolved at the time of his death.[31] Lothario rails against Murr as "a character that greatly offends against all manners and customs" {245} (550). To be sure, Murr soon abandons his slightly ridiculous friends, and there is no reason to suspect that his literary works are politically subversive. Yet Hoffmann's satire *was* considered subversive; as the charges later brought by Kamptz's investigating committee against Hoffmann make clear, condemnations of the student radicals could easily be transferred to those who ridiculed the government's attempts to suppress them.[32] Strict censorship laws could make it impossible for writers to get their works published at all, or only

---

30. "Murr ist jederzeit bereit und bestrebt, sich mit allen seinen Talenten in den Dienst der 'herrschenden Macht' zu stellen" (Singer, "Hoffmann: Kater Murr," 308.) Similar comments in Jones, "Hoffmann and the Problem of Social Reality," 53, and Daemmrich, "Hoffmann: *Kater Murr,*" 85.

31. Segebrecht provides extensive commentary and documentation in his solid account of Hoffmann's troubles with the Prussian censors ("Anmerkungen," *Späte Werke,* 899-920). See also Safranski, *Hoffmann,* 455-71.

32. Among other things, Hoffmann was accused of "öffentliche, grobe Verläumdung eines StaatsBeamten wegen Ausübung seines Amts," namely the enforcement of official measures that Hoffmann publicly represented "als lächerlich und als das Werk der niedrigsten persönlichen Motive" (cited from *Späte Werke,* 906-7.)

after potentially offensive passages had been suppressed, as was the case with "Master Flea." In a letter to his publisher, clearly intended for use in his defense before the courts, Hoffmann applied a sort of self-censorship to his work, as he denied any political significance to obvious allusions to contemporary events.[33] With typical concern for the commercial success of his work, Hoffmann suggested in this same letter to his publisher that the story's notoriety should make for brisk sales, which in fact turned out to be the case.[34] Unfortunately, Hoffmann died before he could profit from the work that caused him such aggravation in his last years; the censored passages were not printed until 1906.

Thus far we have viewed Murr as a representative writer and downplayed Hoffmann's repeated reminders that this author really is a cat. One of Hoffmann's simple but effective techniques for deflating sentimental prose involves substituting the cat's body into clichés: " 'Son—oh son! Come! hasten to my paws!' " {41} (332). "Readers! Youths, men, women, under whose fur beats a feeling heart" {40} (332). "Invisible paws drew me toward her with an irresistible power" {153} (451). Despite Murr's best intentions, he cannot resist his natural desires when attempting to sacrifice his own dinner for his poor starving mother: "O Appetite, thy name is Tomcat!... I ate the fishhead!" {43} (335). As was the case in Jean Paul's *Flegeljahre,* Hoffmann also parodies the romantic belief in the inspired nature of poetic production. The editor Jean Paul insisted that he was merely collecting material for a documentary account of Walt's life, a job that could have been performed by thousands of other professional authors. Hoffmann parodies the same notion by substituting physical reactions for spiritual rapture. At times poetry can actually overcome "all earthly sorrow, even—as someone has claimed—frequently overcoming hunger and toothache" {287} (597), reports Murr. Nevertheless, he is forced to admit that poetic inspiration can come on like an illness, "just as a person who has caught cold involuntarily breaks out in a fit of sneezing" {157} (455). Slightly earlier Murr recalls Meister Abraham's account of a man plagued by a certain *materia peccans* in his body that could only be discharged by writing {150} (449). Although he considers the anecdote "a malicious satire," Murr admits that he too is sometimes overcome with an irresistible urge; "a peculiar feeling, I

---

33. "Indessen wie gesagt, es ist rein unmöglich selbst bey der größten Neigung hämisch mißdeuten zu wollen, etwas aus dem Buche, das keinem Gegenstande entfernter liegt als der Politik, heraus zu finden" (cited from *Späte Werke,* 905; similar comments in Hoffmann's long legal defense, 910-13). Needless to say, the lawyer Hoffmann assumed this posture of indignant innocence as a strategy against the prosecution.

34. *Späte Werke,* 905, 913.

might almost call it a spiritual cramp, goes through me to my paws, which have to write down everything I think" {150-51} (449).

In passages like these Hoffmann uses an old comic technique to parody current literature and philosophy. As Jean Paul had pointed out in the *Vorschule der Ästhetik,* the comic writer focuses on "sensual particulars, and one falls, for example, not onto one's knees, but rather onto one's kneecaps."[35] At other moments Hoffmann hollows out the feline body of his protagonist with the repeated suggestion that Murr is nothing more than a walking quotation. Murr proudly points to his great relative, Tieck's "Puss in Boots," "an ancestor without whom I probably would not have existed" {58} (350). While both Anton Reiser and Walt experience reality as a quotation from fiction, we still tend to view them as figures who could plausibly exist outside the text. Because Murr is a cat who reads and writes, we know from the start that he is a creature of fairy tale, of phantasy, of literature.[36] Although he descends directly from Tieck's literary reworking of a popular fairy tale, Murr makes references to most of the leading writers and philosophers of the eighteenth and early nineteenth centuries, including Goethe, Schiller, Jean Paul, Leibniz, Kant, and Fichte.[37]

The editor E.T.A. Hoffmann expresses moral outrage at Murr's attempts to add luster to the events of his life with references to other fictional heroes: "Oh Murr, my tomcat! Either the point of honor has not changed since Shakespeare's time or I have caught you in a literary lie" {226} (528). Most critics have chosen to follow the editor's lead in condemning Murr for his unauthorized appropriations from other literary texts. As Herman Meyer argues, Murr "trivializes and flogs to death" the texts he cites, whereas Kreisler's quotations "serve as a strengthening illumination of the self, despite all ironic disengagement."[38]

---

35. Jean Paul, *Werke* 5:140.
36. Kofman stresses this aspect of Murr in her interpretation of the novel: "Man kann sogar sagen, daß das ganze 'Leben' des Katers, seine gesamte Erfahrung, ein einziges literarisches Zitat ist, eine Wiederholung dessen, was er in den Büchern gelesen hat.... Der Text des Lebens und der der Schrift sind eng miteinander verschränkt" (*Schreiben wie eine Katze,* 108). Kofman comes to the predictable conclusion that Hoffmann deconstructs the logocentric premises of the autobiography as that which establishes the author's identity: "Effekt dieses Zitatcharakters ist die Tilgung der Signatur des Eigennamens... jeder Text, jede Sprache [ist] mit Anführungszeichen versehen" (*Schreiben wie eine Katze,* 109-10). That is, Kofman uses Hoffmann's novel to reproduce the ahistorical conclusions of her contemporary literary theory. While I agree that Hoffmann subverts organic notions of the self, I am more interested in the question of how his work differs from that of other writers. Here it seems that we must turn to the specifics of his particular literary and political situation.
37. See Meyer for a more complete list of Hoffmann's allusions (*Zitat,* 117-18).
38. Meyer, *Zitat,* 124; also 120.

But can we confidently assume that Kreisler's literary allusions reveal a deeper and more genuine character? Hoffmann tends to use the same sort of hackneyed language to describe the feelings of both protagonists: "Then he [Kreisler] heard Julia singing, and an ineffably sweet sadness [pulsed through his inner being]" {139} (436). "O the sound [pulsed through my innermost being] with a sweet spasm; my pulse throbbed; my blood raced through my arteries; my heart was about to burst; an ineffably painful rapture, which quite overpowered me, poured out in a long, extended meow," echoes Murr in his love for Miesmies {153} (451; translations modified). At this point one could still claim that the same phrases in different contexts reveal contrasting character types.[39] Moreover, Murr clearly parodies Kreisler in the above quotation: Kreisler's "inner being" becomes Murr's "innermost being," one phrase describing Kreisler turns into a half-dozen increasingly passionate outbursts for Murr, all of which are punctured with his long, loud "Meow!"

However, Kreisler himself suffers from the sense that his life is also a quotation of others' lives and experiences. His double, Ettlinger, haunts him, Prince Irenäus chides him for imitating Hamlet {113} (409), and he readily agrees to Julia's suggestion that he resembles Shakespeare's Jacques of *As You Like It* {48, 60} (340, 353). Kreisler even skips over certain details when narrating his youth, "because you can read about something similar in many a stale family novel or play by Iffland" {84} (378). At this point we have to question whether it is really possible to distinguish between Murr's shallow plagiarism and Kreisler's tragic grandeur. While allusions to troubled figures like Hamlet and Jacques give dignity and universality to Kreisler's sufferings, we cannot make the same claim for his reference to Iffland's situation comedy or the tired clichés of popular fiction. Here the quotation tends to undermine rather than intensify Kreisler's sense of self. The comparison does not make Kreisler's life less tragic, but it does reveal a tragedy of a different sort: intense personal suffering yields to the humiliating awareness that even his suffering is half someone else's.

The complex plot structure of Kreisler's biography adds to the impression that his life is in the grasp of forces beyond his control. While Murr's autobiography unfolds linearly in chronological order, Kreisler's

---

39. "Nicht der Wortlaut als solcher, der sich ja gleichbleibt, sondern nur der Kontext ist ausschlaggebend für den gemeinten Sinn.... Was im einen Bereich echte Sprache der Seele ist, wird im anderen in seichter Eitelkeit zerredet" (Meyer, *Zitat*, 116). Citing the same passage, Safranski challenges Meyer's hierarchy: "Original und Parodie sind auswechselbar. Das Original ist schon seine eigene Parodie" (*Hoffmann*, 261).

story begins at the end and circles back to the beginning.[40] Murr progresses in picaresque fashion from one event to the next, while Kreisler reflects on the significance of what has already happened. In the first section of the book Kreisler narrates the story of his childhood and youth. Unlike Wilhelm Meister, who traces the events that have brought him to what he believes is his current triumph, Kreisler explains the sources of his continuing unhappiness. Raised in awe of his uncle, who filled the post of Councillor for Foreign Affairs in the nearby capital city, the young Kreisler felt compelled to repeat his life {88} (382). When he finally realized that he really wanted to be an artist, Kreisler discovered that he had missed his chance. "The liberation occurred too late. I am like that prisoner who, when finally released, was so unaccustomed to the turmoil of the world, even the light of day, that he was unable to enjoy the golden freedom and longed to be back in his prison" {88-89} (383). In the last section of the novel Kreisler's sense of being trapped in the dilemma of his youth gives way to the impression that he is caught up in the intricate web of intrigue spun between the petty court at Sieghartsweiler and the corrupt Italian nobles. Here again Kreisler's fate becomes a sinister variant of Wilhelm Meister's: the Tower Society ultimately grants Wilhelm his bride after having broken his will, whereas Kreisler not only loses Julia but also comes close to losing his life. The fact that these intrigues recall the plots of Gothic novels stretching from Karl Grosse's *Genius* through Tieck's *William Lovell* to Hoffmann's own *Elixiere des Teufels* further depersonalizes Kreisler's biography. From this perspective Kreisler has lost his own life long ago, for he has acted out a role in a script written by someone else.

Kreisler's sense of alienation from his own life carries over to the form in which this life is presented to the reader. While Murr proudly records his "Lebenslauf nach aufsteigender Linie,"[41] Kreisler's unidentified biographer pieces together fragments of his story as they become available: "But such a beautiful, chronological arrangement cannot be used, since only oral accounts, imparted piecemeal, are at the unfortunate narrator's disposal, which he must record at once so as not to lose the whole thing from his mind" {44} (336). The biographer repeatedly interrupts his narrative to apologize for "the complete break in the reports from which

---

40. Singer is very helpful in sorting out the complex interconnections between the two halves of the novel. As he points out, Kreisler's name reflects the circular chronological order of narration in his biography ("Hoffmann: Kater Murr," 325-28).

41. "Life-History on an Ascending Line." I allude to the title of Theodor Gottlieb von Hippel's novel, *Lebensläufe nach aufsteigender Linie* (1778/81). Hippel was influenced by Sterne and in turn influenced Jean Paul and Hoffmann. Incidentally, Hippel was the uncle and benefactor of Hoffmann's life-long friend Theodor Gottlieb Hippel.

he must patch together the present story" {177} (476). As the editor of Murr's autobiography informs us, Kreisler's biography was eventually printed, but most probably not distributed, "so nobody knows anything at all about it" {6} (298). It reaches the market only after having been further fragmented by Murr, who has torn pages out of Kreisler's biography to blot his own manuscript. Like the life of the artist it describes, Kreisler's biography is literally *zerrissen,* torn to pieces. Kreisler already suffers from the sense that his life reenacts the tragedies portrayed in *Trivialliteratur;* now his forgotten biography enters the public sphere as scrap paper used in the production of another text.

Taken together, the two halves of Hoffmann's novel serve as mirror images. Kreisler's life is certainly more tragic than Murr's, but it is not more authentic; its tragedy lies precisely in its inauthenticity. Murr uses classical literature to glorify a trivial life, whereas Kreisler's tragic fate is trivialized by its association with the patterns of popular fiction. In constructing this dilemma Hoffmann generates the most bitterly critical portrait of German society, culture, and politics since Moritz's *Anton Reiser.* We had left Reiser disillusioned, penniless, and distraught about his sudden baldness; here Murr's fragmentary autobiography ends abruptly with the death of its author, and we leave Kreisler with his beloved Julia engaged to an idiot. If anything, the situation is even more depressing in *Kater Murr,* for while Moritz's narrator anticipates an aesthetic order still denied his protagonist, Hoffmann looks back at the unfulfilled promise of Germany's Golden Age. For all its negativity, however, Hoffmann's novel remains the most entertaining *Bildungsroman* of its epoch, not because it formulates a deeply serious Germanic *Humorbegriff,* but because it is simply funny. Without qualifying his critique of the German present and past, Hoffmann displays a stylistic brio and perversely comic imagination that anticipate the vitality of German literature even after the end of the "Age of Goethe." In response to those Anglo-American suspicions regarding the accessibility of the German *Bildungsroman,* Hoffmann enthusiasts will agree that reading *Kater Murr* is one of those rare "infinitely rewarding 'cultural tasks' " that can be performed with pleasure.

Conclusion

9

In my comments on Tieck's *Sternbald* I noted the extraordinary series of coincidences that propel his plot, as a small number of closely related individuals collide unexpectedly in the capitals and provinces of Europe. At the time, I suggested that this artifice revealed the influence of popular fiction on Tieck's Romanticism. Yet when reading the biographies of the authors examined in this study, one often has the sense of moving in Sternbald's world, for the authors' personal and professional lives are remarkably intertwined. Goethe visited with Jung-Stilling in Straßburg, with Moritz in Rome, and with Jean Paul, Tieck, and Novalis in Weimar; he also enabled the publication of Jung-Stilling's *Lebensgeschichte*. Moritz provided enthusiastic support for Jean Paul's first novel, Tieck edited Novalis's works, and Jean Paul wrote the introduction to Hoffmann's first collection of prose. Thus it is not surprising that the novels themselves appear as successive contributions to an ongoing literary conversation. Together these writers took part in the rapid transformation of the German literary institution around 1800; their *Bildungsromane* provide critical commentary on this transformation.

We can get some indication of the extent of this change by contrasting the use of literary quotation in a work that immediately precedes the period examined here with a work that comes at its end. Like later authors, Christoph Martin Wieland already reflects on the relation between individual development and aesthetic form in his *Geschichte des Agathon* (1766/67): by relating her autobiography in an artful narrative, Agathon's lover Danae avoids telling him unpleasant truths about her past, while the narrator distances himself from the improbable events that lead to the resolution of the plot by claiming that he bases his story on documentary evidence.[1] Yet Wieland's work comes at a very early stage in the German literary revolution; as a result, he alludes to a wide range of classical and European literatures, but to almost nothing German.[2] Thus I have chosen to begin with the slightly later works of Jung-Stilling and Moritz, in which we already encounter protagonists in contemporary Germany who are deeply influenced by the recent literature of the *Sturm und Drang*. Less than fifty years later, Kater Murr quotes extensively from newly canonical German classics: "Hoffmann," as Herman Meyer writes, "comes at the end of the literary Golden Age, and in the meantime a substantial body of German poetic writing had emerged which had taken on canonical status among educated readers, and whose sayings and formulations had obviously taken hold in a quite broad reading public."[3]

Goethe and Schiller established their program of German Classicism in deliberate opposition to the growing body of popular literature around them. Having raised German literature to new heights, however, they found themselves isolated from the broad public below. The demanding work of the early Romantics seemed hardly calculated to win back the common reader, and even the popular Jean Paul found himself increasingly isolated in his later years. In the autobiography of Kater Murr, however, we find the new German classics neatly packaged for popular consumption. While Murr's editor feigns indignation over Murr's plagiarisms, readers are more likely to enjoy identifying the sources of his quotations. Unlike Jean Paul, who peppers his novels with references to odd facts in obscure disciplines, Hoffmann makes easily identifiable allusions to popular classics. " 'Kennst du das Land, wo die Zitronen glühn' " (Do you know the land where the lemons glow?) {158} (457) is not likely to stump most readers, even if they are not sure if the quotation is completely accurate (it is not). The encyclopedic range of Novalis's *Allgemeine Brouillon* and Jean Paul's *Flegeljahre* has been

---

1. Swales focuses on the interplay between the two layers of the text: "Agathon is, then, a novel which makes traditional novel fiction (and its attendant expectations) explicitly thematic and challenges them.... Our narrator is able to use this story as a cipher for a mode of unsophisticated narration, for unsophisticated portrayal of the self as a known quantity—and can criticize it in terms of his own (modern) awareness of the psychological (and hence narrative) complexity" (*The German Bildungsroman*, 49-50).

2. "Das Arsenal, aus dem Wieland schöpfte, bestand zum weitaus größten Teile aus der antiken Literatur und aus den ausländischen belles lettres seines Jahrhunderts; seine Zitierkunst war ein Leckerbissen für literarische Kenner" (Meyer, *Zitat,* 117).

3. Meyer, *Zitat,* 117.

reduced to a relatively small canon that would fit nicely behind glass in a German parlor. It would seem that we have an early example of the ability of what Adorno will later call the "culture industry" to blunt the critical edge of art that challenges the status quo. Popularization and vulgarization go hand in hand.[4]

From one perspective, then, Hoffmann's *Kater Murr* records the disappointing end to what Heine terms the "Goethische Kunstperiode." The dream of aesthetic education was not fulfilled. At the same time, however, it is all too easy to bemoan the passing of an untroubled ideal that in fact never existed. As I have argued throughout, these *Bildungsromane* already contain the seeds of their own critique. To be sure, Jung-Stilling's piety, the Tower Society's sententious maxims, and Walt's sentimentality can all test the patience of an unsympathetic reader. Yet Jung-Stilling reveals enough of his social and psychological deprivation to render his overt claims of representative piety questionable. Wilhelm Meister grows impatient with the packaged wisdom of the Tower Society, and Vult abandons his overly sentimental brother. Hoffmann does not so much expose the demise of German literature as help bring out the critical potential already present. His work serves as a healthy corrective to those who would enshrine the works of Goethe and Schiller like the Tower Society embalms Mignon. In *Kater Murr* Hoffmann transforms the common lament over the decline and fall of Germany's Golden Age — a lament still audible in Habermas's theory of the public sphere — into the source of continued creativity. One is reminded of Oskar Matzerath's sarcastic reference in the *Blechtrommel* (Tin Drum) to those writers who proclaim the death of the novel, and then, "so to say behind their backs pump out a fat bestseller, so that they stand there as the last possible novelist."[5]

For the tradition of the German *Bildungsroman* did not come to an end with Hoffmann's *Kater Murr*. Of course, not every German novel is a *Bildungsroman;* recent studies have helped correct the misleading impression generated by earlier literary historiographers.[6] Nevertheless, a significant number of later authors continue to write texts that are routinely discussed in surveys of the genre, and that I would be willing to call *Bildungsromane*. In broad outlines, the *Bildungsromane* of the

---

4. "Murr [ist] der Repräsentant eines Typus, welcher der Literatur zum Unsegen gereicht. Was in seiner Gestalt sichtbar wird, ist die entsetzliche Banalisierung des Dichterwortes, das seichte Zerreden der hohen Inhalte der deutschen Dichtung, schon zur Zeit ihrer großen Blüte selber" (Meyer, *Zitat,* 130). See also Steinecke, "Nachwort," 491.

5. Grass, *Blechtrommel,* 11-12.

6. See in particular Sammons, "The Mystery of the Missing *Bildungsroman,*" and Steinecke, "*Wilhelm Meister* und die Folgen."

nineteenth and twentieth centuries continue two trends already evident in the works examined here.

On the one hand, we can indeed trace in these novels evidence of the continuing disintegration of the bourgeois public sphere and the attendant loss of the emancipatory potential that had been ascribed to art during the classical period. Hans Castorp's seemingly profound insights on the magic mountain are of no use to him as we leave him running across the battlefields of World War I. Both Adrian Leverkühn and Germany collapse together in Mann's account of World War II, while such postwar figures as Oskar Matzerath and Siegfried Lenz's Siggi Jepsen compose their fictional autobiographies in prison. Either art proves impotent in the face of political barbarism or, more sinister still, progressive aesthetics mirror reactionary politics, as when Adrian Leverkühn's strict style in music turns into an unwitting paradigm of the repressive society around him.[7]

On the other hand, the very existence of one *Bildungsroman* after the next argues against those who view the development of the genre solely in terms of the sort of negative teleology ridiculed in Grass's novel. As I have argued, the much-heralded fragmentation of the organic self in the twentieth century is already evident in works of the eighteenth. Anton Reiser anticipates the chameleonlike Felix Krull or Hesse's Steppenwolf, who explores a myriad of past and potential selves in the Magic Theater. More recently, Botho Strauß depicts the individual in an age of "total public consciousness" in *Der junge Mann*.[8] Conceding the impossibility of portraying personal development in a chronological narrative, he seeks to capture what Goethe might have termed a "pregnant moment": "Instead of history he will seek to grasp the historically layered moment, the simultaneous occurrence" (10). The result is a postmodern transformation of the classical and romantic *Bildungsroman:* "Initiation stories. Romantic Reflection Novel. A little conventional, a little innovative" (15). In a novel that resonates with allusions to both *Wilhelm Meister* and *Heinrich von Ofterdingen,* this "Romantic of the electronic age" (369) interrupts the story of his protagonist's theatrical mission with a series of mythical interludes, including the tale of a strange utopian community that celebrates the mystic unity of the termite heap and the semiconductor (137).

This recent addition to a supposedly exhausted genre suggests that we view the *Bildungsroman* as a series of continuing transformations of a constant problematic rather than the record of a progressive decline.

7. See Frank, "Reaction as Progress."
8. Strauß, *Der junge Mann,* 10. Hereafter cited in the text; translations are my own.

"No," writes Strauß, "the concept of decline is only a deception, the ghost of a used-up belief in progress. We transform ourselves, after all, and the one proceeds from the other either as a continuation or a reaction" (12). The genre that emerged as a commentary on the structural transformation of the public sphere in the eighteenth century continues to explore its further transformations at the end of the twentieth. The self that was in a state of crisis from the outset also continues to exist, if only in the form of a persistent commentary on its disappearance. Perhaps, to paraphrase Oskar, authors of the *Bildungsroman* need the myth of its impending demise in order to generate their "last" contribution to the tradition, just as critics go on sounding its death knell in a growing list of publications. Yet the genre will survive as a discursive event as long as writers find it worth parodying and critics insist on its nonexistence. Future readers and writers may well lose interest in the genre, and the *Bildungsroman* could go the way of the medieval pageant or the courtly masque. From Jung-Stilling's autobiography of an extensive reader through Strauß's probing of consciousness in the computer age, at least, the *Bildungsroman* endures as a series of metafictional representations of private lives in the public sphere.

Works Cited

Primary Sources

Goethe, Johann Wolfgang. *Wilhelm Meisters theatralische Sendung.* Vol. 8 of *Gedenkausgabe der Werke, Briefe und Gespräche.* Zurich: Artemis, 1949.
———. *Goethes Werke: Hamburger Ausgabe.* Hamburg: Wegner, 1950.
———. *Briefwechsel Schiller Goethe.* Ed. and introduction Emil Staiger. Insel Taschenbuch 250. Frankfurt: Suhrkamp, 1977.
———. *Gedichte: 1756-1799.* Ed. Karl Eibl. Vol. 1 of *Sämtliche Werke.* Frankfurt: Deutscher Klassiker Verlag, 1987.
———. *Wilhelm Meister's Apprenticeship.* Ed. and trans. Eric A. Blackall and Victor Lange. Goethe's Collected Works 9. New York: Suhrkamp, 1989.
Grass, Günther. *Die Blechtrommel.* Darmstadt: Luchterhand, 1959.
Hegel, Georg Wilhelm Friedrich. *Ästhetik.* Ed. Friedrich Bassenge. Frankfurt: Europäische Verlagsanstalt, 1955.
Hoffmann, E.T.A. *Briefwechsel.* 3 vols. Ed. Fr. Schnapp. Munich: Winkler, 1967-69.
———. *The Life and Opinions of Kater Murr.* Vol. 2 of *Selected Writings of E.T.A. Hoffmann.* Ed. and trans. Leonard J. Kent and Elizabeth C. Knight. Chicago: University of Chicago Press, 1969.
———. *Lebens-Ansichten des Katers Murr.* Including "Nachwort" by Walter Müller-Seidel. Munich: Winkler, 1977.
———. *Werke.* 6 vols. Munich: Hanser, 1959.
Jean Paul. *Sämtliche Werke: Historisch-Kritische Ausgabe.* Ed. Eduard Berend. Berlin: Akademie, 1960.
———. *Werke.* 6 vols. Munich: Hanser, 1959.
Jung-Stilling, Johann Heinrich. *Lebensgeschichte.* Vol. 1 of *Sämmtliche Schriften.* Stuttgart: Henne, 1835.
Kant, Immanuel. *Schriften zur Anthropologie, Geschichtsphilosophie, Politik und*

Pädagogik 1. Vol. 11 of *Werkausgabe*. Ed. Wilhelm Weischedel. Frankfurt: Suhrkamp, 1978.
Moritz, Karl Philipp. *Andreas Hartknopf: Eine Allegorie. Andreas Hartknopfs Predigerjahre. Fragmente aus dem Tagebuch eines Geistersehers*. Faksimiliedruck der Originalausgabe. Ed. Hans Joachim Schrimpf. Stuttgart: Metzler, 1968.
———. *Werke in zwei Bänden*. Berlin: Aufbau, 1981.
Novalis (Friedrich von Hardenberg). *Schriften*. Ed. Paul Kluckhohn and Richard Samuel. Stuttgart: Kohlhammer, 1960.
———. *Henry von Ofterdingen: A Novel*. Trans. Palmer Hilty. New York: Ungar, 1964.
Schiller, Friedrich. *Schillers Briefe: 1794-95*. Vol. 27 of *Schillers Werke: Nationalausgabe*. Ed. Günter Schulz. Weimar: Böhlaus, 1958.
———. *Sämtliche Werke*. Eds. Gerhard Fricke and Herbert G. Göpfert. Munich: Hanser, 1960.
Schlegel, Friedrich. *Kritische Friedrich-Schlegel-Ausgabe*. Ed. Ernst Behler. Munich: Ferdinand Schöningh, 1967- .
Strauß, Botho. *Der junge Mann*. Munich: Hanser, 1984.
Tieck, Ludwig. *Franz Sternbalds Wanderungen: Studienausgabe*. Ed. Alfred Anger. Stuttgart: Reclam, 1979.

General

Abrams, M. H. *The Mirror and the Lamp: Romantic Theory and the Critical Tradition*. Oxford: Oxford University Press, 1953.
———. *Natural Supernaturalism: Tradition and Revolution in Romantic Literature*. New York: Norton, 1971.
Albertsen, Leif Ludwig. "Internationaler Zeitfaktor Kotzebue: Trivialisierung oder sinnvolle Entliterarisierung und Entmoralisierung des strebenden Bürgers im Frühliberalismus?" *Sprachkunst* 19 (1978): 220-40.
Alter, Robert. *Partial Magic: The Novel as a Self-Conscious Genre*. Berkeley and Los Angeles: University of California Press, 1975.
Bakhtin, M. M. "Discourse in the Novel." In *The Dialogic Imagination: Four Essays*, ed. Michael Holquist; trans. Caryl Emerson and Michael Holquist. Austin: University of Texas Press, 1981.
Becker, Eva D. *Der deutsche Roman um 1780*. Germanistische Abhandlungen 5. Stuttgart: Metzler, 1964.
Behler, Ernst. *Klassische Ironie, romantische Ironie, tragische Ironie: Zum Ursprung dieser Begriffe*. Darmstadt: Wissenschaftliche Buchgesellschaft, 1972.
Berghahn, Klaus. "Volkstümlichkeit ohne Volk: Kritische Überlegungen zu einem Kulturkonzept Schillers." In his *Schiller: Ansichten eines Idealisten*, 99-124. Frankfurt: Athenäum, 1986.
Blackall, Eric A. *The Novels of the German Romantics*. Ithaca: Cornell University Press, 1983.
Blumenberg, Hans. *Die Lesbarkeit der Welt*. Frankfurt: Suhrkamp, 1981.
Bruford, Walter Horace. *Die gesellschaftlichen Grundlagen der Goethezeit*. Literatur und Leben 9. Weimar: Böhlaus, 1936.

Bürger, Christa. *Der Ursprung der bürgerlichen Institution Kunst im höfischen Weimar: Literatursoziologische Untersuchungen zum klassischen Goethe.* Frankfurt: Suhrkamp, 1974.
———. "Literarischer Markt und Öffentlichkeit am Ausgang des 18. Jahrhunderts in Deutschland." In *Aufklärung und literarische Öffentlichkeit,* ed. C. Bürger, P. Bürger, and J. Schulte-Sasse, 162-213. Edition Suhrkamp 40. Frankfurt: Suhrkamp, 1980.
Bürger, Peter. *Theory of the Avant-Garde.* Trans. Michael Shaw. Theory and History of Literature 4. Minneapolis: University of Minnesota Press, 1984.
Culler, Jonathan. *On Deconstruction: Theory and Criticism after Structuralism.* Ithaca: Cornell University Press, 1982.
Curtius, Ernst Robert. *European Literature and the Latin Middle Ages.* Trans. Willard R. Trask. Princeton: Princeton University Press, 1973.
Darnton, Robert. *The Literary Underground of the Old Regime.* Cambridge: Harvard University Press, 1982.
———. *The Great Cat Massacre and Other Episodes in French Cultural History.* New York: Vintage, 1985.
———, and Daniel Roche, eds. *Revolution in Print: The Press in France 1775-1800.* Berkeley and Los Angeles: University of California Press, 1989.
Eagleton, Terry. *The Rape of Clarissa: Writing, Sexuality and Class Struggle in Samuel Richardson.* Oxford: Basil Blackwell, 1982.
———. *The Function of Criticism: From the Spectator to Post-Structuralism.* Norfolk: Thetford, 1984.
Engelsing, Rolf. *Der Bürger als Leser: Lesergeschichte in Deutschland 1500-1800.* Stuttgart: Metzler, 1974.
Foucault, Michel. "What Is an Author?" In *Language, Counter-Memory, Practice: Selected Essays and Interviews,* ed. Donald F. Bouchard, 113-38. Ithaca: Cornell University Press, 1977.
Frank, Joseph. "Reaction as Progress: Thomas Mann's *Doktor Faustus.*" In his *The Widening Gyre: Crisis and Mastery in Modern Literature,* 131-61. Bloomington: Indiana University Press, 1968.
Furst, Lilian R. *Fictions of Romantic Irony.* Cambridge: Harvard University Press, 1984.
Germer, Helmut. *The German Novel of Education from 1764 to 1792: A Complete Bibliography and Analysis.* German Language and Literature 550. Bern: Lang, 1982.
Girard, René. *Deceit, Desire, and the Novel: Self and Other in Literary Structure.* Trans. Yvonne Freccero. Baltimore: Johns Hopkins University Press, 1965.
Greenblatt, Stephan. *Renaissance Self-Fashioning: From More to Shakespeare.* Chicago: University of Chicago Press, 1980.
Habermas, Jürgen. *Strukturwandel der Öffentlichkeit: Untersuchungen zu einer Kategorie der bürgerlichen Gesellschaft.* Neuwied: Luchterhand, 1962.
Hadley, Michael. *The German Novel in 1790: A Descriptive Account and Critical Bibliography.* German Language and Literature 87. Frankfurt: Lang, 1973.
Haferkorn, Hans Jürgen. "Der freie Schriftsteller: Eine literatursoziologische Studie über seine Entstehung und Lage in Deutschland zwischen 1750

und 1800." *Archiv für Geschichte des Buchwesens* 5 (1963), columns 523-712.
Heiderich, Manfred W. *The German Novel of 1800: A Study of Popular Prose Fiction.* Canadian Studies in German Language and Literature 25. Bern: Lange, 1982.
Hohendahl, Peter Uwe. "Critical Theory, Public Sphere and Culture: Jürgen Habermas and His Critics." *New German Critique* 16 (1979): 89-118.
———. *The Institution of Criticism.* Ithaca: Cornell University Press, 1982.
Holub, Robert. *Reception Theory: A Critical Introduction.* New York: Methuen, 1984.
Huyssen, Andreas. *After the Great Divide: Modernism, Mass Culture, Postmodernism.* Bloomington: Indiana University Press, 1986.
Kittler, Friedrich A. *Aufschreibesysteme 1800/1900.* Munich: Fink, 1985.
König, Dominik von. "Lesesucht und Lesewut." In *Buch und Leser,* ed. Herbert G. Göpfert, 89-113. Hamburg: Hauswedell & Co., 1977.
Lepenies, Wolf. *Melancholie und Gesellschaft.* Suhrkamp Taschenbuch 63. Frankfurt: Suhrkamp, 1972.
Lyotard, Jean-François. *The Postmodern Condition: A Report on Knowledge.* Trans. Massumi Bennington. Theory and History of Literature 10. Minneapolis: University of Minnesota Press, 1984.
Mahoney, Dennis F. *Der Roman der Goethezeit (1774-1829).* Sammlung Metzler 241. Stuttgart: Metzler, 1988.
Mann, Thomas. *Schriften und Reden zur Literatur, Kunst und Philosophie.* Vol. 2. Frankfurt: Fischer, 1968.
Mellor, Anne K. *English Romantic Irony.* Cambridge: Harvard University Press, 1980.
Meyer, Herman. *Das Zitat in der Erzählkunst: zur Geschichte und Poetik des europäischen Romans.* Second revised edition. Stuttgart: Metzler, 1967.
Pascal, Roy. *The German Novel.* Toronto: University of Toronto Press, 1968.
Rosenthal, Mark. *Anselm Kiefer.* Philadelphia: Philadelphia Museum of Art, 1987.
Rosmarin, Adena. *The Power of Genre.* Minneapolis: University of Minnesota Press, 1985.
Sauder, Gerhard. "Erbauungsliteratur." In *Hansers Sozialgeschichte der deutschen Literatur,* vol. 3, ed. Rolf Grimminger, 251-66. Munich: Hanser, 1980.
Schlaffer, Heinz. *Der Bürger als Held: Sozialgeschichtliche Auflösungen literarischer Widersprüche.* Edition Suhrkamp 624. Frankfurt: Suhrkamp, 1973.
Schmidt, Siegfried J. *Die Selbstorganisation des Sozialsystems Literatur im 18. Jahrhundert.* Frankfurt: Suhrkamp, 1989.
Schulte-Sasse, Jochen. "Das Konzept bürgerlich-literarischer Öffentlichkeit und die historischen Gründe seines Zerfalls." In *Aufklärung und literarische Öffentlichkeit,* 83-115. Edition Suhrkamp 40. Frankfurt: Suhrkamp, 1980.
Strohschneider-Kohrs, Ingrid. *Die romantische Ironie in Theorie und Gestaltung.* Tübingen: Niemeyer, 1960.
Szondi, Peter. *Antike und Moderne in der Ästhetik der Goethezeit.* In *Poetik und Geschichtsphilosophie I.* Vol. 2 of *Studienausgabe der Vorlesungen.* Suhrkamp Taschenbuch Wissenschaft 40. Frankfurt: Suhrkamp, 1974, 11-265.
Todorov, Tzvetan. *Theories of the Symbol.* Trans. Catherine Porter. Ithaca: Cornell University Press, 1982.

Voßkamp, Wilhelm. "Gattungen als literarisch-soziale Institutionen." In *Textsortenlehre-Gattungsgeschichte,* ed. Walter Hinck, 27-44. Heidelberg: Quelle & Meyer, 1977.
Ward, Albert. *Book Production, Fiction, and the German Reading Public: 1740-1800.* Oxford: Clarendon Press, 1974.
Waugh, Patricia. *Metafiction: The Theory and Practice of Self-Conscious Fiction.* London: Methuen, 1984.
Woodmansee, Martha. "The Interests in Disinterestedness: Karl Philipp Moritz and the Emergence of the Theory of Aesthetic Autonomy in Eighteenth-Century Germany." *Modern Language Quarterly* 45, 1 (1984): 22-47.
Wuthenow, Ralph-Rainer. *Im Buch die Bücher oder Der Held als Leser.* Frankfurt: Europäische Verlagsanstalt, 1980.

Bildungsroman

Amrine, Frederick. "Rethinking the *Bildungsroman.*" *Michigan Germanic Studies* 13 (1987): 119-39.
Beddow, Michael. *The Fiction of Humanity: Studies in the Bildungsroman from Wieland to Thomas Mann.* Cambridge: Cambridge University Press, 1982.
Borcherdt, Hans Heinrich. *Der Roman der Goethezeit.* Stuttgart: Port, 1949.
―――. "Der deutsche Bildungsroman." In *Wege der Forschung,* ed. Selbmann, 182-238.
Dilthey, Wilhelm. *Das Erlebnis und die Dichtung: Lessing Goethe Novalis Hölderlin.* 4th edition. Leipzig: Teubner, 1913. Abbreviated in *Wege der Forschung,* ed. Selbmann, 120-22.
Gerhard, Melitta. *Der deutsche Entwicklungsroman bis zu Goethes 'Wilhelm Meister.'* 1926; second edition. Bern: Francke, 1968.
Jacobs, Jürgen. *Wilhelm Meister und seine Brüder: Untersuchungen zum deutschen Bildungsroman.* Munich: Fink, 1972.
―――, and Markus Krause, eds. *Der deutsche Bildungsroman: Gattungsgeschichte vom 18. bis 20. Jahrhundert.* Munich: Beck, 1989.
Janz, Rolf-Peter. "Bildungsroman." In *Deutsche Literatur: Eine Sozialgeschichte,* vol. 5, ed. Horst Albert Glaser, 144-63. Reinbeck: Rowohlt, 1980.
Köhn, Lothar. *Entwicklungs- und Bildungsroman: Ein Forschungsbericht. Erweiterter Sonderdruck aus Deutsche Vierteljahrsschrift für Literaturwissenschaft* 42, nos. 3 and 4 (1968). Abbreviated version in *Wege der Forschung,* ed. Selbmann, 291-373.
Martini, Fritz. "Der Bildungsroman: Zur Geschichte des Wortes und der Theorie." *DVJS* 35 (1961): 44-63. In *Wege der Forschung,* ed. Selbmann, 239-64.
Mayer, Gerhart. "Zum deutschen Antibildungsroman." *Jahrbuch der Raabe-Gesellschaft* (1974): 41-64.
Miles, David H. "The Picaro's Journey to the Confessional: The Changing Image of the Hero in the German Bildungsroman." *PMLA* 89 (1974): 980-92.
Morgenstern, Karl. "Ueber das Wesen des Bildungsromans (1820)." In *Wege der Forschung,* ed. Selbmann, 55-72.

Ratz, Norbert. *Der Identitätsroman: Eine Strukturanalyse.* Untersuchungen zur deutschen Literaturgeschichte 44. Tübingen: Niemeyer, 1988.
Sammons, Jeffrey L. "The Mystery of the Missing *Bildungsroman,* or: What Happened to Wilhelm Meister's Legacy?" *Genre* 14 (1981): 229-46.
Selbmann, Rolf. *Der deutsche Bildungsroman.* Sammlung Metzler 214. Stuttgart: Metzler, 1984.
——, ed. *Zur Geschichte des deutschen Bildungsromans. Wege der Forschung* 640. Darmstadt: Wissenschaftliche Buchgesellschaft, 1988.
Smith, John H. "Sexual Difference, *Bildung,* and the *Bildungsroman.*" *Michigan Germanic Studies* 13 (1987): 206-25.
Sorg, Klaus-Dieter. *Gebrochene Teleologie: Studien zum Bildungsroman von Goethe bis Thomas Mann.* Heidelberg: Winter, 1983.
Stahl, Ernst Ludwig. "Die Entstehung des deutschen Bildungsromans im achzehnten Jahrhundert (1934)." In *Wege der Forschung,* ed. Selbmann, 123-81.
Stanitzek, Georg. "Bildung und Roman als Momente bürgerlicher Kultur: Zur Frühgeschichte des deutschen 'Bildungsromans.'" *DVJS* 62 (1988): 416-50.
Steinecke, Hartmut. "*Wilhelm Meister* und die Folgen: Goethes Roman und die Entwicklung der Gattung im 19. Jahrhundert." In *Goethe im Kontext,* ed. Wolfgang Wittkowski, 89-118. Tübingen: Niemeyer, 1984.
Swales, Martin. *The German Bildungsroman from Wieland to Hesse.* Princeton: Princeton University Press, 1978.

Jung-Stilling: *Lebensgeschichte*

Arnold, Gottfried. *Vitae Patrum oder Das Leben der Altväter und anderer gottseligen Personen.* Potsdam: 1699.
Blanckenburg, Friedrich von. *Versuch über den Roman: Faksimiledruck der Originalausgabe von 1774.* Including an essay by Eberhard Lämmert. Stuttgart: Metzler, 1965.
Boeschenstein, Hermann. *Die Grundlagen, 1770-1830.* Vol. 1 of *Deutsche Gefühlskultur.* Bern: Haupt, 1954.
Cunz, Dieter. "Nachwort" to Johann Heinrich Jung-Stilling, *Heinrich Stillings Jugend, Jünglingsjahre, Wanderschaft und häusliches Leben,* 367-422. Stuttgart: Reclam, 1968.
Günther, Hans R. G. *Jung-Stilling: Ein Beitrag zur Psychologie des Pietismus.* Second revised edition. München: Reinhardt, 1948.
Gutzen, Dieter. "Johann Heinrich Jung-Stilling." In *Deutsche Dichter des 18. Jahrhunderts: Ihr Leben und Werk,* ed. Benno von Wiese, 446-61. Berlin: Schmidt, 1977.
Hahn, Otto W. *Jung-Stilling zwischen Pietismus und Aufklärung: Sein Leben und sein literarisches Werk 1778 bis 1787.* Europäische Hochschulschriften, Reihe 13 (Theologie) 344. Frankfurt: Lang, 1988.
Pfeiffer-Belli, Wolfgang. "Nachwort." In Jung-Stilling, *Lebensgeschichte,* 540-51. Ed. Pfeiffer-Belli. Munich: Winkler, 1968.
Reitz, Johann Henrich. *Historie der Wiedergebohrnen.* 3rd ed. Berlenburg: Haug, 1726; Offenbach a. M.: de Launoy, 1691-1701.

Ritschl, Albrecht. *Geschichte des Pietismus in der reformirten Kirche.* Bonn: Marcus, 1880. Rpt. Berlin: de Gruyter, 1966.
Stecher, G. *Jung-Stilling als Schriftsteller.* Berlin: Mayer & Müller, 1913.
Vinke, Rainer. *Jung-Stilling und die Aufklärung: Die polemischen Schriften Johann Heinrich Jung-Stillings gegen Friedrich Nicolai (1775/76).* Stuttgart: Steiner, 1987.
Willert, Albrecht. *Religiöse Existenz und literarische Produktion: Jung-Stillings Autobiographie und seine frühen Romane.* Europäische Hochschulschriften, Reihe 1 (Deutsche Sprache und Literatur) 471. Frankfurt: Lang, 1982.

Moritz: *Anton Reiser*

Boulby, Mark. *Karl Philipp Moritz: At the Fringe of Genius.* Toronto: University of Toronto Press, 1979.
Catholy, Eckehard. *Karl Philipp Moritz und die Ursprünge der deutschen Theaterleidenschaft.* Tübingen: Niemeyer, 1962.
Fürnkäs, Josef. *Der Ursprung des psychologischen Romans: Karl Philipp Moritz' 'Anton Reiser'.* Stuttgart: Metzler, 1977.
Kestenholz, Claudia. *Die Sicht der Dinge: Metaphorische Visualität und Subjektivitätsideal im Werk von Karl Philipp Moritz.* Munich: Fink, 1987.
Minder, Robert. *Glaube, Skepsis und Rationalismus: Dargestellt aufgrund der autobiographischen Schriften von Karl Philipp Moritz.* Suhrkamp Taschenbuch Wissenschaft 43. Frankfurt: Suhrkamp, 1974. Originally *Die religiöse Entwicklung von Karl Philipp Moritz aufgrund seiner autobiographischen Schriften.* Berlin: Junker und Dünnhapt, 1936.
Müller, Lothar. *Die kranke Seele und das Licht der Erkenntnis: Karl Philipp Moritz' Anton Reiser.* Frankfurt: Athenäum, 1987.
Schrimpf, Hans Joachim. "Moritz: Anton Reiser." In *Der deutsche Roman: Vom Barock bis zur Gegenwart,* ed. Benno von Wiese, 95-131. Düsseldorf: Bagel, 1963.
Stemme, Fritz. "Die Säkularisation des Pietismus zur Erfahrungsseelenkunde." *Zeitschrift für deutsche Philologie* 72 (1953): 144-58.

Goethe: *Wilhelm Meisters Lehrjahre*

Alewyn, Richard. "'Klopstock!'" *Euphorion* 73 (1979): 357-64.
Baioni, Giuliano. "Märchen—Wilhelm Meisters Lehrjahre—Hermann und Dorothea: Zur Gesellschaftsidee der deutschen Klassik." *Goethe Jahrbuch* 92 (1975): 73-127.
Barner, Wilfried. "'Die Verschiedenheit unserer Naturen': Zu Goethes und Schillers Briefwechsel über 'Wilhelm Meisters Lehrjahre.'" In *Unser Commercium: Goethes und Schillers Literaturpolitik,* ed. Wilfried Barner, Eberhard Lämmert, and Norbert Oellers, 379-404. Stuttgart: Cotta, 1984.

Behler, Ernst. "*Wilhelm Meisters Lehrjahre* and the Poetic Unity of the Novel in Early German Romanticism." In *Goethe's Narrative Fiction: The Irvine Goethe Symposium,* ed. William J. Lillyman, 110-27. New York: de Gruyter, 1983.
Bennett, Benjamin. *Goethe's Theory of Poetry: 'Faust' and the Regeneration of Language.* Ithaca: Cornell University Press, 1986.
Berger, Albert. *Ästhetik und Bildungsroman: Goethes 'Wilhelm Meisters Lehrjahre.'* Vienna: Braumüller, 1977.
Blackall, Eric. *Goethe and the Novel.* Ithaca: Cornell University Press, 1976.
Böhler, Michael. "Die Freundschaft von Schiller und Goethe als literatursoziologisches Paradigma." *Internationales Archiv für Sozialgeschichte der deutschen Literatur* 5 (1980): 33-67.
Bollnow, Otto Friedrich. "Vorbetrachtungen zum Verständnis der Bildungsidee in Goethes 'Wilhelm Meister.'" *Die Sammlung* 10 (1955): 445-63.
Brandt, Helmut. "Die 'hochgesinnte' Verschwörung gegen das Publikum: Anmerkungen zum Goethe-Schiller Bündnis." In *Unser Commercium,* 19-35. See Barner.
Conrady, Karl Otto. *Goethe: Leben und Werk.* Königstein/Ts: Athenäum, 1985.
Eichner, Hans-Egon. "Zur Deutung von 'Wilhelm Meisters Lehrjahren.'" *Jahrbuch des freien deutschen Hochstifts* (1966): 165-96.
Gerhard, Melitta. "Goethes 'Geprägte Form' im Romantischen Spiegel: Zu Friedrich Schlegels Aufsatz 'Über Goethe's Meister.'" In her *Leben im Gesetz: Fünf Goethe-Aufsätze,* 64-78. Bern: Francke, 1966.
Gille, Klaus Friedrich. *'Wilhelm Meister' im Urteil der Zeitgenossen: Ein Beitrag zur Wirkungsgeschichte Goethes.* Leiden: van Gorcum, 1971.
Hass, Hans-Egon. "Wilhelm Meisters Lehrjahre." In *Der deutsche Roman: Vom Barock bis zur Gegenwart,* ed. Benno von Wiese, 1:132-210. Düsseldorf: Bagel, 1963.
Immerwahr, Raymond. "Friedrich Schlegel's Essay 'On Goethe's *Meister.*'" *Monatshefte* 49 (1957): 1-21.
Janz, Rolf-Peter. "Zum sozialen Gehalt der 'Lehrjahre.'" In *Literaturwissenschaft und Geschichtsphilosophie: Festschrift für Wilhelm Emrich,* ed. Arntzen, Balzer, Pestalozzi, and Wagner, 320-40. Berlin, New York: de Gruyter, 1975.
Kittler, Friedrich A. "Über die Sozialisation Wilhelm Meisters." In *Dichtung als Sozialisationsspiel: Studien zu Goethe und Gottfried Keller,* 13-124. Göttingen: Vandenhoeck & Ruprecht, 1978.
Kontje, Todd Curtis. *Constructing Reality: A Rhetorical Analysis of Friedrich Schiller's Letters on the Aesthetic Education of Man.* New York University Ottendorfer Series 25. New York: Lang, 1987.
Mandelkow, Karl Robert. "Einleitung." In *Goethe im Urteil seiner Kritiker: Dokumente zur Wirkungsgeschichte Goethes in Deutschland: Teil I 1773-1832.* Munich: Beck, 1975.
———. "Der Roman der Klassik und Romantik." In *Neues Handbuch der Literaturwissenschaft.* Vol. 14, *Europäische Romantik I,* 393-428. Wiesbaden: Akademische Verlagsgesellschaft, 1982.
May, Kurt. "'Wilhelm Meisters Lehrjahre': ein Bildungsroman?" *Deutsche Vierteljahrsschrift* 31 (1957): 1-37.
Pütz, Peter. "Werthers Leiden an der Literatur." In *Goethe's Narrative Fiction:*

The Irvine Goethe Symposium, ed. William J. Lillyman, 55-68. New York: de Gruyter, 1983.
Pyritz, Hans. "Der Bund zwischen Goethe und Schiller: Zur Klärung des Problems der sogenannten Weimarer Klassik." In Pyritz, *Goethe-Studien,* 34-51. Cologne: Böhlau, 1962.
Reed, T. J. "Ecclesia militans: Weimarer Klassik als Opposition." In *Unser Commercium,* 37-53. See Barner.
Roberts, David. *The Indirections of Desire: Hamlet in Goethes 'Wilhelm Meister.'* Heidelberg: Winter, 1980.
Scherpe, Klaus R. *Werther und Wertherwirkung: Zum Syndrom bürgerlicher Gesellschaftsordnung im 18. Jahrhundert.* Bad Homburg: Gehlen, 1970.
Schings, Hans-Jürgen. "'Agathon,' 'Anton Reiser,' 'Wilhelm Meister': Zur Pathologie des modernen Subjekts im Roman." In *Goethe im Kontext,* ed. Wittkowski, 42-68. Tübingen: Niemeyer, 1984.
Schlaffer, Heinz. "Exoterik und Esoterik in Goethes Romanen." *Goethe Jahrbuch* 95 (1978): 212-26.
Schlechta, Karl. *Goethes Wilhelm Meister.* Frankfurt: Klostermann, 1953.
Schulz, Günter. *Schillers Horen: Politik und Erziehung: Analyse einer deutschen Zeitschrift.* Deutsche Presseforschung 2. Heidelberg: Quelle & Meyer, 1960.
Strack, Friedrich. "Selbst-Erfahrung oder Selbst-Entsagung? Goethes Deutung und Kritik des Pietismus in 'Wilhelm Meisters Lehrjahre.'" In *Verlorene Klassik? Ein Symposium,* ed. Wolfgang Wittkowski, 52-78. Tübingen: Niemeyer, 1986.
Vaget, Hans Rudolf. "Der Schreibakt und der Liebesakt: Zur Deutung von Goethes Gedicht 'Das Tagebuch.'" *Goethe Yearbook* 1 (1982): 112-37.
———. "Die Leiden des jungen Werthers (1774)." In *Goethes Erzählwerk: Interpretationen,* ed. Paul Michael Lützeler, 37-72. Stuttgart: Reclam, 1985.
Waniek, Erdmann. "*Werther* lesen und Werther als Leser." *Goethe Yearbook* 1 (1982): 51-92.
Weisinger, Kenneth D. *The Classical Façade: A Nonclassical Reading of Goethe's Classicism.* University Park: Pennsylvania State University Press, 1988.
Zantop, Susanne. "Eignes Selbst und fremde Formen: Goethes 'Bekenntnisse einer schönen Seele.'" *Goethe Yearbook* 3 (1986): 73-92.

Tieck: *Franz Sternbalds Wanderungen*

Alewyn, Richard. "Ein Fragment der Fortsetzung von Tiecks 'Sternbald.'" *Jahrbuch des freien deutschen Hochstifts* (1962): 58-68.
Anger, Alfred. "Nachwort." In *Franz Sternbalds Wanderungen: Studienausgabe,* 545-83. Stuttgart: Reclam, 1979.
Fink, Gonthier-Louis. "L'Ambiguïté du message romantique dans *Franz Sternbalds Wanderungen* de L. Tieck." *Recherches Germaniques* 4 (1974): 16-70.
Geulen, Hans. "Allegorie im Erzählvorgang von Ludwig Tiecks Roman 'Franz Sternbalds Wanderungen.'" *Germanisch-Romantische Monatsschrift,* n. s. 18 (1968): 281-98.

Gundolf, Friedrich. "Ludwig Tieck." In *Romantiker: Neue Folge*, 5-139. Berlin: Keller, 1931.
Haym, Rudolf. *Die romantische Schule: Ein Beitrag zur Geschichte des deutschen Geistes*. Berlin, 1870; rpt. Hildesheim: Olms, 1961.
Hibberd, J. L. "The Idylls in Tieck's *Sternbald*." *Forum for Modern Language Studies* 12 (1976): 236-49.
Hillmann, Heinz. "Ludwig Tieck." In *Deutsche Dichter der Romantik: Ihr Leben und Werk*, ed. Benno von Wiese, 111-34. Berlin: Schmidt, 1971.
Kern, Johannes P. *Ludwig Tieck: Dichter einer Krise*. Heidelberg: Stiehm, 1977.
Lillyman, William J. *Reality's Dark Dream: The Narrative Fiction of Ludwig Tieck*. Berlin: de Gruyter, 1979.
Minder, Robert. *Un Poète Romantique Allemand: Ludwig Tieck (1773-1853)*. Diss. Paris 1936. Paris: Les Belles Lettres, 1936.
Paulin, Roger. *Ludwig Tieck: A Literary Biography*. Oxford: Clarendon Press, 1985.
Ribbat, Ernst. *Ludwig Tieck: Studien zur Konzeption und Praxis romantischer Poesie*. Kronberg/Ts: Athenäum, 1978.
Sammons, Jeffrey L. "Tieck's *Franz Sternbald:* The Loss of Thematic Control." *Studies in Romanticism* 5 (1965): 30-43.
Schweikert, Uwe, ed. *Dichter über ihre Dichtungen: Ludwig Tieck*. Munich: Heimeran, 1971.
Staiger, Emil. "Ludwig Tieck und der Ursprung der deutschen Romantik." In *Stilwandel: Studien zur Vorgeschichte der Goethezeit*, 175-204. Zürich: Atlantis, 1963.
Thalmann, Marianne. *Ludwig Tieck: Der romantische Weltmann aus Berlin*. Dalp Taschenbücher 318. Bern: Francke, 1955.

Novalis: *Heinrich von Ofterdingen*

Beck, Hans-Joachim. *Friedrich von Hardenberg 'Oeconomie des Styls': Die 'Wilhelm Meister'—Rezeption im 'Heinrich von Ofterdingen'*. Bonn: Bouvier, 1976.
Frühwald, Wolfgang. "Nachwort." In *Heinrich von Ofterdingen: Ein Roman*, 229-45. Stuttgart: Reclam, 1965.
Heftrich, Eckhard. *Novalis: Vom Logos der Poesie*. Frankfurt: Klostermann, 1969.
Hiebel, Friedrich. *Novalis: Deutscher Dichter, europäischer Denker, christlicher Seher*. Second, revised and expanded edition. Bern: Francke, 1972.
Kesting, Marianne. "Aspekte des absoluten Buches bei Novalis und Mallarmé." *Euphorion* 68 (1974): 420-36.
Kittler, Friedrich A. "Die Irrwege des Eros und die 'Absolute Familie.'" In *Psychoanalytische und Psychopathologische Literaturinterpretation*, ed. Bernd Urban and Winfried Kudzus, 421-70. Darmstadt: Wissenschaftliche Buchgesellschaft, 1981.
———. "'Heinrich von Ofterdingen' als Nachrichtenfluss.'" In *Novalis: Beiträge zu Werk und Persönlichkeit Friedrich von Hardenbergs*, ed. Gerhard Schulz, 480-508. Darmstadt: Wissenschaftliche Buchgesellschaft, 1986.
Kluckhohn, Paul. "Friedrich von Hardenbergs Entwicklung und Dichtung." In

Novalis, *Schriften,* vol. 1, 1-67. Ed. Paul Kluckhohn and Richard Samuel. Stuttgart: Kohlhammer, 1960.
———. and Richard Samuel. "Einleitung der Herausgeber" to Novalis, *Heinrich von Ofterdingen.* In *Schriften,* vol. 1, 183-92.
Kuzniar, Alice A. *Delayed Endings: Nonclosure in Novalis and Hölderlin.* Athens: University of Georgia Press, 1987.
Link, Hannelore. *Abstraktion und Poesie im Werk des Novalis.* Stuttgart: Kohlhammer, 1971.
Mähl, Hans Joachim. *Die Idee des goldenen Zeitalters im Werk des Novalis: Studien zur Wesensbestimmung der frühromantischen Utopie und zu ihren ideengeschichtlichen Voraussetzungen.* Heidelberg: Winter, 1965.
———. "Einleitung" to Novalis, *Das allgemeine Brouillon.* In *Schriften,* vol. 3, 207-41.
Mahr, Johannes. *Übergang zum Endlichen: Der Weg des Dichters in Novalis' Heinrich von Ofterdingen.* Munich: Fink, 1970.
Molnár, Géza von. *Romantic Vision, Ethical Context: Novalis and Artistic Autonomy.* Theory and History of Literature 39. Minneapolis: University of Minnesota Press, 1987.
Samuel, Richard. "Einleitung" to Novalis, *Dialogen und Monolog.* In *Schriften,* vol. 2, 655-60.
———."Novalis: Heinrich von Ofterdingen." In *Der deutsche Roman: Vom Barock bis zur Gegenwart,* ed. Benno von Wiese, 1:252-300. Düsseldorf: Bagel, 1963.
Schreiber, Jens. *Das Symptom des Schreibens: Roman und absolutes Buch in der Frühromantik (Novalis/Schlegel).* Europäische Hochschulschriften 649. Frankfurt: Lang, 1983.
Stadler, Ulrich. *Die theuren Dinge: Studien zu Bunyan, Jung-Stilling und Novalis.* Bern: Francke, 1980.

Jean Paul: *Flegeljahre*

Berend, Eduard. *Jean Pauls Ästhetik.* Forschungen zur neueren Literaturgeschichte 35. Berlin: Duncker, 1909.
———. "Einleitung." In *Sämtliche Werke: Historisch-Kritische Ausgabe,* vol. 10. Weimar: Böhlaus, 1934.
———. "Jean Paul—der meistgelesene Schriftsteller seiner Zeit?" *Imprimatur,* n.s. 2 (1958/60): 172-83.
———. "Jean Pauls Handschriftlicher Nachlaß: Seine Eigenart und seine Geschichte." *Jahrbuch der Jean-Paul Gesellschaft* 3 (1968): 13-22.
de Bruyn, Günter. *Das Leben des Jean Paul Friedrich Richter.* Halle: Mitteldeutscher Verlag, 1975.
Freye, Karl. *Jean Pauls Flegeljahre: Materialien und Untersuchungen.* Berlin: Mayer & Müller, 1907.
Gansberg, Marie-Luise. "Welt-Verlachung und 'das rechte Land': Ein literatursoziologischer Beitrag zu Jean Paul's 'Flegeljahre.'" *DVJS* 42 (1968): 373-98.
Harich, Walther. *Jean Paul.* Leipzig: Haessel, 1925.

Köpke, Wulf. *Erfolglosigkeit: Zum Frühwerk Jean Pauls.* Munich: Fink, 1977.
Lindner, Burkhardt. *Jean Paul: Scheiternde Aufklärung und Autorrolle.* Darmstadt: Agora, 1976.
Maurer, Peter. *Wunsch und Maske: Eine Untersuchung der Bild- und Motivstruktur von Jean Pauls Flegeljahren.* Palestra 273. Göttingen: Vandenhoeck & Ruprecht, 1981.
Mayer, Gerhart. "Die humorgeprägte Struktur von Jean Pauls 'Flegeljahren.'" *Zeitschrift für deutsche Philologie* 83 (1964): 409-26.
Meyer, Herman. "Jean Paul: Flegeljahre." In *Der deutsche Roman: Vom Barock bis zur Gegenwart,* ed. Benno von Wiese, 211-51. Düsseldorf: Bagel, 1963.
Müller, Götz. *Jean Pauls Exzerpte.* Würzburg: Königshausen & Neumann, 1988.
Neumann, Peter Horst. *Jean Pauls 'Flegeljahre.'* Palaestra 245. Göttingen: Vandenhoeck & Ruprecht, 1966.
Ohly, Friedrich. "Das Buch der Natur bei Jean Paul." In *Studien zur Goethezeit: Erich Trunz zum 75. Geburtstag,* ed. Hans-Joachim Mähl and Eberhard Mannack, 177-232. Heidelberg: Winter, 1981.
Rehm, Walter. "Jean Pauls vergnügtes Noten leben oder Notenmacher und Notenleser." In his *Späte Studien,* 7-96. Bern, Munich: Francke, 1964.
Soffke, Günther. *Jean Pauls Verhältnis zum Buch.* Forschungsstelle für Buchwissenschaft in der Universität Bonn. Kleine Schriften 7. Bonn: Bouvier, 1969.
Sprengel, Peter. *Innerlichkeit: Jean Paul oder Das Leiden an der Gesellschaft.* Munich: Hanser, 1977.
Theiss, Winfried. "Garlieb Merkel als Rezensent Jean Pauls." *JJPG* 8 (1973): 78-99.
Tönz, Leo. "Das Wirtshaus 'Zum Wirtshaus': Zu einem Motiv in Jean Pauls 'Flegeljahren.'" *JJPG* 5 (1970): 105-23.
Wiethölter, Waltraud. "Jean Paul: Flegeljahre." In *Romane und Erzählungen der deutschen Romantik: Neue Interpretationen,* ed. Paul Michael Lützeler, 163-93. Stuttgart: Reclam, 1981.
Wuthenow, Ralph-Rainer. "Gefährdete Idylle." Cited from Jean Paul, *Des Luftschiffers Giannozzo Seebuch.* Insel Taschenbuch 144. Frankfurt: Insel, 1975.

Hoffmann: *Kater Murr*

Daemmrich, Horst S. "E.T.A. Hoffmann: *Kater Murr (1820/22).*" In *Romane und Erzählungen zwischen Romantik und Realismus: Neue Interpretationen,* ed. Paul Michael Lützeler, 73-93. Stuttgart: Reclam, 1983.
Feldges, Brigitte, and Ulrich Stadler, eds. *E.T.A. Hoffmann: Epoche—Werk—Wirkung.* Munich: Beck, 1986.
Hartmann, Anneli. "Geschlossenheit der 'Kunst-Welt' und fragmentarische Form: E.T.A. Hoffmanns 'Kater Murr.'" *Jahrbuch der deutschen Schillergesellschaft* 32 (1988): 148-90.
Jones, Michael T. "Hoffmann and the Problem of Social Reality: A Study of *Kater Murr.*" *Monatshefte* 69 (1977): 45-57.

Kofman, Sarah. *Schreiben wie eine Katze: Zu E.T.A. Hoffmanns 'Lebens-Ansichten des Katers Murr.'* Ed. Peter Engelmann. Trans. Monika Buchgeister and Hans-Walter Schmidt. Graz: Böhlaus, 1985.
Mayer, Hans. "Die Wirklichkeit E.T.A. Hoffmanns: Ein Versuch." In Hoffmann, *Poetische Werke*, v-lv. Berlin: Aufbau, 1958.
Müller-Seidel, Walter. "Nachwort." In Hoffmann, *Lebens-Ansichten des Katers Murr*, 667-89. Munich: Winkler, 1977.
Safranski, Rüdiger. *E.T.A. Hoffmann: Das Leben eines skeptischen Phantasten.* Munich: Hanser, 1984.
Schnapp, Friedrich, ed. *E.T.A. Hoffmann in Aufzeichnungen seiner Freunde und Bekannten.* Munich: Winkler, 1974.
Segebrecht, Wulf, ed. "Anmerkungen" to Hoffmann, *Späte Werke.* Munich: Winkler, 1969.
Singer, Herbert. "Hoffmann: Kater Murr." In *Der deutsche Roman: Vom Barock bis zur Gegenwart,* ed. Benno von Wiese, 301-28. Düsseldorf: Bagel, 1963.
Steinecke, Hartmut. "Nachwort." In Hoffmann, *Lebens-Ansichten des Katers Murr,* 486-511. Stuttgart: Reclam, 1972.
von Wiese, Benno. "E.T.A. Hoffmanns Doppelroman 'Kater Murr.'" In his *Von Lessing bis Grabbe: Studien zur deutschen Klassik und Romantik,* 248-67. Düsseldorf: Bagel, 1967.

Index

Abrams, M. H., 19, 37
Adorno, Theodor, 163
Apel, Karl-Otto, 98
Arnold, Gottfried, 23
Auerbach, Erich, 54
Augustine, Saint,
 Confessions, 19, 48, 62, 135

Baioni, Giuliano, 77
Bakhtin, Mikhail, 136
Bible, 2, 19, 23, 26, 44, 55, 64 n. 30, 70,
 101-2, 104, 106, 111, 120, 138
Blackall, Eric, 55
Borcherdt, Hans Heinrich, 14
Bräker, Ulrich, 130
Büchner, Georg, 49
Bunyan, John, 25
Bürger, Peter, 9

Calvin, John, 23
Chamisso, Adalbert, 146

Dante, 108
Derrida, Jacques, 97-98
Dickens, Charles, 143
Dilthey, Wilhelm, 12, 13, 14
Duchamp, Marcel, 10

Dümmler, Ferdinand, 152

Eagleton, Terry, 5
Eckermann, Johann Peter, 77
Engelsing, Rolf, 1
Eugen, Karl, 4

Fichte, Johann Gottlieb, 97, 156
Fleischbein, Johann Friedrich von, 33
Foucault, Michel, 49
Fouqué, Friedrich de la Motte, 146
Francke, August Hermann, 21
Freud, Sigmund, 49

Goethe, Johann Wolfgang, 4, 6, 13, 20, 27,
 29, 30, 42, 45, 89, 104, 124, 140,
 156, 161, 162, 163, 164
 "Das Tagebuch," 63
 "Dauer im Wechsel," 76
 "Epistel," 57, 58, 76
 Faust, 59, 62, 71, 77, 108
 "Hermann und Dorothea," 58
 "Literarischer Sansculottismus," 59
 "Maximen and Reflexionen," 76
 "Myrons Kuh," 43
 "Römische Elegien," 62-63
 "Über Laokoon," 43

Goethe, Johann Wolfgang (continued)
 Die Leiden des jungen Werther, 6,
  44-46, 54-55, 58, 61, 67-68, 83
 Wilhelm Meisters Lehrjahre, 6, 12, 13,
  14, 15, 51-78, 95, 101, 103, 106,
  107, 109, 111, 114, 123-24, 130-31,
  133, 145, 158, 163, 164
 Wilhelm Meisters theatralische Sendung,
  55-56, 60-61, 63, 67-69
 "Winckelmann," 76
 "Xenien," 58-59
Gottfried von Straßburg, 118
Gozzi, Carlo, 127
Grabbe, Christian Dietrich, 49
Grass, Günter,
 Blechtrommel, 163, 164, 165
Greenblatt, Steven, 8, 9, 22
Grimm, Hans, 14
Grimmelshausen, Hans Jakob Christoffel,
 11
Grosse, Karl, 158
Gundolf, Friedrich, 80

Habermas, Jürgen, 2, 5, 98, 163
Hamann, Johann Georg, 152
Haym, Rudolf, 79
Hegel, Friedrich, 13
Heine, Heinrich, 163
Heinse, Wilhelm, 89
Herder, Johann Gottfried, 24, 136
Herodotus, 130
Hesse, Hermann, 164
Hillmann, Heinz, 80-81
Hippel, Theodor Gottlieb, 146
Hoffmann, E.T.A., 7, 9, 161, 162
 Das Fräulein von Scuderi, 147
 Elixiere des Teufels, 158
 Fantasiestücke, 146
 Kater Murr, 6, 7, 13, 143-59, 162-63
 "Meister Floh," 154-55
 Undine, 146, 147
Hölderlin, Friedrich, 12, 97
Homer, 46, 130
 Odyssey, 54, 55, 108

Iffland, August Wilhelm, 157

Jean Paul, [Friedrich Richter], 7, 9, 153,
 156, 161, 162
 Die unsichtbare Loge, 124, 136, 137

Flegeljahre, 6, 7, 123-41, 148, 151,
 155, 156, 162, 163
Grönländische Prozesse, 124, 125, 139
Hesperus, 124, 137
Siebenkäs, 124, 137
Teufelspapiere, 124
Titan, 124
Vorschule der Ästhetik, 127, 135, 138,
 139, 140, 156
Jung-Stilling, Heinrich, 6, 37, 39, 47, 48,
 55, 104, 161, 162, 163, 165
 Lebensgeschichte, 13, 19-31, 33, 34, 35,
  41, 44, 62, 134, 161

Kafka, Franz, 36, 147
Kant, Immanuel, 4, 42, 49, 57, 104, 156
 Kritik der reinen Vernunft, 26, 37
 "Was ist Aufklärung?," 3
Kittler, Friedrich, 63
Kleist, Heinrich, 26, 49
Klopstock, Friedrich Gottlieb, 45, 54
Kofman, Sarah, 152
Körner, Christian Gottfried, 52, 53
Kuzniar, Alice, 97

Leibniz, Gottfried Wilhelm, 26, 156
Lenz, Siegfried, 164
Lepenies, Wolf, 149
Lessing, Gotthold Ephraim,
 Emilia Galotti, 25, 54
Lichtenberg, Georg Christoph, 152
Luther, Martin, 23
Lyotard, François, 10, 11

Mann, Thomas, 8, 164
Marx, Karl, 49
Mayer, Hans, 146
Merkel, Garlieb, 123
Meyer, Herman, 126, 139, 156, 162
Miles, David, 53-54
Milton, John, 123
Molnár, Géza von, 97-98, 110
More, Thomas, 22
Morgenstern, Karl, 12, 14
Moritz, Karl Philipp, 4, 6, 23, 26, 161, 162
 Andreas Hartknopf, 37, 38
 Anton Reiser, 6, 33-49, 67, 114, 133,
  135, 156, 159, 164
 Fragmente aus dem Tagebuche eines
  Geistersehers, 35

Moritz, Karl Philipp (continued)
  Magazin zur Erfahrungsseelenkunde, 48
  "Über den Begriff des in sich selbst
    Vollendeten," 42
  "Über die bildende Nachahmung des
    Schönen," 42, 46, 62
Motte-Guyon, Jeanne Marie Bouvier de la,
  33, 34, 36, 38, 42
Müller, Lothar, 49

Nicolai, Friedrich, 20, 79, 123
Novalis [Friedrich von Hardenberg], 7, 52,
  124, 145, 150, 161
  Die Lehrlinge zu Saïs, 101, 104, 105
  Das Allgemeine Brouillon, 101, 103,
    106, 138-39, 162
  Dialog, 102-4, 111-12, 121
  "Glauben und Liebe," 100
  Heinrich von Ofterdingen, 6, 97-121,
    123, 124, 139, 141, 164
  "Hymnen an die Nacht," 104
  "Monolog," 105

Oppel, Julius Wilhelm von, 99
Ossian, 54, 61

Pascal, Roy, 143

Rabelais, François, 127
Rabener, Gottlob Wilhelm, 123
Rambach, Friedrich Eberhard, 79
Rehm, Walter, 140
Reitz, Johann Henrich,
  Historie der Wiedergebohrenen, 19, 20,
    23, 25
Richardson, Samuel, 5
Roberts, David, 70
Roche, Sophie de la, 30
Rosmarin, Adena, 14, 16

Sammons, Jeffrey, 12, 13, 143
Schiller, Friedrich, 4, 6, 42, 51-60, 71,
  104, 117, 156, 162, 163
  Ästhetische Erziehung, 11, 56-60, 66,
    76, 145
  "Ankündigung der Rheinischen Thalia," 4

Die Horen, 3, 56-59, 63, 106
Kabale und Liebe, 24
Schlaffer, Heinz, 52
Schlechta, Karl, 14, 52
Schlegel, Caroline, 53, 106
Schlegel, Friedrich, 51, 53, 100-102, 106,
  116, 124, 126-28
Schleiermacher, Friedrich, 106
Scott, Walter, 143
Seconda, Joseph, 145, 146
Shakespeare, William, 6, 44, 45, 67, 70,
  111, 156
  As You Like It, 157
  Hamlet, 6, 45, 56, 70-71, 157
Spangenberg, August Gottlieb, 21
Spener, Philipp Jakob, 21
Sprengel, Peter, 129
Sterne, Laurence, 127
Strauß, Botho,
  Der junge Mann, 11, 164-65
Swales, Martin, 15, 17
Swift, Jonathan, 124

Tasso, Torquato, 60
Tieck, Ludwig, 7, 124, 146, 153, 161
  Franz Sternbalds Wanderungen, 7,
    79-95, 107, 161
  Peter Lebrecht, 81, 91
  Der gestiefelte Kater, 156
  William Lovell, 158

Unger, Johann Friedrich, 57

Vieweg, Hans Friedrich, 58
Virgil,
  Aeneid, 108, 118
Voltaire, François, 124, 127

Wackenroder, Wilhelm Heinrich, 89, 91
Waugh, Patricia, 11
Wezel, Johann Karl, 123
Wieland, Christoph Martin,
  Agathon, 161-62
Wolff, Christian, 26
Wolfram von Eschenbach, 11
Woodmansee, Martha, 4

www.ingramcontent.com/pod-product-compliance
Lightning Source LLC
Chambersburg PA
CBHW031552300426
44111CB00006BA/283